D1614411

For Ann and Peter

Contents

Contents

SOCIALISM: CRITICAL AND CONSTRUCTIVE

Contents

DANIEL DERONDA: *'There will still remain the danger of mistaking a tendency which should be resisted for an inevitable law that we must adjust ourselves to. . . .'*

Acknowledgements

I should like to thank Professor Gwyn Williams, who made my research possible, and the Social History Seminar at York University which first heard and discussed the arguments advanced in the introduction; Professor Keith Robbins for his criticism of the various drafts; Mr V. A. C. Gatrell of Gonville and Caius College for his tireless encouragement and hospitality; Professor Bernard Crick for reading the manuscript; Mrs Lucy Middleton for her recollections and friendship; Mr Malcolm MacDonald for his support and permission to cannibalize his father's work; and my parents for reading the proofs. Without my wife, of course, I would never have begun.

Abbreviations

ILP   Independent Labour Party
LCC   London County Council
LRC   Labour Representation Committee
SDF   Social Democratic Federation
TUC   Trades Union Congress

The Political Setting

Born the illegitimate son of an agricultural labourer in 1866 at Lossiemouth, a small Morayshire fishing village, James Ramsay MacDonald was an unlikely political theorist, and an even more unlikely Prime Minister. He remains today, more than thirty-five years after his death and a century after his birth, the only Labour Prime Minister not to have had an Oxford education. He had to be content with Free Kirk Sunday School and a spell as a pupil teacher. Thus spared a classical education, MacDonald was able to write in 1906: '... the *Waverley Novels*, in conjunction with Scottish history, opened out the great world of national life for me and led me on to politics'.*

He came to London in 1886, and almost starved himself, on a diet of boiled water and dry bread, in an effort to win a scientific scholarship. His health broke, and when he came back it was to support himself by clerical, secretarial and journalistic work. He joined the Fabian Society in 1886 and the Independent Labour Party (ILP) in 1894, and at once devoted himself to winning over the working class movement to 'slow socialism', based on rational discussion and persuasion rather than hopes of revolution or capitalist decay. As he told the 1909 ILP Conference in his farewell address as chairman: 'Socialism is not to come from the misery of the people. ... I know that there is a belief still fairly prevalent amongst one school of socialist theorists that the more capitalism fails, the clearer will the way to Socialism be. I have never shared that faith. ... Poverty of mind and body blurs the vision and does not clarify it.' MacDonald's

* In *Review of Reviews*, W. T. Stead (ed.), vol. 33, January–June 1906, p. 577.

own clarity of mind earned him the post of secretary to the newly formed Labour Representation Committee (LRC) in 1900.

Socialism and Society, published in 1905, a year before he was elected to Parliament for the first time, and written mostly while he was representing Central Finsbury on the LCC, argued comprehensively and learnedly that Labour should only attempt to do what people wanted it to do, or could be persuaded to want it to do. It was immensely influential, and ILP study circles up and down the country examined every page in weekly sessions. The Party faithful had been desperate for an intellectual to tell them that their attitude to poverty was rational, a legitimate political response that might be the basis for change. The phrase 'evolutionary socialism' caught on, and provided the Labour Movement with a well-thought-out and respectable alternative to the extremists of the Social Democratic Federation* and the British Socialist Party. The instincts of Keir Hardie were made rational in the self-taught erudition of MacDonald.

MacDonald was rapidly becoming something more than a theorist or even a politician, although his performance in the Commons soon distinguished him from the predominantly trade union group of MPs returned under the auspices of the LRC in 1906. He was a handsome man, a fine orator (although it is almost impossible to infer this from transcripts of his speeches) with a deep organ-like voice and an unflinchingly emotional and romantic style. He was later accused of falling into the aristocratic embrace, but in the early days the movement was proud of his fine bearing and ability to meet nobleman and labourer with equal ease. It would be misleading to call him a demagogue, but his Scottish timbre and fluency strongly appealed to the sentimental, ethical socialists of the ILP, and epitomized their aspirations, which were as fine and vague as he was himself.

Socialism appeared in 1907, shortly after the LRC had adopted the title 'Labour Party'. It was a historical survey, an

* The SDF was the Marxist group led by the old Etonian, H. M. Hyndman.

exercise in legitimization and justification, and instruction for the new Party. Although he took a keen interest in foreign affairs, it was in socialist text books like this that he succeeded in influencing a new generation.

Between 1911 and 1914 MacDonald was leader of the Parliamentary Labour Party, and earned considerable criticism from the left for behaving as he had argued Labour ought to act. He supported the Liberal Government, which after two elections in 1910 over the Parliament Act was dependent upon Labour and Irish votes. He accepted the contributory principle in Lloyd George's proposals for national insurance, and exchanged Labour support for a measure of trade union protection. His view was that Labour should move no faster than the possibilities of the situation; what could not be won at the ballot box should not be seized by direct action (i.e. strikes). MacDonald also attempted to minimize the number of parliamentary election contests, in so far as he, and Arthur Henderson,* were able to do so. There was always the danger that a cautious determination to win over public opinion might lead to an under-estimate of actually existing support. MacDonald was one of the last to agree that Labour ought to assert its independence and discard compromises with the Liberals.

War in 1914 disrupted MacDonald's career and Labour's rather hesitant progress, but by the time it was over it had presented Labour with a great opportunity, in the shape of a franchise increased from seven and a half millions to twenty-one millions, and a Liberal Party hopelessly divided, one half tied to Lloyd George by the Coalition coupon and the remainder still loyal to Asquith and a rather dated Edwardian Liberalism.

MacDonald was dubbed a pacifist by public opinion, and subsequently Horatio Bottomley† devoted a page in *John Bull* to

* Arthur Henderson, one of the first prominent Labour leaders to reach Parliament (in 1903), had taken over as secretary of the Party in 1911, a post he held until 1934. His trade union background, his common sense, his loyalty to the Party, and his dismissal from the Lloyd George cabinet endeared him to all sections of the Movement.
† A jingoistic journalist whose 'patriotism' led him to pursue a private vendetta against pacifists and conscientious objectors.

a photograph of his birth certificate. In fact, his position was little different from Henderson's. He blamed Sir Edward Grey's foreign policy and 'secret diplomacy' for the war,* but realized that once the war was on, it had to be fought, if not to a successful conclusion, then at least to successful negotiations. The Labour Party decided to support the Government, and Henderson even joined the Cabinet in the second war-time Coalition under Lloyd George. MacDonald felt that he could not endorse the conduct of Grey and Asquith, and resigned the leadership in 1914, to become the darling of the ILP and the left, and the bogeyman of press and public.

But Labour's split was not as deep or as bitter as that of the Liberals. When war-weariness set in, MacDonald drafted a War Aims memorandum which was adopted by the TUC and the Labour Party, and published in December 1917. Around this peace plan, similar to President Wilson's Fourteen Points (1918),† the various elements of the Party were able to reunite. The loss of working men in the trenches probably saddened the possible protagonists in any internal squabble to a point beyond bitterness. By November 1918 Labour was able to vote heavily in favour of leaving the Coalition and fighting the election as an independent party.

In the short run this policy was unsuccessful. Most of the soldiers did not vote, and the 58 per cent of the electorate who did gave the Conservative-weighted Coalition a massive majority. The principal Labour men, including MacDonald himself, were badly beaten. But the 1922 election, fought with the Coalition broken by its own impossible internal tensions, and on a much higher poll (71 per cent) showed the decision to have been wise.

* Grey was Foreign Secretary from 1905–16. His undeclared support for the French was blamed for the war, especially by the anti-French elements on the left.
† The American President's Fourteen Points brought false optimism to bear on the Peace Settlement at Versailles. His proposals, which included self-determination and national independence, were thwarted during the Conference by Lloyd George and Clemenceau, the French leader.

Between 1918 and 1922 MacDonald worked hard to re-habilitate himself with the rest of the Party, and produced *Parliament and Revolution* in 1919 and *Parliament and Democracy* in 1921. These were classic statements of the case for social democracy, answering the arguments of G. D. H. Cole and the other Guild Socialists,* as well as the pressures for direct action, syndicalism and violence which had been puffed up by the post-war boom and the appalling inactivity of the Coalition. Having declared the need for at least a million homes for heroes, Lloyd George contrived 1200 by 1920. It was a difficult period, although war-exhaustion had probably drawn any real revolutionary sting. The miners fought a series of battles with the Government, over nationalization and pay reductions, but talk of revolution seemed hopelessly unrealistic when the promised support of the railwaymen and transport workers failed to materialize, and they were left to their fate. The unions could barely coordinate a strike, let alone capture the machinery of government. MacDonald's efforts held the ILP steady (it turned sharply leftwards as soon as his attentions were diverted), and his books and speeches provided the ammunition for the intellectual battle with the Communists, who tried to exploit the failure of the unions to support the miners. Mary Hamilton, subsequently a Labour MP and confidante of Mac-Donald's, gives him credit for having destroyed the 'Communist infection' in the Party during this period.

When MacDonald returned to Parliament in 1922 the Party, now expanded to 142 MPs, paid tribute to his singular breadth of appeal to the left (as an opponent of war) and to the right (as a 'slow' Socialist) by electing him leader once more. J. H. Thomas, the railwaymen's leader, who had been expected to support J. R. Clynes, the trade union 'nominee' who had filled MacDonald's place after the war, decisively voted for MacDonald. The Party had missed him more than it had

* The Guild Socialists wanted to base the new society on workers' control, exercised through unions of producers and consumers. MacDonald was specific in rejecting Cole's argument that 'the transformation required is fundamentally not political but economic'.

5

realized. The colourless loyalty of Clynes could not compete with MacDonald's serious, romantic, albeit unspecific, socialism. MacDonald has been under-estimated as a Party manager, although probably not by the people who voted for him. He was good at balancing interests and men, and talked brilliantly at a moment when Labour did not quite know how to ask for what it wanted.

Baldwin, the new Tory leader, decided to seek a popular endorsement for his protectionist policy, and found his large majority whittled down to nothing in the 1923 election. Labour, with 191 members, was the largest opposition party, and with Asquith's acquiescence took office as a minority Government on 22 January 1924. There was little that the Party could do on the domestic front, entirely dependent as it was upon Liberal votes. There was a notable success by the Clydesider John Wheatley, in housing policy,* and Fred Jowett† had his own way with the inscription on Edith Cavell's statute ('Patriotism is not enough'). In foreign affairs, however, there was more room for manœuvre, and it was in anticipation of this that MacDonald yielded to a round-robin from the ILP (pressing him to take the Foreign Office to prevent it going to J. H. Thomas) and combined the premiership with Foreign Affairs. There was some progress in the negotiations with Russia, and MacDonald was generally rated a success. But in the end the Government's very existence was its real justification. It proved that the working man could sit in the Cabinet and that the old order could be overthrown if the people wanted it badly enough, even if the engine driver carried a cocked hat with him when he went to see the King.‡ MacDonald's own career was something like that. He knew that in his lifetime the victories could only be symbolic, but he

---

* Wheatley, as Minister of Health, introduced a system of Government housing subsidies, which provided for an annual grant of £9 over forty years for houses built to let at controlled rents.

† Jowett was a leading figure in the Bradford ILP, an MP from 1906, and Minister of Works in the 1924 Government.

‡ J. H. Thomas was much abused for seeming to enjoy court ceremonial.

devoted many hours of writing and speaking to explaining how the symbols might come alive.

Socialism; Critical and Constructive, first published in 1921 as a major theoretical argument on the nature of production and distribution, was reissued in 1924, partly to capitalize on public interest in Socialism, and partly to point the moral of the Government's existence.

The first Labour Government did not last out the year. J. R. Campbell, acting editor of the *Workers' Weekly*, was arrested over an article that was alleged to be an incitement to mutiny. The case was withdrawn after questions from Labour MPs. The Conservatives criticized the Government for dropping the charges, and the Liberals called for a Select Committee of Inquiry. The Cabinet decided to treat these motions as matters of confidence, and so when the Liberal motion was supported by the Tories, the Government was doomed. For MacDonald, weary of minority, the issue was an excuse for a dissolution. The 1924 Election produced a large Tory majority, and Labour subsequently blamed the 'red scare' provoked by the Zinoviev letter* for its defeat. Even so, Labour's total vote rose, despite the loss of forty seats.

MacDonald led the Party through the years of oppositions resisting all pleas for a more aggressively socialist programme, and declining the increasingly vocal ILP plans for action. His insistent moderation helped thwart Baldwin's 'Safety First'† appeal in 1929, and to secure the election of the largest number of Labour MPs ever. But even with 288 members, the Parliamen-

---

* During the election campaign several papers, including *The Times*, published a letter, allegedly from Zinoviev, President of the Communist International, urging the British Communists to pressurize the Labour Party into ratifying the Russian Treaty. This seemed to associate Labour's foreign policy with revolution, an impression heightened by confusion over the letter's authenticity and MacDonald's handling of it.

† Baldwin's 1929 General Election appeal was based on his own calm and complacent manner and epitomized in the slogan 'Safety First'. The intended contrast was, of course, with wild Socialism. Apparently this was the basis of Tory election tactics throughout the Twenties.

tary Labour Party was still in a minority, and still crippled by the need to win Liberal support. The Party was unable to take positive initiatives on unemployment or social policy, although once again Foreign Affairs were handled with distinction, this time by Arthur Henderson. But on this occasion the fall of the Government was not induced by the Liberals.

In July 1931 a run on the pound led to a serious financial crisis. Bankers advised that it was due to lack of confidence in the Government, and called for a balanced budget. This meant substantial cuts in Government expenditure, including a considerable reduction in the over-stretched unemployment benefit. MacDonald wanted to carry the measures with the Labour Party and the Opposition, but after a meeting of the General Council of the TUC it was clear that although most members of the Cabinet had initially seen the necessity for the economies, at least nine would resign rather than vote for them. The idea of a National Government under MacDonald's leadership was only mooted after it emerged that Labour could not carry on, and that the Liberals and Tories did not want the single-handed responsibility and unpopularity involved. The King, Baldwin and Samuel (the Liberal leader) all pressed MacDonald to stay and see out the crisis, and he eventually agreed, expecting it to be a temporary expedient. His own attitude is perhaps reflected in a letter he wrote to J. S. Middleton (the Party's assistant secretary) on 29 August: 'I know I have done the right thing for both the country and the Party, and I am much encouraged by the support I am having from the older friends in the Socialist Movement. So soon as I am freed from my day to day burdens, I shall turn my attention to Party opinion without in any way dividing the organization or making strife. I hate the kind of praise I am getting for the moment and place no value upon it. . . . It looks as though we have saved the country from a general Act of Moratorium. . . .'*

In fact, MacDonald stayed well beyond the needs of the moment, and clinched the myth that he had betrayed the

* J. R. MacDonald to J. S. Middleton, 29 August 1931, *J. S. Middleton Papers.*

Movement by presiding, with Philip Snowden* and J. H.
Thomas, over a General Election in October 1931, which saw
Labour reduced to an ignominious rump of 52, and himself
the prisoner of an overwhelming Conservative majority. The
Labour Party expelled them all as soon as the National Govern-
ment was formed, and bitterness and disillusionment set in
which was to last a generation. MacDonald continued as Prime
Minister until 1935, steadily more incoherent, isolated and
unhappy. He died at sea in 1937, after two years as Lord
President of the Council.

The rejection of MacDonald in 1931, and the legend of his
betrayal had a profound effect upon the Labour Movement.
The man who, more than any other, embodied the ideals of
hundreds of thousands of ordinary Labour Party supporters,
seemed to have abandoned them for aristocratic company and
the pleasures of office. The longer he stayed, presiding over
Tory cabinets, the more firmly was the legend entrenched. The
romantic, gentlemanly idealism had turned sour, and was rejected. But although MacDonald was vilified and spurned, his
ideas were not. The controversy over MacDonald's treachery
inhibited any genuine discussion of his ideas, or even an understanding of the underlying continuity in the Party's development. It is this false emphasis on 1931 which this essay is intended to correct.

* Snowden was a Yorkshire ILP agitator and Chancellor of the
Exchequer in the Labour Governments of 1924 and 1929. Although
he hated MacDonald, his opinions and political career followed the
same path. In the 1931 Election campaign he denounced a Labour
Party manifesto he had helped draft, calling it 'Bolshevism run mad'.
This was even more bitter for some Labour followers than Mac-
Donald's defection. But it is not true to say, as a Colne Valley heckler
did, that Snowden was 'nowt but a Liberal'. Like MacDonald, he
was impressed by Thomas Kirkup's *Inquiry into Socialism*, and in the
only House of Commons debate on Socialism (March 1923) reduced
the Government side to tatters with his brilliant advocacy, which
reads impressively to this day.

Introduction

Ramsay MacDonald has been frequently blamed for the alleged weakness or paralysis of the Labour Party. For a while, at least, a denunciation of him was one way of establishing a reputation for loyalty to the 'movement'. The events of 1931 and a penchant for convoluted English earned him a good deal of odium, personal and political. Even writers who have avoided vindictiveness have seen dire consequences for the Labour Party in his style of leadership. Tom Nairn (1965, p. 185), for example, argues that the Party's right-wing in Parliament let it down: 'Nor was this betrayal the result of individual hypocrisy or moral degeneration, as the left has too often said; it followed logically from the whole orientation of Fabianism. Evolutionism, or "gradualism" divorces the end-state of socialism from the actual steps taken to achieve it.' More recently MacDonald has been identified as a utopian socialist whose eyes, fixed on the golden dawn of a new age, were quite unable to see the sensible solutions offered by radical economists like Maynard Keynes.*

These cataclysmic accounts at least acknowledge the importance of MacDonald's contribution to the Party, both as leader and theorist. His intellect, now so heavily sneered at,† was once respected and admired. Contemporaries were anxious to proclaim his influence and power. Bruce Glasier, for example, felt that MacDonald was an integral part of the 'political developments of our time', and claimed that: '. . . his extraordinary

* Skidelsky (1967, p. xii). For a full survey of these critics see R. Harrison, 'Labour Government: then and now', *Political Quarterly*, vol. 41, no. 1.
† As in F. Williams (1965, p. 67).

political capacity, and his high seriousness as a protagonist, are recognized wide over Europe and the world' (1919). He felt that: 'No socialist writer, not even Kautsky, has more thoroughly digged down to the roots of political institutions or searched out the implications of socialist dogmas', (ibid.).' A more academic critic, Max Beer, was no less impressed, and he gave up several pages of his 1919 *History of British Socialism* to friendly comment: 'Next to Bruce Glasier stands James Ramsay MacDonald, who from a Scottish pupil-teacher and London journalist has risen to the front rank of writers and leaders of the Socialist movement. His favourite studies were biological. Spencer's works and Ritchie's *Darwinism and Politics* appear to have influenced him most ... and in giving his best to the movement he has been adding much to his own intellectual stature ...' (1919, p. 312). M. A. Hamilton, a perceptive journalist and subsequently author of a solid work on Arthur Henderson, found him different 'not only intellectually, but morally, from his competitors' (1925, p. 9). Later, she reflected that: 'In the days when he gave himself the intensive schooling in history and general science, which furnished his well-stored mind, economics was in its infancy' (1944, p. 125). *The Times* seemed to accept Lord Elton's opinion that: 'While other future leaders were struggling with the Labour theory of value, or the problem of trade union organization, MacDonald was lecturing for the ethical societies, studying Swedenborg.'* H. W. Nevinson was reported to have commented on MacDonald's 1924 election tour: 'The trained intellect is there, the record of hard, intellectual toil, the wide and accurate knowledge of the world and its problems' (Hamilton, 1925, p. 105), while the London correspondent of *Vorwarts* declared that he was 'beyond question the outstanding figure of international socialism' (Wertheimer, 1929, p. 174). Even his critics noted that he 'took broad views and was far-sighted' and 'argued on broad principles' (Kirkwood, 1935, p. 222). Beatrice Webb frequently denounced MacDonald in her diary for his lack of

* In a review of Lord Elton's *Life of James Ramsay MacDonald*, *The Times*, 21 March 1939.

sincerity, incipient Liberalism and disloyalty, but admitted he was a 'leading propagandist socialist' (1952, 12 December 1923). Howard Gray of the *Observer* thought he was 'one of the best educated men in public life' and spoke of the 'high intellectual quality of some of his utterances' (19 March 1939).

After 1922 the Labour Party seems to have been well satisfied with its leader, anxious to install him as a writer and thinker of the first order. Whatever authority and stature MacDonald achieved with his dozen volumes of social and political theory between 1905 and 1921 was certainly enhanced by the desire of many labour supporters to establish a legitimate tradition of British Socialism, with its own prophets and interpreters. MacDonald's view of Marx, and his attempt to provide a realistic alternative, struck a true note among his Labour audiences up and down the country. As he put it: 'The mechanical and formal conception of social evolution which Marx held, together with the inadequate reason he assigned for the conduct of individuals and of classes are seed unfitted for our historical soil' (1905, p. xix). It was feeling like this that made Wilfrid Whiteley, a Huddersfield Socialist, say of Marx: 'His line of thought and that of the SDF – they didn't appeal to me as much as the ILP type of socialism with its "human brotherhood" and its ethical side and the "class war" side didn't appeal to me at all' (1969).

MacDonald's reputation, in part, was a function of the Labour Party's desire for acknowledgement and respectability, as well as an indication of the real influence he had. His social theory, on the other hand, had a widespread impact upon his contemporaries and probably upon the development of the Labour Party itself which was infinitely more complex and subtle than the utopianism or biological Socialism normally found in the lists against him. Although his books contain confusions and misunderstandings, sitting uneasily balanced between analysis and advocacy, they nevertheless represent a coherent, systematic and sustained attempt to formulate a theory of Socialism that would work in England, an alternative to the ideas of the SDF urgently required by the nascent labour Movement. Mac-

Donald's reasons for seeking to develop such a theory, and the role he hoped his ideas would play in the party's growth, should help balance the orthodox picture of the man, and substantially aid our understanding of his contribution to the future of British Socialism.

A straightforward exposition of MacDonald's argument is, however, hindered by his awareness of his place in a tradition of British Socialist writing, of which he saw himself as the leading exponent and interpreter. He was not the only Socialist to be preoccupied with traditions, influence and cross-fertilization between thinkers. The pages of E. R. Pease and Sidney Webb are heavily laden with a similar burden of attempts to establish a self-contained and self-confident pedigree, and remind the reader of MacDonald's habit of filling his books with recitations about the history of socialist ideas. This effort to create a British Socialism with roots of its own, respectable and authoritative, reflects the search for a distinct identity and the need to reassure the electorate about the intentions of Socialists. It was as if the very number of Socialist writers and the weight of their non-revolutionary pages were expected to prove that Socialism was neither wild nor irresponsible. There was also a pedagogic element. Works like *Socialism* were intended to be read by young workmen, and to feed the flames of anti-capitalist discontent.

This poses a number of problems for the historian. It is easy to build up an attractive genetic pattern for English Socialism on the strength of sentences like this one from Webb: 'Owing mainly to the efforts of Comte, Darwin and Herbert Spencer we can no longer think of the ideal society as an unchanging state' (1889, p. 31). Later he is even more comprehensive: 'Then came Maurice, Kingsley, Ruskin and others who dared to impeach the current middle-class cult; until finally, through Comte, and John Stuart Mill, Darwin and Herbert Spencer, the conception of the Social Organism has at last penetrated to the minds, though not yet to the books, even of our professors of Political Economy' (ibid., p. 46). E. R. Pease's (1918) chapter on the sources of Fabian Socialism contrives to catalogue the names of Darwin, Spencer, Huxley, Comte, J. S. Mill, Harrison, Lavelaye, Henry George, Owen, Marx, Hyndman, Headlam, Maurice, Kingsley, Shaw, Champion, Olivier, Marson and Moll in fourteen pages. Such a tradition would defy interpretation, whether it cohered or not. The Fabians, in other words, were desperate for an intellectual pedigree free from the Marxist taint, and to establish an 'English' background for Socialism. The evolutionary ideas of Comte or Spencer were a good deal more congenial than the drastic analysis Marx and Engels offered. This prejudice has helped distort the origin and the substance of British Socialist ideas. The historian, before pursuing evolutionary Socialism through the pages of Webb, Pease, Comte and Ritchie* has to reflect whether or not he is chasing a myth. The danger is that a critic will spend more time tying down the source of an idea than the idea itself, and will analyse generalities about the influence of one man upon another rather than set out the distinctive features and development of particular ideas. It must always be remembered that whatever the Fabians said about the derivation of their ideas was in itself part of the propaganda for those very ideas. They were committed to building a pantheon, not to close analysis in the history of political thought. However, an understanding of the connections MacDonald saw between his 'authorities', and the emphasis he gave their ideas will throw considerable light on the emergence of his own Socialism and its relationship to the consensus view of Socialism within the Labour Party.

MacDonald's contact with ideas was often second-hand, and the details he gives in his various volumes on the different thinkers† have often been lifted directly from someone else. His unacknowledged debt to Thomas Kirkup, an *Encyclopaedia*

---

* D. G. Ritchie, the author of *Darwinism and Politics* (see Select Bibliography).

† Textbook accounts, with potted biographies and gentle praise, appear in *Socialism, Socialism; Critical and Constructive, The Socialist Movement*, etc., of Saint-Simon, Fourier, Owen and Marx. Others making their appearance include Louis Blanc, Proudhon, Godwin and William Thompson.

Britannica contributor from Wooler, in Northumberland, is best demonstrated by comparing MacDonald's account of Saint-Simon in *Socialism; Critical and Constructive* (1921b, p. 36) with Kirkup's in his *History of Socialism* published twenty-nine years earlier in 1892 (pp. 22–3).* MacDonald's accounts of Marx also occasionally resemble those of Kirkup. The wording and content of many passages in Kirkup's resumé of Socialist thinking are sufficiently like those of Mac-Donald to establish a prima facie case of plagiarism. When MacDonald discusses learnedly the labour theory of value and the views of Rodbertus, Locke, Petty, Adam Smith and Ricardo, while saying nothing that does not appear in the slightly different language of Kirkup, the case is strengthened. Similarly, the flavour of Comte or Saint-Simon in MacDonald's work reminds the critic of Kirkup. More literally than he would have cared to admit, MacDonald shared Kirkup's general view of Socialism: 'Socialism, then, simply means that the normal social organization of the future will and should be an associated or cooperative one. It means that industry should be carried on by the free associated workers. The development of Socialism will follow the development of the large industry; and it will rationally, scientifically and systematically use the mechanical appliances evolved during the industrial revolution for the promotion of a higher life among the masses of the people'

* MacDonald's text said: 'Comte Henri de Saint-Simon belonged to the French aristocracy and was born in 1760 in Paris. He was of the romantically quaint type of humanity, more common then than now. He was visited in his dream by his ancestor, Charlemagne, who told him that his life was to be notable, and he instructed his valet to address him, the first thing every morning, with the reminder: "Remember, monsieur le comte, that you have great things to do." ...'

Kirkup's account of the same episode ran: 'Comte Henri de Saint-Simon, the founder of French Socialism, was born at Paris in 1760. He belonged to a younger branch of the family of the celebrated Duke of that name .... His valet had orders to awake him every morning with the words, "Remember, monsieur le comte, that you have great things to do"; and his ancestor Charlemagne appeared to him in a dream, foretelling a remarkable future for him.'

(Kirkup, 1892, pp. 414–15). Kirkup's stress upon an ethical force ensuring that progress moves along the right lines, and upon the rejection of revolution as upturning 'the fundamental laws of human nature' is echoed in MacDonald's writing. Kirkup also analysed the central problem for those who wished to extend the biological metaphor; 'Is not competition, therefore, the prime condition of social progress? And is not Socialism, therefore, inconsistent with progress?' (ibid., pp. 416–17). His answer is the same as MacDonald's. Social progress is not entirely governed by the 'struggle for existence' – there is an ethical development working parallel with nature, and this ensures that Socialism will work – the ethical component will remove the struggle to a higher plane of social activity.

This plagiarism is unremarkable, and should not be given undue emphasis. It would have been more surprising had an active politician engaged in forming a new party actually had first-hand contact with the writings discussed by MacDonald. His borrowings serve merely to illustrate the argument that lines of influence are seldom direct. Max Beer, for example, asserted that: 'Comte was introduced to the British public by the indefatigable Miss Harriet Martineau and G. H. Lewes. But it was J. S. Mill who brought Comte's influence to bear upon political economy' (1919, p. 232). Evidence from Mill's *Autobiography* appears to clinch it: '. . . the writers by whom, more than by any others, a new mode of political thinking was brought home to me, were those of the Saint-Simonian school in France . . . but I was greatly struck with the connected view which they for the first time presented to me of the natural order of human progress' (1873, p. 163). But in fact MacDonald, who learned a great deal from Comte and Saint-Simon, acquired his knowledge from Kirkup rather than Mill or G. H. Lewes. It is, however, the use he made of ideas that were 'in the air' that matters, rather than their precise derivation.

The contribution of Comte and Saint-Simon to Socialist or radical thought has always been assessed in terms of either development or evolution. MacDonald himself speaks rather slightingly of Saint-Simon, suggesting that he was an out-of-date utopian Socialist whom Darwin had up-staged. In fact, there are some very modern ideas in the arguments of both Comte and Saint-Simon, which MacDonald develops and elaborates for his own purposes. Sidney Pollard has taken the view that: '. . . it is the recognizably Saint-Simonian type of Socialism which has held the stage since his day, and still offers itself as the most credible alternative to capitalism at the present time' (1968, p. 100) and argues that: 'Those who, like Saint-Simon, were driven to join with the working classes, could henceforth do so under the banner of a *dirigiste*, expert-controlled state Socialism' (ibid., p. 99). MacDonald obtained two important ideas from the positivist 'tradition'. The first of these is the conception of an industry which will, in the course of its own natural development in line with the laws of history, resolve its own problems. Antagonisms between capital and labour can only obstruct progress. The second notion is of the role to be played by science as a principle of social organization. Man must understand the laws of historical development so that he can be in harmony with the unfolding of society: intellectual reform must precede social reform. Although MacDonald probably picked up the broad outlines of these ideas from his London contacts during the nineties, and perhaps by reading Kirkup, it is necessary to turn to Comte and Saint-Simon to see these conceptions in their clearest form.

Saint-Simon and Comte have competing claims to originality in the development of positivism. They collaborated, and Comte has been seen alternatively as either the power behind the throne, or the hard-working propagandist disciple. However, the publication of the *Mémoire sur la science de l'homme*, written in 1813 but not published until 1859, shows that Saint-Simon had already developed a positivist programme before he met Comte. On the other hand, while Saint-Simon was still searching for a universal conception to hold his positivist synthesis together, perhaps the laws of physics or gravity, Comte showed that the unifying factor was scientific method itself.

Saint-Simon shared with Comte a conception of a science of

history based on discoverable laws, producing inevitable and predictable results. As Comte put it: 'I showed them that the crucial discovery of sociological laws made by me in 1822 gave me, at the age of twenty-four, true cerebral unity, by effecting complete convergence of the two sets of tendencies, scientific and political, which, till then, had divided my attention' (1851, vol. I, p. ix). Comte's argument is that the discovery of sociological laws provides the basis for a synthesis on the plan laid down by science, which is now concentrated on the study of humanity. In other words, industry is developing along certain lines and through the application of sociological study man can come to understand the laws of its development, and align himself accordingly. Comte contends that the predominant tendency in all animal life is towards species forming themselves into collective organisms. He sees no clash between the interests of capital and labour: his emphasis is upon the unity of human nature. Social change is not going to come through the antagonisms of class society, as Marx held, but through the unfolding of industry itself, according to the laws of history. Human conflict, of whatever kind, can only obstruct progress. Comte's view is of the development and concentration of industry, and of the accumulation of wealth. Raymond Aron has described it in these terms: 'Material civilization can advance only if each generation produces more than it needs to survive and consequently transmits to the following generation a greater accumulation of capital than it received' (1965, p. 71). The study of historical laws in the light of the positivist synthesis convinced Comte that: '. . . the grand object of human existence was the constant improvement of the natural order that surrounds us; of our material condition' (quoted in Bowle, 1954, p. 123). It is a case of the organic world combining to exploit the inorganic world. His study of the laws of history gives him faith in the development of society in the right direction, and he urges that man must ensure harmony between himself and the laws of society. Saint-Simon's position is similar: 'Toute la société doit travailler à l'amélioration de l'existence morale et physique de la classe la plus pauvre; la société doit s'organiser de la manière la plus convenable pour lui faire atteindre ce grand but' (ibid., p. 113).

MacDonald's position resembles this view of industry growing in complexity yet providing within its own development the solution to present problems. He insists on the unity of industry: the Socialist frowns on 'recent developments in the conflicts between capital and labour... he believes they are both immoral and uneconomic and will lead to disaster' (1921b, p. vii; p. 169 in this volume). He often refers to the necessary evolution of industry, and frequently denounces revolutionary means as disruptive of natural development. MacDonald objected to strikes not because they disrupted the economy but because they delayed 'socialism'. There would be nothing remarkable in this if all MacDonald had acquired was a vague idea about the evolution of industry. What is unusual is the readiness with which he absorbed the positivist notion that industry is progressing in a beneficial direction, and that very development, even if it at present creates misery and suffering, contains the solution to social problems within itself. He accepts, in effect, the positivist offering of a scientific notion of progress in the place of a providential one.

Saint-Simon's closing remark in the *Nouveau Christianisme*, that society must organize itself, is the key to the principle of social organization which the positivists 'discovered'. Saint-Simon's important contribution was to realize the social function of technology; he saw that applied science was of vital importance in creating a civilization of the mass. MacDonald was well aware of Saint-Simon's pioneer work on this principle of social organization: 'He would put men of science into the position of the medieval church, and the available labour of the community was to be organized and controlled by them' (1921b, p. 37). In MacDonald's hands this principle of social organization becomes socialism itself: 'The Socialist doctrine systematizes these industrial changes. It lays down a law of capitalist evolution. It describes the natural history of society' (1921b, p. 3). This idea is closely related to Comte's, as described by Raymond Aron: 'It is not by the accidents of revolution nor by violence that a society in crisis will be reorganized, but through a synthesis of the sciences and by the creation of positive politics' (1965, pp. 60–61). Once the scientist has grasped the essential development of society, it is his responsibility to achieve the intellectual reform of society which is essential if there is to be harmony between men and nature. The philosopher will work with the people for this purpose. The positivist position is essentially a propagandist one; to achieve harmony between human will and the laws of development requires active propaganda. Comte's fundamental interest was to spread a way of thinking which would automatically lead to the just organization of society and the state.

Comte and MacDonald draw similar conclusions from the belief that the order of nature necessarily contains within itself the germ of all possible progress. Comte argues: 'The effective impulse towards social regeneration depends, then, on one ultimate condition; the formation of a firm alliance between philosophers and proletaries' (1851, p. 119). MacDonald's method of putting the principle of social organization into practice follows the same path: 'To establish an organic relationship has now become the task of society. This task, become the subject of political propaganda and the guide of social change, is known as Socialism' (1905, p. 35). Comte's point is that: '... the primary object ... of positivism ... is to generalize our scientific conceptions and to systematize the art of life' (Bowle, 1954, p. 121). MacDonald's conclusion is that: '... the preparation before the revolution must be one of political propaganda, which creates the new society in the bosom of the old' (1919(b), p. 31) for 'If the people cannot construct Socialism in their minds they cannot build it into their institutions' (ibid., p. 59; p. 223 in this volume). For Comte the object of the alliance between his philosophers and workers will be 'to set in motion the force of public opinion ... the principle feature of the State to which we are tending will be the increased influence which public opinion is destined to exercise' (1851, p. 110). In *Socialism and Society* MacDonald envisages a moral sense in the individual constantly attacking a morally

inefficient state of society. The state of public opinion is, therefore, of critical importance to those who wish to bring the
principle of social organization into practice. Propaganda will
be the central weapon in bringing men into harmony with the
evolution of industry. The Marxist, believing in the self-
destructiveness of capitalism, would resort to propaganda only
as a way of rescuing political agitators from the armchair during
a pre-determined revolution. For MacDonald, though, propaganda is central, for he retains an eighteenth-century faith
in moral will, which can keep pace with industrial development,
and which only needs summoning into action.

MacDonald's emphasis upon propaganda, as the prime form
of political activity, is discussed below. It is sufficient here to
note that the positivists were equally insistent about a parallel
movement of will and development, working through public
opinion.

In developing his argument from these positivist roots
MacDonald turned to the state of classical political economy, with
its anti-collectivist bias, and its happy optimism about a natural
identity of interests between the producer and consumers.
Liberal economics had to be discredited before he could introduce his alternative. For his criticism of *laisser-faire* he went
to Ruskin, rather than Mill, who is generally supposed to have
applied the brakes to philosophic radicalism. This preference
was probably stimulated by his friend J. A. Hobson, who had
written a long book praising Ruskin's contribution to the
understanding of the 'new' industry, but it was sustained by
Ruskin's emphases in the study of society. This is remarkable,
because Ruskin was never popular with the leading radical/
Labour writers. E. R. Pease is quite explicit in denying Ruskin
as an influence on Fabian circles: 'I think that the value of his
social teachings was concealed from most of us at that time by
reaction against his religious medievalism, and indifference to
his gospel of art. Books so eminently adapted for young ladies
at mid-Victorian schools did not appeal to modernists educated
by Comte and Spencer' (1918, p. 27). Bernard Shaw agreed
with him. 'It is a curious fact that of the three great propagandist

Ramsay MacDonald's Political Writings

amateurs of political economy, Henry George, Marx and Ruskin, Ruskin alone seems to have had no effect on the Fabians ... Ruskin's name was hardly mentioned in the Fabian Society' (ibid., Appendix I, p. 278). Yet Ruskin's ideas were important. Hobson believed that: 'Ruskin's work will hereafter be recognized as the first serious attempt in England to establish a scientific basis of economic study from the social standpoint' (1898, p. 106–7). Perhaps it was because Ruskin himself was not a professional economist that his dissatisfaction with the generalization of ends implicit in the utilitarian case, and his reluctance to believe in the coincidence of interest between employer and employed led where they did. He did not change economics, but he showed the social relevance of economic study, and gave practical advice to those who were working for Keir Hardie's 'new moral world'. The aesthetic tone of his condemnation of liberalism did little to popularize his ideas, but while the Fabians were still leaning on Ricardo's theory of rent he was offering a two-pronged attack on classical economics, which revealed the work economists could and should be doing in a modern industrial state.

In the first place he argued that utility was no longer an adequate criterion for social judgement, that quality was as important as quantity, and that what was really needed was a concept of value. In the second, he insisted that attention should be turned from production to what today would be called 'the quality of life'.* Together these involved a scientific approach to society, intent on the preservation of human values in the centre of the industrial machine.

Ruskin begins with an attack on the individualism of the orthodox writers: 'It can never be shown generally either that the interests of master and labourer are alike, or that they are opposed; for, according to circumstances, they may be either' (1862, p. 7). He disapproves of the attempt to balance human interests by expediency, and to predict human actions on the basis of motives of greed and idleness. He argues that man has a soul which is beyond the reach of the economists' equations.

* This notion would include the idea of social or distributive justice.

22

Introduction

The 'buy cheap/sell dear' mechanism is demonstrably inadequate: 'We do not sell our prime-ministership by Dutch
auction; nor, on the decease of a bishop, whatever may be the
general advantages of simony . . . offer his diocese to the higher
bidder . . .' (ibid., p. 18). Ruskin does not deny that a science
may be constructed on these assumptions as to the nature and
aim of man, and may be consistent and logical in its internal
organization, but he will not accept this science as applicable
to actually existent men and their conduct. 'Economic man' is
a hypothesis, and to study man from the viewpoint of the industrial machine in competition is to lose sight of the real man
in favour of the model. Hobson pin-points the source of Ruskin's refutation of the model: 'Mr Ruskin had early come to
recognize that work is not an evil to be shunned but a good to
be desired, provided it is in kind and quantity desirable' (1898,
p. 67). The willingness of Professor Marshall and other modern
writers to consider 'disturbing influences' and the role of the
'affections' was all very well, but such writers were only prepared to consider such influences in so far as they could be placed
upon a common economic footing with the main driving forces
of idleness and greed.

He concedes that J. S. Mill had already covered some of this
ground: 'He deserves honour among economists by inadver-
tently disclaiming the principles which he states, and tacitly
introducing the moral consideration with which he declares his
science has no connection . . .' (1862, p. 110). 'It appears, then,
according to Mr Mill, that usefulness and agreeableness underlie the exchange value, and must be ascertained to exist in the
thing, before we can esteem it an object of wealth' (ibid., p. 112).
This shift of emphasis from an object's use to its value clearly
demands a new understanding of the role of economics. Ruskin's definition of value is an exacting one: 'The value of a
thing, therefore, is independent of opinion and quantity . . .'
(ibid., p. 118) '. . . it depends on the person, much more than
on the article, whether its usefulness or ab-usefulness will be
the quality developed in it' (ibid., p. 124). Hobson underscored
the significance of this change: 'His full, final conception of

23

Ramsay MacDonald's Political Writings

Political Economy, as a science of human welfare, includes within its scope not merely the processes by which men gain a livelihood, but all human efforts and satisfactions. . . . Now Mr Ruskin insists that the organic unity of man as a conscious, rational being, with a capacity for regarding his life as a whole and forming a place for its conduct, imposes a corresponding unity upon the science which is to treat of human conduct' (1898, pp. 74-5).

The shift from utility to value involves a parallel shift from the problems of the maximization of production to the difficulties of a distributive mechanism that places welfare before profit and value before money. In Hobson's view the biologists and sociologists who were giving an intellectual form to science and the art of life owed a great deal to Ruskin, although he lacked an adequate sense of continuous development. His view is moral, ethical and human, and his argument is that the country's prosperity can be as much advanced by educating the consumer as by improving the 'arts of the producer'. Ruskin's sees society as an organic and interdependent whole, and it is this view which demands the consideration of the social consequences of economic action. It is easy to see how these arguments must have commended themselves to MacDonald, especially as he probably saw them through Hobson's eyes. Ruskin demonstrated that there was an alternative to classical political economy, and provided the 'science of human welfare'. The potentiality of this idea was not lost on MacDonald, who was searching for an alternative to the Marxist formulation of socialist economics. But the line of influence was not direct.

J. A. Hobson was not wholly satisfied with Ruskin's case, and added to it a conception of progress and development which seemed to be founded in observation of the growing complexity and evolution of modern industry. It was in this developmental form that these ideas reached MacDonald, and had their greatest impact on his thought. Hobson's quarrel was with Ruskin's belief that man is a constant, and that there was one specific ideal of society, independent of race, place and age. As an alternative to Ruskin's 'specific types' Hobson offered an

24

evolving society in which old values were constantly adjusted to new conditions, and new objects were assigned their true value. He believed that Ruskin's ethical arguments would have been stronger with biological support, and tried to make good this deficiency himself, supplying the notion of a struggle for existence passing through various phases: '. . . this identity and continuity of organic processes, which by continuous strengthening of social forces raises the struggle for life to a higher plane, in which the struggle of societies plays a more important part, imposing a more social test of "fitness" upon the struggles of individuals, are essential for the realization of rational order in the universe' (1898, p. 105). It is true that Ruskin lacked a view of human development, and retained a utilitarian notion of the fixity of human nature. However, his discontent with industrial conditions, and the constructive policy he proposed, do not suggest a complete absence of an evolutionary dimension. His refusal to divorce work and enjoyment, his insistence on value, his protest against the division between producer and consumer, and the science of human welfare he recommended represent an essentially original argument, developed beyond the road block of prolonged industrial disorder and squalor which *laisser-faire* economics had imposed on itself. Hobson's anxieties about the transition from competition to co-operation lead him to biological analogies for reassurance. Although his own view of development almost certainly arose from his observation of the working of industry and its organization, he lacked Ruskin's conviction that the rational application of the findings of a science of welfare would be sufficient to ensure co-operation. He wanted to reconcile the naturalist's contention that progress came through competition with the sociologist's belief that the natural development of industry was towards co-operation. He tried to bridge parallel arguments, but did not depend upon the biological analogy for his view of progress. The essential stimulus to a science of society was Ruskin's shift from utility to value, and from production to distribution, not the application of the biological evidence.

Bernard Porter has convincingly argued that Ruskin was not

the source of Hobson's ideas on the organic integrity and unity of human activities, or on the organic nature of the co-operation of social units (1968, p. 173). Porter makes the point that Hobson uses biology, the 'new knowledge', to shore up democratic liberalism, but in fact he did no more than illustrate independently argued propositions with this 'Darwinian' evidence.

Hobson argues, for example, that social evolution will be achieved when society learns to '. . . bring its conscious will to bear upon the work of constructing new social and industrial forms to fit the new economic conditions . . .' (quoted in Porter, 1968, p. 174). There can be no conscious will in biology, and the direct application of biology to social studies would lead to outright determinism. The possibility of a fully integrated society acting according to the criterion of an ethically and rationally conceived standard of 'social utility' owes more to the development of political economy through Mill and Ruskin, and Hobson's own observation of detailed developments in industry, than to any biological platitudes current in the thought of his time. Porter probably goes too far in arguing that Ruskin's only important contribution was the notion that the pursuit of wealth was not always beneficial for everyone, and consequently that old style individualism needed to be abandoned. No doubt many people felt dissatisfied with the atomistic structure of nineteenth-century political thinking, without analysing the deficiencies or offering an alternative. Ruskin did both of these things, and therein lies his importance.

Hobson believed that men could consider their own rational interests and act upon them: that the economics of even nineteenth-century society was within the sphere of human volition. If the 'laws' of economics were beyond human control, the social problem was insoluble. It is in this context that Ruskin's insistence on value is so important. The ethical basis was essential to an approach which argued that a science of society could yield results that were usable. Hobson also drew on Ruskin's prognosis about the continued pursuit of production for profit. Ruskin's answer was to shift the locus of study from production to distribution and co-operation. Hobson's thesis, the statement of the 'evolution of capitalism', which will be examined below, depended upon the possibility of men guiding the system. And that possibility hinged upon the shift to co-operation. Hobson's saving and underconsumption theories, which made his name, were essentially devices for restoring human values in the field of distribution, and in establishing a relationship between production and distribution that rested on human need rather than the workings of the market.

The alternative critique of political economy which was open to MacDonald was, of course, the Marxist analysis. MacDonald frequently referred to Marx, although he appears to have read only the *Communist Manifesto*. His attitude towards Marx is direct enough: '... while fully accepting the collectivist and Socialist conclusions of Marx, we must explain and defend them with a different conception of society in our minds ...' (1905, p. 109; p. 81 in this volume). This different conception is generally expressed in the old formula of revolution versus evolution. The British Socialist, reluctant to accept the class struggle, is alleged to have swallowed 'evolutionary Socialism' in one mouthful. The danger of this argument is that it leads into a general view of democratic Socialism as a sweetly reasonable and pragmatic position where idealists hang their hats, and wait for society to 'grow'. It would be much more accurate to characterize the distinction between Marx and MacDonald by saying that while Marx was interested in the development of capitalism, MacDonald concerned himself with the growth of industry. The *Communist Manifesto* is a sociological statement, while *Socialism and Government* provides an account of social institutions that will accompany the development of industry. This difference in subject matter led to quite distinct social analyses. One critic has noticed that: 'The problems of production and distribution could not be divorced from political theory: production raises the question of the functions of government and the limits of its intervention in trade and industry: distribution involves questions of property, justice and equality' (Bury, 1932, p. 172).

This separation of production and distribution is a characteristic of the political economists. MacDonald took up the position that when industry had developed, and had overcome the problems of production, it would then turn to solve the problems of distribution. His interest is indeed 'property, justice and equality'. The instrument of social change is to be the increasing technical capacity of industry. Marx, on the other hand, would not have acknowledged production and distribution as separate categories. For him they are part of the same process, and are both subject to the same laws. For Marx, the agent of social change is the antagonism within the capitalist mode of production. As Raymond Aron has interpreted this point (1965, p. 114), the capitalist system is able to produce more and more, but in spite of this increase in wealth, poverty remains the lot of the majority. This contradiction, in Marx's view, will eventually produce a revolutionary crisis.

It was precisely this revolutionary crisis, and its apparent inevitability, that British Socialists were most anxious to deny. The term 'evolutionary Socialism' was invented to suggest the possibility that socialism could come by other than revolutionary means, and to discredit Marx as unnecessarily fond of bloodshed and class war. The notion that there are two types of Socialism, 'revolutionary' and 'evolutionary', and that they are opposing views of society, has therefore been established. MacDonald's frequent use of biological parallels and examples* has been taken as proof that he differed from Marx on precisely this point – 'evolution' versus 'revolution'. It seems that MacDonald himself thought that this was the centre of his difference with Marx. Yet, ironically, there is no shortage of evidence that both Marx and Engels regarded themselves as both scientists and evolutionists. For example, Marx wanted to dedicate *Capital* to Darwin, who refused because he did not wish to be associated with attacks on Christianity and Theism.† Engels, apparently,

---

* *Socialism and Society* for example is well-larded with biological allusions, e.g. p. xix, 'the process of organic nutrition is paralleled in the process of social nutrition', or p. 13, 'the work of organic nervous systems is paralleled in society by political functions'.

† Sir Gavin de Beer quoted by Robert Young (1969, p. 138).

'... sometimes referred to Marxist socialism as a theory, a theory of which he says that it is not a dogma, but the exposition of a process of evolution, that it is a "theory of evolution"' (Bottomore and Rubel, 1956, p. 30). Marx and Engels, like MacDonald, wanted to embrace Darwin because they thought that *Origin of Species* confirmed the possibility of endless progress. When Marx first read Darwin's book in 1860 he wrote to Engels that: '... although it is developed in the crude English style, this is the book which contains the basis in natural history for our view' (Young, 1969, p. 138). The aim was to prove progress with biological evidence, but neither MacDonald nor Marx were prepared to accept the pessimistic possibilities of Darwin's theory, with which it had been endowed by Malthus.

MacDonald was sufficiently clear about his superiority here to declare that Marx and Engels had been 'handicapped by having been guided by the metaphysics of Hegelianism rather than by the science of Darwinism' (1909, vol. 2, p. 113).* But his own contribution does not leave the reader much wiser about the precise nature of this 'science of Darwinism'. There is no exposition of natural selection, no talk about 'nature bloody in tooth and claw', no precise discussion of genetics or of the evidence one way or the other, and the structure of Darwin's case is ignored. There is no insistence on man's position in the animal kingdom, no demand that physical and mental phenomena should be treated alike, and certainly no view of progress depending on the selective effects of Malthusian food scarcity. Indeed, MacDonald does not come to terms with any of the problems posed by Darwin, and the state of his knowledge suggests a vague familiarity with the clichés current since

* His extraordinary note on pages 36–7 of *Socialism and Society* reveals his complete failure to understand what Marx was writing about: 'Marx's insistence that each epoch has its own characteristic law of development is inconsistent with the assertion that economic considerations are at the basis of all historical evolution except that of primitive folk.' That MacDonald should have regarded this as Marx's weak spot reflects his general incapacity to come to terms with the concept of the alienation of labour.

Lamarck rather than an awareness of the importance of *Origin of Species*. If anything, MacDonald was closer to those who believed that man was exempt from natural selection because he was socially organized. Of Socialism he wrote: '... it is those very processes themselves applied to human society with such modifications as are necessitated by the fact that they now relate to life which can now consciously adapt itself to its circumstances and aid natural evolution by economizing in experimental waste ...' (Preface to Ferri, 1909, p. vii). If men are exempt, it is nonsense to talk about the importance of Darwin's discoveries for society. MacDonald's optimism is pre-Darwinian, pre-Malthusian, and probably unrelated to any biological data. His conclusion that: '... the Socialist change must be gradual and must proceed by stages, just as the evolution of an organism does' (1905b, p. 73) owes the example only, not the analysis, to biology. He used biology to confirm *a priori* assumptions about social change, derived from other sources. Since this is precisely what Marx was trying to do, it is clearly not satisfactory to describe their disagreement as the opposition of a model of organic growth to a materialistic dialectic of struggle and revolution. MacDonald was no doubt very anxious to impress the public with his 'scientific' researches, and perhaps he believed in this utterly false dichotomy himself. But the fact remains that the arguments he uses about economics and industry are derived from Comte and the English political economists, not Darwin or Lamarck.

Nevertheless, Marx and MacDonald do seriously diverge in their attitudes to revolution. But the dividing line is the sociological analysis of labour, not 'evolution' or materialism. For MacDonald social conflicts are obstructing progress; even the dole is a danger to progress, as it may make the poor lazy. Social confrontations, in his argument, are mere incidents on the way to a higher place of existence. Marx, on the other hand, believes that revolution is the inevitable consequence of capitalism's self-negation. MacDonald accepts that there is a polarity between capital and labour* but retains a tacit faith in the in-

* MacDonald (1921b) e.g., 'Labour considers that it produces for

Introduction

dustrial machinery itself, and believes that it will naturally lead through its own development to the next stage of society. The distributive machinery will be put to rights by labour representation in Parliament, but there is no fundamental critique of the role of Labour. The antagonisms of capital and labour will be left behind by growing technology. The beneficial direction of the development of technical society is assured by the moral claims of individuals, democratically expressed. Socialism's stance is a moral one, and the development of ethical will side by side with technology takes the place of Marxist class struggle, which is repudiated. MacDonald argues: 'The combination that Socialism seeks is not one between the economic interests of labour and capital in the capitalist system, but one between the moral interests of labour and capital in the community' (1921, pp. 109–10). 'Today we are in the economic stage. Yesterday we were in the political stage. Tomorrow we shall be in the moral stage' (1905, p. 36). In this way it emerges that MacDonald did not use biology to close the gap between capital and labour on one hand, and the gradual development of society on the other. He found himself analysing will and industry in the place of capital and labour. He believed that technical change guided by will and expressed in socialism would lead to progress.

Marx, however, places his critique of labour at the centre of the problem, in sharp contrast to MacDonald, who possesses no sociology of labour, and barely mentions the misery and poverty created by the industrial system. Marx maintained that in capitalism the relation of man to his work is unnatural and inhuman. As he put it: '. . . the realization of labour appears as negation to such an extent that the worker is negated to the point of starvation' (quoted in Marcuse, 1941, p. 277). Man works with tools that do not belong to him on products which someone else will sell and which he himself cannot afford. Labour in the capitalist system therefore leads to the alienation

---

capital, not for society . . .' (p. 100; p. 195 in this volume) or 'Labour and capital cannot be reconciled within the capitalist system' (p. 112).

Ramsay MacDonald's Political Writings

of man from his product and hence from himself. The social order progresses through the contradictions inherent in it. The advance of technology reduces the ingredient of labour power, and also reduces the value of labour by increasing competition. This takes out the factor which made capital increase possible through the appropriation of surplus value, and leads to falling profits.

The negativity of the social world is the dynamic of the Marxian dialectic, and carries forward the contradictions of class society, and is the motor of social progress. Marx argues: 'Capitalist production begets, with the inexorability of a law of nature, its own negation ...' (Marx and Engels, 1968, p. 237). 'Centralization of the means of production and socialization of labour at last reach a point where they become incompatible with their capitalist integument' (ibid.). There is no escaping Shlomo Avineri's conclusion that: 'For Marx the question of the inevitability of revolution is a tautology. Since the revolution needs a conscious urge and motor in the form of revolutionary praxis (a self-change in the proletarian *pari passu* with his striving for the revolutionary goal) the dilemma of determinism versus voluntarism is transcended by the dialectical nature of this revolutionary consciousness' (1969, p. 144). MacDonald did not have such an analysis. He regarded Hegel as an incomprehensible mystic, and would not have appreciated Marx's observation: 'The outstanding achievement of Hegel's "Phenomenology" ... is first, that Hegel grasps the nature of Labour and conceives of objective man ... as the result of his own labour' (quoted in Bottomore and Rubel, 1956, p. 18). MacDonald was not much interested in poverty, and his notions about the labour theory of value go no further than text-book summaries. Lacking this perspective MacDonald was forced to fall back on the development of technology as the instrument for social change, complementing it with a rather Rousseauesque conception of human will. The internal developments of political economy, which had oriented it more towards human need, and had emphasized distribution rather than the production that had so absorbed nineteenth-century liberals,

32

clearly provided him with a sound basis for the formulation of his version of 'gradual' socialism.

MacDonald and Marx do not, then, appear in the contra-distinctive light sketched by their followers. It can be seen that Marx's revolution is an inevitable result of his sociological approach to capitalism. It is a further analysis of the problem of social development, not a process distinct from evolution. MacDonald's repudiation of class struggles and revolution is a product of his focus on industry rather than labour and capital. Therefore, although he introduces biological concepts like continuity and growth to fortify his conclusions, the break comes far earlier than he himself seems to have realized. In his hands socialism is a form of descriptive methodology, rather than the full analysis it becomes in the Marxist account.

Once it has been established that Marx and MacDonald are divided on their point of focus rather than on revolution and biology, and that because he lacks an analysis of labour Mac-Donald is forced to depend upon a vision of technical change supplied by positivism, it becomes of critical importance to analyse the developments in English political economy which made this point of view tenable.

Herbert Spencer, more than anyone else, developed the positivist view of society in England, although his concern was with bolstering up utilitarianism, not with urging the creation of a collectivist state. The work of Hobson and Ruskin, on the other hand, showed how man might regain control of the industrial machine, and in so doing, demonstrated how technology might be the source of its own salvation. MacDonald drew heavily on the conclusions of both these lines of argument.

In spite of his protestations of originality,* Spencer is slipped into the same mouthful as Comte and Darwin by Pease, Webb, Shaw and, of course, later historians. He was highly esteemed in radical circles, where *Man versus the State* (Spencer, 1884) tended to be set aside as an old man's spluttering at a new age,

* See the Preface to the 4th edition (May 1880) of *First Principles*, p. v–vi.

and was a close friend of Beatrice Webb. When she married Sidney, Spencer asked her about changing his will, in which he had made her his literary executor. He could not, for the sake of his reputation, be openly connected with a socialist (Muggeridge and Adam, 1967, p. 128). J. A. Hobson, a fellow native of Derby, read Spencer's *Study of Sociology* and was impressed (Hobson, 1938, p. 23). MacDonald's opinion was that Spencer's philosophy had 'contributed to the stability of Socialist thought, mainly by his clear exposition of the fact of social evolution' (1905, p. 156). It can, therefore, be inferred that even if MacDonald had not read Spencer at all closely, the philosopher's ideas were very much 'in the air' in radical circles, as Pease recalls (1918, p. 18). This opinion is confirmed by J. B. Bury who argues that *First Principles* 'probably did more than any other work, at least in England, both to drive home the significance of the doctrine of evolution, and to raise the doctrine of progress to the rank of a commonplace truth in popular estimation, an axiom to which political rhetoric might effectively appeal' (1932, p. 341).

Spencer's idea of development comes from Lyell, and depends upon two key concepts Lyell was adumbrating in his geological treatises. Lyell was putting forward the idea of natural causation, in other words, eliminating divine intervention from earthly affairs, and of continuity in the natural world, which undermined the Neptunist and Catastrophist* positions. Spencer acknowledged this: 'The result of reading this† was that rejecting his adverse arguments, I adopted the hypothesis of development' (Duncan, 1908, p. 536). Lyell's exposition of the Lamarckian case had appealed to many of his contemporaries, but there was not a shred of doubt about his own conclusion that: '. . . the popular theory of the successive development of the animal and vegetable world, from the simplest to the most

---

* The Neptunists (floods) and the Catastrophists (disasters) offered rival geological theories which denied the operation of natural causes. Lyell's formulation insisted that geological history was the result of presently existing forces operating at their present intensity.

† Sir Charles Lyell, *The Principles of Geology*, vol. 1, 1830–33.

perfect forms, rests on a very insecure foundation' (1830, p. 147).
But this was precisely the position Spencer took up, arguing
that progress was a development from the homogeneous to the
heterogeneous, and from the simple to complex. As he put it:
'Evolution, then, under its primary aspect, is a change from
a less coherent form to a more coherent form, consequent on
the dissipation of motion and integration of matter' (1862,
p. 327). In the *Filiation of Ideas*, which is a review of his own
work, Spencer argues that man's moral nature is modifiable,
and capable of progressive adaptation to the social state. This is
the crux of his 'improvement' of the utilitarian case: 'Civilization is described as a continuous moulding of human beings to
the social state, and of the social state to human beings as they
become moulded' (1908, p. 540). The reason that Spencer
denounces the state, and demands freedom for the individual,
is not as inconsistent with his belief that evolution is carrying
itself towards a more perfect social organization as is generally
believed. His argument is that if progress is inevitable the state
is unnecessary, and can only obstruct progress. Spencer's view
of the modifiability of human nature contains more than hints of
relativism. He remarks: '. . . there is . . . an adaptation between
the ideas of right and wrong and the kind of life which inherited
nature and environing conditions produce' (1908, p. 575). Under
such a dispensation the beneficence of evolution is inevitable.
The possibility of determinism is eliminated by his willingness
to extend his conception of social evolution to accommodate
every intervention and non-determined act as part of the
process.

In *Social Statics* Spencer writes: 'Man himself obeys the
law of indefinite variation. His circumstances are ever altering
and he is ever adapting himself to them' (1851, p. 33). Progress,
then, is the mutual adaptation of environment and organism
which at the same time are moving forwards on the simple to
complex continuum. Biology supports his efforts to replace the
utilitarian legislator with an evolutionary process. He sees an
analogy between a society formed of individuals and an animal
formed of living cells. The movement from simple to complex,

Ramsay MacDonald's Political Writings

which he calls differentiation, is the single law of progress, with universal applicability. He argues: 'This differentiation is just what takes place during the evolution of a civilized society . . .' (1860, p. 283), and elsewhere: 'Alterations of structure in human beings and concomitant alterations of structure in aggregates of human beings jointly produce corresponding alterations of structure in all those things which humanity creates' (1862, p. 319). However, there are difficulties in persuading biology to support these social conditions. Bury remarks that: 'Evolution itself, it must be remembered, does not necessarily mean, applied to society, the movement of man to a desirable goal. It is a neutral, scientific conception, compatible with either optimism or pessimism' (1932, p. 335). Spencer himself only allows natural selection a role in the earlier stages of development: he appreciated that once you have admitted natural selection as the critical factor, there is no way of guaranteeing progress. He assumes that progress will be beneficial. The fact of progress itself proves the beneficence of evolution. He extends the Lamarckian evolutionary mechanism from the individual to the whole race, and underpins his hopes for men with science. As he puts it: 'Always towards perfection is the mighty movement, towards a complete development and a more unmixed good; subordinating in its universality all petty irregularities and fallings back, as the curvature of the earth subordinates mountains and valleys' (quoted in Bury, 1932, p. 340).

The difference between Darwin and Spencer is sharply illustrated by their phraseology. Spencer writes of the 'survival of the best' which is in direct contrast with Darwin's 'survival of the fittest'. Spencer, then, is not interested so much in biology as in rescuing utilitarianism. His vision of progress provides a model for MacDonald's analysis of industry, supplementing and fortifying his Comte-ist ideas, and stressing the possibility of man's moral adaptation to a new state of society. The influence of Spencer's ideas is again suggested by the willingness with which MacDonald adopted biology as the paradigm for his analysis of social change. MacDonald saw in the relationship between biological science and evolutionary theory a parallel to the relationship between technology and socialism for which he himself was arguing. As he said: 'Darwin had to contribute the work of his life to human knowledge before Socialism could be placed on a definitely scientific foundation' (1905, p. 98–9; p. 74 in this volume). Evolution, like Socialism, was a principle of organization which reformers had to apply critically to society. The methodological foundation upon which both the improvements in the utilitarian case and the innovations in biological and natural science depended, should not be overlooked. It was the implications of the scientific methodology common to both biological study and political 'science' which MacDonald was in fact discussing when he talked about 'biology'. For him the vision of man as a conscious agent, intervening in his environment, represented the convergence of biology and politics in a methodological formula: '. . . human progress is not the result of the natural law of the survival of the fittest but the human art of the making of the fittest . . .' (1911, p. 246). The 'making of the fittest' and the 'survival of the best' had common roots.

MacDonald, like Spencer, wanted to guarantee social progress with biology. Spencer's necessary progression and social evolution was more a concession to history, necessitated by the impasse reached by nineteenth-century utilitarianism once it had abandoned the belief that the science of man could be deduced from basic propositions about human nature,* than an offshoot of biological discoveries. Spencer's conception of necessary and beneficial progress, from simple to complex, illustrates the point that 'evolutionary' Socialism owed more to the work of the utilitarians bolstering up their view of human nature than to developments in biology.

Many of the strands discussed above come together in J. A. Hobson's work, and here, at least, there is relatively concrete evidence of the influence and derivation of ideas. Hobson and

* The best discussion of the relationship between social and evolutionary theory is contained in Burrow (1966). Young (1969) explores the same issues in an earlier context.

MacDonald were first connected in the London Ethical movement, beginning an association which continued until the latter's death. Although Hobson remained on the fringes of political activity, supporting the 'New Liberalism' of the nineties, and acting as chairman of one of the Labour Party's advisory committees after the war (Webb, 1952, 16 June 1918), there is no doubt that he influenced MacDonald a great deal. *Labour and the Empire* (MacDonald, 1907a) followed Hobson's *Imperialism* fairly closely, and many of Hobson's economic and social arguments are echoed in MacDonald's work.

MacDonald joined the East London Ethical Society in 1898, and wrote a regular column for the *Ethical World*. Hobson's position seemed to be converging with MacDonald's by the turn of the century. He gave as his reason for leaving the London Ethical Society the fact that it was 'committed so strongly to the stress on individual moral character, as the basis of social progress, as to make it the enemy of that politico-economic democracy which I was coming to regard as the chief instrument of social progress and justice' (Hobson, 1938, p. 56). MacDonald's early Socialism was not far removed from this. Stanton Coit was sanguine enough to write to MacDonald in 1899: 'Is there no possibility that the I L P would change its name to the "Democratic Party" and introduce some new ethical elements into its principles and programmes?' (*MacDonald Papers*, 1 December 1899, quoted in Porter, 1968, p. 163).

The atmosphere of the Ethical movement was congenial to MacDonald, and the 'Manifesto of the First Congress of the International Ethical Union' offered a programme with which he was much in sympathy: 'The good of the individual was dependent upon the good of society, and both depended in turn on the permeation of rational morality through all aspects of life' (Porter, 1968, p. 160). It was in the 'Rainbow Circle' that MacDonald and Hobson came into closer contact: 'There were J. A. Hobson, who was to win much distinction as an economist of original views . . . Charles Trevelyan, an active Liberal and one of my closest friends. For a number of years the secretary

Introduction

of the Rainbow Circle was a young Labour politician and journalist named Ramsay MacDonald' (Samuel, 1945, p. 24). A
circular issued in August 1894 said that the circle would discuss
' the reasons why the old Philosophic Radicalism and the Manchester School of Economics can no longer furnish a ground of
action in the political sphere' (Porter, 1968, p. 164). MacDonald
was also secretary to the short-lived *Progressive Review* which
published the ideas of the group. Unfortunately the capital ran
out, and MacDonald rowed with the editor, Clarke. Hobson
commented on the demise of the review: 'The *Progressive
Review* was definitely opposed to such a general Socialist policy
as Keir Hardie was allowed to advocate in one of its early
numbers. The term "New Liberalism" was adopted by Samuel
and others as rightly descriptive of its aims ... The early
collapse of this review was, I think, a great misfortune. Had it
lived, it might have had a most useful influence in moulding the
thought, policy and structure of the new Labour–Socialist
party which was just beginning to emerge from the clouded
counsels and mixed interests of diverse "progressive" movements' (1938, p. 54). He also noted that MacDonald's earliest
standing was that of an 'independent radical with Socialist
sympathies' (ibid., p. 51).

Hobson focused on the development of modern industry, and
the inadequacy of the old-style *laisser-faire* individualism
confronted with the conditions of monopoly capitalism. For
him, Socialism is a development of industry itself; the growth
of public control is an aspect of industrial change. Public control
is the only alternative to the pursuit of self-interest; the failure
of the *laisser-faire* case makes reform of the distributive mechanism essential. In the *laisser-faire* society an unseen hand is
expected to regulate the mechanism of production for the mutual
benefit of individual and society: in the Socialist society, the
state is brought into the system to ensure that distribution is
just, or at least sets human needs before those of machine
technology. Of course, this analysis depends upon the self-
movement of industry. Hobson argues that 'the efficient causation of the evolutionary process may be found in the application

of scientific inventions to the industrial arts' (1894, p. 25). So far as he is concerned, 'The chief material factor in the evolution of capitalism is machinery. The growing quantity and complexity of machinery applied to the purposes of manufacture and conveyance, and the extractive industries, is the great special fact in the narrative of the expansion of modern industry' (ibid., p. 27).

Hobson argues that this development has sacrificed human needs to those of production, and that the time is ripe for a re-assessment both of the machine and the values it represents. Social morality was more important than anything 'else. Porter argues that Hobson was anxious to 'dethrone political economy from its privileged position above the law' (1968, p. 170).

MacDonald's position is almost exactly the same. He too sees the development of industry overruling human wants and needs, and believes that the answer lies in the reform of political economy. He argues: 'But here I must point out that the vast and intricate mechanism of production, exchange and distri-bution – of factory, market and shop – has become as though it were a thing good and complete in itself' (1921, p. 14). The concentration, the growing complexity and the increasing self-sufficiency of industry has upset the philosophic radical apple-cart. The need to humanize the industrial machine necessarily leads to an attack on the natural identity of interests. Hobson argues: 'That machinery subject to the unrestricted guidance of the commercial interests of an individual or a class cannot be safely trusted to work for the general welfare, is already conceded by all those who admit the desirability or necessity of the res-trictive factory acts ...' (1894, p. 406). The Factory Acts represent an admission of a genuine antagonism between the apparent interests of individuals and of the whole community, which it is the business of society to guard against. This attack is echoed by MacDonald: 'The free competition of the theoretical text-books does not exist. It is as much an abstrac-tion as the economic man' (1921b, p. 86; p. 183 in this volume). And elsewhere: 'But at last the falseness of this individualistic emphasis is being recognized. On its moral side it is not bringing peace ... on its political side ... it now stands baffled by the problems of State authority; on its industrial side it has divorced economics from life' (1905, p. 26). The force of Hobson and MacDonald's criticism of individualism is derived, as noted above, from Ruskin, whose re-emphasis of value and quality in opposition to utility and quantity was of such fundamental importance. The State must, therefore, intervene to secure just and fair distribution, and to see that the further development of industry is for the benefit of all. MacDonald points this out clearly: 'Labour's quarrel with capitalism is not in the sphere of production but in that of distribution' (1907, p. 55; p. 134 in this volume).

Hobson's answer is public control. The application of a scientific sociology to industrial organization, unemployment, poverty and imperialism would ensure social progress through the development of industry. Once economic laws are controlled by man, instead of the reverse, rational social reform along the lines suggested by wider judgements, based firmly on criteria derived from a standard of 'social utility' which was ethical, 'organic' and qualitative, becomes possible. Complexity will lead to control. MacDonald accepts this evaluation: 'Thus we can see that in industry there is a law of concentration by which not merely do small businesses of the same kind tend to unite into large ones, but different processes with the same inevitability tend to be co-ordinated so that they become related parts of one industrial unit' (1921, p. 79; p. 176 in this volume). From this Hobson sees the emergence of social control: 'The need of a growing social control over the modern machine production in cases where that production is left in the main to the direction of individual enterprise, is admitted on every side' (1894, p. 407). And later: 'When it is said that modern industry is becoming essentially more collective in character and therefore demands collective control, what is meant is that under modern industrial development the interest of the industrial society as a whole, and of the consuming public in each piece of so-called private enterprise, is greater than it was ever before, and

41

requires some guarantee that this interest shall not be ignored' (ibid., p. 409).

MacDonald is even more explicit in his vision of this development in the direction of state control: 'As the organization of capital has proceeded in an increasingly large scale, and as the relationship between employer and employed has become, in consequence, more impersonal, more economic and less human, the State as such has passed a series of laws asserting its right to protect the weak and to adjust the admitted inequality established by modern capitalism' (1907b, p. 2; p. 100 in this volume). Hobson foresees two circumstances in which this extension of public control may take place; where the size and structure have eliminated the benefits given to the public by competition, and where the waste and damage done by excessive competition outweighs the loss of enterprise caused by the removal or restriction of the incentive of individual gain.

In this way the reassertion of human needs assists the natural process of industry solving its own problems. With man in control of the industrial machine, its beneficial development is assured. The evolution in the structure of capitalism 'facilitates the work of social control' (Hobson, 1894, p. 410). The natural process is assisted by an ethical will which is informed by study: 'To the question how far and how rapidly may this extension of collective control proceed, no more definite answer is possible than this, that as a larger and larger amount of industry passes into the condition of the most highly evolved machine industries of today, and develops along with the corresponding economies ... larger portions will pass under restrictive legislation or state-management' (ibid.). Competition is supplanted by public control because the well-being of the community is the assumed target, and selfishness cannot guarantee this in modern conditions. The well-being of the community is the inevitable goal of a democratic society, and in this way it becomes democracy rather than biology which guarantees the peaceful development of a stage of co-operation. The extension of the franchise ensures that the community will be more important in deciding social priorities than it has been before. Hobson makes this point emphatically: 'But all the same it is to this associated Labour power that we must look for the rudiments of any coming art of democracy' (1910). MacDonald is equally confident: 'Society in this country, with our free institutions and machinery which can respond to the least impulse of the popular will so soon as the people care to express themselves, progresses by an assimilation of ideas and circumstances' (1905, p. xix). Associated Labour, or the popular will, ensure that the public interest is the governing criterion in society. The only way to guarantee communal well-being in modern society is through public control of trusts and monopolies. Democracy therefore becomes the guarantor of the beneficial development of industry, once man has regained control of the economic machinery, which had previously been self-sufficient.

This view of a self-moving industry, which can be brought under social control if we pay as much attention to distribution as the *laisser-faire* economists formerly paid to production,* is central to MacDonald's argument. He seeks to apply the findings of the study of society and its institutions to industry. Rationality, applied through democracy, can, with this new knowledge, guarantee social progress in line with the development of industry itself. If democracy is to fulfil this new role satisfactorily, and if the people are to express themselves with effect, then a programme of propaganda and education becomes of crucial importance. For MacDonald, this is Socialism. 'But the industrial and economic inevitability of Socialism is mere fancy. It is inevitable only if intelligence makes it so. It is inevitable only if we are to develop on rational lines: it is inevitable, not because men are exploited or because the fabric of capitalism must collapse, under its own weight, but because men are rational' (1905, p. 126; p. 92 in this volume).

His case now begins to fall into place. It represents the begin-

* MacDonald's emphasis on distribution is unmistakable: for him socialism is 'the organization which includes distribution as well as production within its scope . . . extending the economy of the trust until it is merged into the greater economy of socialism' (1907b, p. 84; p. 152 in this volume).

ning of the argument that social reform depends upon efficiency, planning, organization, science; upon the understanding of economic change and the conscious pursuit of greater wealth. His specific contribution is to adapt the themes of development and progress to the notion of an expanding and growing technology, so providing an alternative to the Marxist analysis of capitalism and labour. Dialectic and revolution are irrelevant if the source of social change is technology alone. It is not that MacDonald specifically set out to avoid revolution. His intellectual background simply predisposed him to reject or misunderstand Marxist sociology. His own idea of sociology left him ill-equipped to cope with the problems of modern society, and he was forced to fall back on the very utilitarian arguments he had sought to supplant, and to make use of what they said about the character of economic and social change. The result is a version of Socialism which is a philosophy of industrial rather than social change. MacDonald made this argument respectable, and provided it with a biological vocabulary, which greatly assisted its popularization, and obscured its origins. His suggestion that prosperity would come through Socialism amounted to no more than the claim that the evolution of industry would, itself, bring material well-being. This argument placed great weight upon the education of democracy for the higher stage of society to come, and insisted that in order to reap the benefits of an expanding technology, the people should wait and prepare themselves.

MacDonald's theory of education is at the core of his argument about industrial change, and constitutes his most significant contribution to political thought. He uses the words education and propaganda interchangeably to define the primary task of Socialism and socialists. According to him, education is a natural concomitant of political reform and democracy, and the only way to recover the social harmony destroyed by modern capitalism. The education of labour is presented as the only viable alternative to the Marxist sociology of labour, and the only means by which people might be equipped for the higher stages of social organization to come. The growing complexity of industry requires an objectivity in the individual to match it. The rationality of modern industry is never in doubt; the rationality of the individual can only be secured by extensive political propaganda. If education does not reconcile men and machines, only revolution can result.

The revolution for which MacDonald hopes is one of 'opinion and not of class' (1919b, p. 36). He believes that while a revolution by force may lead to a temporary dictatorship of the intelligent democracy, 'continued progress must before long come back to its source in the minds of the masses' (ibid., p. 58; p. 222 in this volume). The only foundation for a socialist state is 'intelligence, which is the only reliable power in society' (1920, p. 65). His constitutional proposals are designed to ensure that political activity of every kind, both party and parliamentary, should be geared to this end. Parliament is, after all, 'the will of the people embodied in an institution' (1919b, p. 63; p. 226 in this volume). MacDonald's arguments for constitutional reform are, therefore, aimed at enabling opinion to be more easily represented or mobilized. In an industrial society these problems are very complex, but unless some way is found of bringing opinion to bear upon technical change, good government is impossible. MacDonald reasons: 'The necessity for improving public intelligence, for organizing moral forces, and for doing communal business . . . increases with the complexity of society and with the expansion of the economic activity of the State' (1909, vol. 2, p. 118). Socialism, from this point of view, is a propaganda mission, setting out to convince people of the need to adopt a higher mode of existence, in tune with technological developments. Politics, similarly, becomes a form of education, rather than an administrative or organizational function. This is, perhaps, the origin of MacDonald's 'wait and see' approach to government. He rated persuasion so highly that he even saw the task threatened by power and office. 'Nothing', he argued, 'will be more damaging to Labour than to take office in the midst of shifting sands or to be presented with political power by the masses who vote for it because other parties are for the time being unpopular' (1919a). Macdonald's pride in ILP propaganda* suggests that he was genuinely afraid that office might distract the Labour Party from its primary educative role. In 1919 he claimed that the 'only action which is possible at the moment is that of changing opinion and awakening intelligence' (1919b, p. 89; p. 229 in this volume). When the ILP showed signs of independent life, as with its new programme for 1920–21 his reply in the *Labour Leader* (11 November 1920) was that: 'I should like to find a greater emphasis placed upon Socialist propaganda and education' (quoted in Lyman, 1963, p. 158).

Essentially, MacDonald's view of persuasion, of education, of Socialist theory and of political activity in general can be reduced to what he likes to call sociology. The parliamentary work of Socialism must be supplemented 'by educational propaganda, the chief aim of which is to induce the intellectual portions of the community to adopt new modes of sociological thought' (MacDonald, 1907b, p. 117; p. 159 in this volume). This is the sociological inheritance MacDonald draws from Spencer and Hobson. Failing to make anything of Marx's analysis of labour, MacDonald is left with the task of ensuring the active participation of human beings in the development of industry. It is the only way he can retain both evolution and human rationality. Education has to be the corner-stone of his thought. Socialism is a principle of social organization which must be apprehended and put into practice; to see that this is done is the task of the ILP and the Labour Party propagandists and educators. Moral will is brought into the self-movement of technical change through political activity. MacDonald, therefore, does not need to exempt man from evolution to retain human rationality. The participation of intelligence guarantees the beneficial direction of industrial evolution. Revolution is thus avoided, and social cohesion maintained. 'Historical forces may impose these things

* See for example his 'Outlook' in the *Socialist Review*, April–June 1918: 'The strength of the Labour Party depends very largely on money spent week by week in propaganda done almost exclusively by the ILP.'

on other countries but the ILP has believed that the political organization and enlightenment of the workers here will turn the revolution into smoother channels . . .' (MacDonald, 1921a). The work had been begun in the schools and colleges, but was paralleled by an 'educational movement from within the working masses. Socialist and labour propaganda had aroused interest in social and economic subjects' (1921b, p. 104; p. 198 in this volume). This teaching aroused the students and stopped them from submitting to their fate: 'No longer was Trade Union propaganda confined to defensive work against capitalism . . . the structure of the capitalist system was studied and understood, the relationship between capital and labour was grasped, the historical evolution of industry was known . . . the forces within it working for its transformation were calculated and explored' (ibid.). Even in his explanation of the Labour unrest of 1910 MacDonald returns to this educational theme. Experience and education together had taught the workman the economic faults of society, and the idea of social justice had unsettled 'the sensitive thinking minority and an intensified struggle for life had stirred up the more passive crowds' (1913, p. 49).

This, then, was the situation facing Socialists. It was their task to 'make enlightenment come quick . . . to coordinate in a movement all the forces that make for organic change' (Mac-Donald, 1919b, p. 99; p. 237 in this volume). With the power of Socialism lying in 'public opinion, not in strikes' (1919a) the problem for the Socialist was to create 'by strenuous propaganda the higher and truer conception of a social unity which in a well-ordered society would embrace in harmonious working all those rivalries' (1920, p. 65). This could only be achieved by 'educational propaganda from the outside, and hard construc-tive thinking within our own ranks' (1919a). The social order that is to come is dimly perceived by every working man, and it is only a question of realizing this 'potential', which finds its strength in the instinctive hankering after equality and justice.

MacDonald's explicit rejection of class is an essential part of this attitude. He claims that: 'Socialism is no class movement. Socialism is a movement of opinion, not an organization of status. It is not the rule of the working class; it is the organization of the community' (1907b, p. 122; p. 162 in this volume). He steadfastly refused to exploit class consciousness for political purposes: 'The man through whom Socialism is to come is not the economic man, the class conscious man, the man toiling with the muck. He is to be the man of ideals, of the historical spirit, the man in whose intelligence religion and sense of what is of good report will have a dominating influence' (1909, vol. 1, p. xxviii). It is a strong feature of MacDonald's work that he hardly ever accumulates the facts of poverty, as, for example, the Fabians had done in *Why are the Many Poor?** He is even more insistent about the irrelevance of class in repudiating the Marxist challenge to the bourgeois state. He argues that: 'The state is, therefore, not the instrument of a class but an organ of society' (1909, vol. 2, p. 117). Opinion is MacDonald's substitute for class struggle, and it depends upon the essential unity of the modern industrial state and the people who live in it. Lacking an economic analysis of society, MacDonald adopted a Rousseauesque, Owenite notion of a general will and social harmony, which he combined with adaptation and development to produce his version of British Socialism.

The analysis of MacDonald's work in this setting demonstrates how serious a mistake has been the concentration on the alleged 'evolutionary' character of British Socialism. British Socialism was no more biological or evolutionary than anyone else's, and the repeated description of it in those terms has dazed even the most serious critics into believing that that was enough. When the Labour Party threw out revolution, it threw out sociology as well. This left it in the awkward position of seeking to humanize the economic machine without a critique of capitalism. Instead of the Marxist analysis of Labour, British Socialists were obliged to take a second look at traditional political economy, and at what improvements could be made on it. This path led through Spencer, Ruskin and Hobson to MacDonald.

* The first Fabian tract.

References

ARON, R. (1965), *Main Currents in Sociological Thought*, Weidenfeld & Nicolson.

AVINERI, S. (1969), *The Social and Political Thought of Karl Marx*, Cambridge University Press.

BEER, M. (1919), *History of British Socialism*, Norton, 1920.

BOTTOMORE, T. B., and RUBEL, M. (1956), *Karl Marx: Selected Writings in Sociology and Social Philosophy*, Penguin, 1961.

BOWLE, J. (1954), *Politics and Opinion in the Nineteenth Century*, Cape.

BURROW, J. W. (1966), *Evolution and Society: A Study in Victorian Social Theory*, Cambridge University Press.

BURY, J. B. (1932), *The Idea of Progress*, Dover Books, 1960.

COMTE, A. (1851), *A System of Positive Polity*, B. Franklin, 1966.

DUNCAN, D. (1908), *Life and Letters of Herbert Spencer*, Methuen.

FERRI, E. (1909), *Socialism and Positive Science*, Preface by J. R. MacDonald, Socialist Library.

GLASIER, J. B. (1919), *Labour Leader*, 16 October.

HAMILTON, M. A. (1925), *J. R. MacDonald: Labour's Man of Destiny*, written under pseud. Iconoclast, Leonard Parsons.

HAMILTON, M. A. (1944), *Remembering My Good Friends*, Cape.

HOBSON, J. A. (1894), *The Evolution of Modern Capitalism: A Study of Machine Production*, Contemporary Science Series, Walter Scott.

HOBSON, J. A. (1898), *John Ruskin, Social Reformer*, Nisbet.

HOBSON, J. A. (1910), 'The General Election: A Sociological Interpretation', *Sociological Review*.

HOBSON, J. A. (1938), *Confessions of an Economic Heretic*, Macmillan.

KIRKUP, T. (1892), *A History of Socialism*, revised and edited by E. R. Pease, 1913, A. & C. Black.

KIRKWOOD, D. (1935), *My Life of Revolt*, Harrap.

LYELL, C. (1830–33), *The Principles of Geology*, 9th edn, London, 1853.

LYMAN, R. W. (1963), 'J. R. MacDonald and the Leadership of the Labour Party', *Journal of British Studies*, vol. 2, no. 2, May.

MACDONALD, J. R. (1905), *Socialism and Society*, Independent Labour Party.

MACDONALD, J. R. (1907a), *Labour and the Empire*, Independent Labour Party.

MACDONALD, J. R. (1907b), *Socialism*, Social Problems Series, ed. O. Smeaton, T. C. & E. C. Jack.

MACDONALD, J. R. (1909), *Socialism and Government*, 2 vols., Independent Labour Party.

MACDONALD, J. R. (1911), *The Socialist Movement*, Independent Labour Party.

MACDONALD, J. R. (1913), *The Social Unrest: Its Cause and Solution*. Independent Labour Party; Foulis, 1924.

Ramsay MacDonald's Political Writings

MACDONALD, J. R. (1919a), 'Outlook' column, *Socialist Review*, October–December.

MACDONALD, J. R. (1919b), *Parliament and Revolution*, National Labour Press.

MACDONALD, J. R. (1920), *Parliament and Democracy*, National Labour Press.

MACDONALD, J. R. (1921a), 'Outlook' column, *Socialist Review*, January–March.

MACDONALD, J. R. (1921b), *Socialism: Critical and Constructive*, Cassell, 1924.

MARCUSE, H. (1941), *Reason and Revolution*, Routledge & Kegan Paul, 1969.

MARX, K. and ENGELS, F. (1968), *Selected Works*, Lawrence & Wishart.

MILL, J. S. (1873), *Autobiography*, ed. Helen Taylor, London.

NAIRN, T. (1965), 'The Nature of the Labour Party', in P. Anderson and R. Blackburn, eds., *Towards Socialism*, New Left Review.

PEASE, E. R. (1918), *History of the Fabian Society*, Cass, 1962.

POLLARD, S. (1968), *The Idea of Progress: History and Society*, Watts.

PORTER, B. (1968), *Critics of Empire*, Macmillan.

RUSKIN, J. (1862), *Unto this Last: Four Essays on the First Principles*, Smith, Elder & Co., 1900.

SAMUEL, H. (1945), *Memoirs*, Cresset Press.

SKIDELSKY, R. (1967), *Politicians and the Slump*, Macmillan.

SPENCER, H. (1851), *Social Statics: or the Conditions Essential to Human Happiness Specified, and the First of Them Developed*, London.

SPENCER, H. (1860), 'The Social Organism', *Westminster Review*, in *Essays: Scientific, Political and Speculative*, Williams & Norgate, 1891.

SPENCER, H. (1863), *First Principles: A System of Synthetic Philosophy*, 3rd edn, New York, 1876.

SPENCER, H. (1884), *Man versus the State*, Williams & Norgate.

WEBB, B. (1952), *Diaries 1912–24*, ed. M. I. Cole, Longmans.

WEBB, S. (1889), *Fabian Essays*, Fabian Society, 1908.

WERTHEIMER, E. (1929), *A Portrait of the Labour Party*, trans, P. Kirwan, Putnams.

WHITELEY, W. (1968), 'Interview with Cyril Pearce', *Bulletin of the Society for the Study of Labour History*, no. 18.

WILLIAMS, F. (1965), *A Pattern of Rulers*, Longmans.

YOUNG, R. (1969), 'Malthus and the Evolutionists', *Past and Present*, May, no. 43.

SOCIALISM AND SOCIETY

Chapter I

The Problem

Poverty still challenges the reason and the conscience of men, and instead of becoming less acute as national wealth increases, it becomes more serious. The results of such investigations as those of Mr Charles Booth and Mr Rowntree, and of the Committees which inquired into the prevalence of child labour and the extent of physical deterioration, shatter with the rudest indifference any complacency that one may have built upon figures showing the astounding totals of national wealth, or the satisfactory averages of personal income. It may not be true literally that the rich are growing richer at a time when the poor are becoming poorer;* but it is an undeniable fact that the lot of the poverty-stricken becomes more deplorable as the advance of the well-to-do becomes more marked, and that modern conditions of life press with increasing weight upon the propertyless classes. Never was it more true than it is today that two civilizations exist side by side in every industrial country—the civilization of the idle or uselessly employed rich, and the civilization of the industrial poor.

Pauperism is perhaps the least alarming form and the most misleading index of poverty. Wrecks lifting their broken spars up to heaven are less woeful than unseaworthy ships tossing helplessly on stormy waters. Moreover, the existence of numerous charitable and subsidizing agencies, together with the increasing expenditure of municipal authorities upon work which is in the nature of relief, show that the flood of poverty has

* This depends upon the length of the period of comparison. If we compare the fourteenth century with the nineteenth it is true literally; if we compare 1800 with 1900 it is not true.

altogether overflowed the embankments which the Poor Law has provided to contain it.

When we survey modern conditions in search of a point from which to begin and trace out the weedy and tortuous path of poverty, we naturally fix upon the silent village and the deserted field. Our rural districts are depopulated; the rural districts of every commercial country are emptying their people into the cities, and as the sources of healthy manhood are depleted, the reserve forces of the race are drained off. Commissions sit and report upon the physique of the people, and their conclusions, bad enough in all conscience, might be worse. For, the nerves of the people, not being subject to foot-rule measurement or pound avoirdupois weighing, are not taken into account, and the morals of the people are left to be gossiped about by sensation-mongers or to be sported with by sectarians, and are not made the subject of cold, impartial investigation.*

The whole subject of the vital condition of the people is too often supposed to be thoroughly dealt with when satisfactory figures of death rates† and enticing photographs of improved houses are given, and thus the fact is obscured that, in spite of all sanitary and similar improvements, the vital energies, the stamina, the mental cleanliness, the moral robustness of our people are suffering, not for this or that special reason, but because the complete setting of life is barren, wearisome and exhausting to human beings.

I need mention but one cause of this. The better organization of the functions of production has been of necessity attended by a quickening of pace and by a heavier draft upon the energies of the producers. More life is consumed in production – in fact, so much life is consumed in this, that little is left to be spent

* Only the fringe of this question is touched in the investigations which Mr Booth has carried on in London and Mr Rowntree in York. Police court records and lunatic asylum reports form a considerable literature upon the subject however.

† But, be it noted, that one of the most important sections of vital statistics, the rates of infant mortality, shows no improvement for the last half-century.

in other concerns. Old age and the inefficiency of years come sooner than they used to do. The squeezing of the orange is done more quickly and more thoroughly now.

Nor is this merely a workman's grievance, for everyone affected by the industrial changes which have marked the liberal* epoch has suffered in the same way. The workman suffers from periodic unemployment and from a chronic uncertainty of being able to make ends meet. This reacts upon his personal habits so that he follows the allurements of intemperance or seeks pleasure in the risks of gambling, loses his sense of craftsmanship and his unwillingness to work dishonestly, is driven into the loafing habit through frequent unemployment, and finally becomes a machine which turns out a minimum amount of work at a maximum price. We may regret this as much as we like, and blame the workman as much as we care, but this is the natural consequence of a state of society in which private interests control industrial capital, in which the land and the instruments of production belong to a class different from that which uses them, in which the predominant relationship between the employer and the workman is that of a contract to do work at a price, and in which there is no response and no appeal to moral and spiritual motives. The capitalist also suffers from insecurity caused, not by mistakes or faults of his own, but by the competitive moves of his rivals. In France,† 20 per cent of the businesses started to disappear at once: in America,‡ 90 per cent of business men fail either absolutely or relatively; and though Marshall contends§ that business risks are decreasing in this country, the

---

* It may be advisable to state definitely that I am frequently to use the word 'liberal', as I do here, not in its political but epochal sense. It indicates that period of social evolution when capital, freed from the political and social dominance of feudalism, developed a political, economic and social policy in accordance with its own nature. The keynote of the epoch is individual liberty of the unreal, atomic kind; its political characteristic is enfranchisement, its economic is competition, and its social is wealth.

† Leroy Beaulieu, *Répartition des Richesses*, ch. 11.

‡ Wells, *Recent Economic Changes*, London, 1891, p. 351.

§ Marshall, *Principles of Economics*, London, 1898, p. 703.

probable truth is that they are only changing their character, as financial cases in the Law Courts appear to show. Moreover, the improvements in methods of production, the concentration of capital, the development of means of communication, the opening up of the world's markets, and the increasing number of nations taking part in international competition, put an ever tightening pressure upon the capitalist, and demand that more and more of his life's energies shall be spent in business. Although the statute book teaches him business morality and protects him against certain forms of unprincipled and anti-social competition (like adulterated goods and long hours), he is compelled to drive the sharpest bargains, to adopt methods in business which he could not employ honourably in personal relations, and to cross far too frequently the line of dishonesty. He can indulge in few sentiments; he cannot enjoy very much of the luxury of morality. Business is a war in which he whose nerves are not always well strung, whose eye is not always fixed upon the vigilant enemy, and whose heart is not always prepared to drive home every advantage, is likely to be overborne. The purpose which must dominate the morality and the thought of the business man is a favourable balance sheet, and only in so far as an exercise of the finer sentiments does not adversely influence that summary of trading operations can he give way to them.

The result is inevitable. The arts languish, the vulgar empire of plutocracy extends its gilded borders, luxurious indulgence takes the place of comfort, selfish pursuits that of public spirit, philanthropic effort that of just dealing.

We are accustomed to regard the present as a state of individualism, but no delusion could be more grotesque. Nothing is rarer in society today than individuality, and it is doubtful if ever there was less individuality amongst us than there is at the present moment. One has only to look on whilst the sons of the *nouveaux riches* spend their money, or whilst the crowds which our industrial quarters have disgorged enjoy themselves, to appreciate the meaningless monotony of our pleasure. From our furniture, made by the thousand pieces by machines, to our religion, stereotyped in set formulae and pursued by clock-work methods, individuality is an exceptional characteristic. In the production of wealth, owing to the differentiation of processes, there is less and less play for individuality, and as this more exclusively occupies the time and thought of both employers and employed, uniformity spreads its deadening hand over society, imitation becomes a social factor of increasing power, respectability becomes more securely enthroned as the mentor of conduct, and a drab level of fairly comfortable mediocrity is the standard to which we conform. Nothing is, indeed, more absurd than an argument in support of the present state of society, based on the assumption that as we move away from it in the direction of Socialism we are leaving individuality and individual liberty behind.

Liberty and regular employment – the fitting of men to the work which they can do best – can be secured only when the various functions of the social organism – the capitalistic and labouring, the consuming and producing – are all coordinated. At present each function is self-centred. It is as though the appetite, the head or the muscles of the human body worked each for itself – as indeed sometimes happens in the case of gluttons, hair splitters or slaves. But then we know the consequences. There is an interruption in the general health and growth. There is a dwarfing of some parts and an abnormal development of others. The body rebels periodically, and teaches the functions that only when they take their proper places in the whole, and act obedient, not to their own appetites, but to the needs of the complete organism, do they enjoy an unbroken and a full satisfaction.

We can best express this failure of present-day society to enrich all its classes not merely with worldly possessions, but with character and capacity to employ leisure time, by describing modern conditions as being poverty-stricken. For to judge the prevalence of poverty merely by returns of income or deposits in savings banks, is like judging a piece of architecture by the size of the stones used in the building.

We have a vast accumulation of actual physical want. Mr

Booth says that about 30 per cent of the London population must be classified amongst that accumulation; and if it is not relatively growing, it is not actually decreasing. We seem to have reached the maximum of improvement which the existing social organization can yield. Further ameliorative efforts of a purely reforming character can produce little fruit. Our social machinery apparently cannot employ more than $97\frac{1}{2}$ per cent of the willing workers at best, and it cannot raise more than from 70 to 80 per cent of our people above the 'poverty line'. In addition to that, our society bears a still greater accumulation of mental and moral poverty, and apparently this is increasing rather than decreasing.

Such are the conditions which challenge the social reformer. They cannot be the final state of social evolution. There must be another state ahead of us less marked by failure, less chaotic, better organized, and the question is, how are we to move into it? It appears to be the special task of the twentieth century to discover a means of coordinating the various social functions so that the whole community may enjoy robust health, and its various organs share adequately in that health. But this is nothing else than the aim of Socialism.

Chapter IV

Utopian and Semi-Scientific Socialism

Before the idea of biological evolution regulated the thought and methods of social reformers, proposals for social reconstruction took the form of creations of a new earth and new men, made by the fiat of someone whose authority was equal to the task. The man who judged social results by his ideas of right and wrong was driven to plant his ideal community, wherein dwelt righteousness, on some undiscovered island in some unknown sea; and when, in times nearer to our own, the reformer did not merely write of Utopias, but tried to make them, he bought land in the hopes of founding a society modelled on a plan devised from his own intelligence.

I

The fundamental mistake of the Utopia builders was that they did not understand that society develops in accordance with laws of social life, and that it could not be rebuilt right away like a house on plans designed by the moral consciousness and administrative acuteness of individuals. They did not see that the reforming operations of the individual will are limited by the fact that society progresses by the readjustment of its existing organization. They assumed that the social relations were casual, and that the group life offered the very slightest resistance to total readjustment. They had not grasped the idea that society at any given time had been moulded and fixed by the experiences of the social group up to that time, – that it had inherited its form from the past, and that therefore it could not be made the plaything of men's imagination. Society could no more return to primitive bliss than man could return to the arboreal habits

59

of his ancestors. They hoped to build anew, when all they could do was to aid in modifying structures and in changing relationships. They approached their task as though they were men considering whether a house is adapted to their needs, whilst, by the nature of the problem, they should have approached it as men who desire to restore to health their ailing bodies. They regarded society as though it were an architectural construction of fixed parts, not as an organism maturing by the laws of variation and growth.

Sir Thomas More's *Utopia* and Robert Owen's experiments illustrate this error.

More was an apostle of the liberal thought of his time, such as it was. Guided by the humanism of the New Learning, he cast his eyes over the state of England, when the evolution of national industry was destroying the peasantry. The English manor system was being transformed into private ownership of land inspired by commercial considerations. The stream from the country to the towns had started. The landlords, responding to the alluring temptations of commerce, were beginning to regard their lands not as the instrument of territorial power but as a source of income, and the demand for wool made them turn their tilled acres to grazing, and put sheep on the fields instead of men. Society was moving from the territorial and agricultural stage to that of world markets and commerce. Capital was concentrating and slowly organizing itself into a function separate and apart from labour, and the guild ordinances which protected the older methods of trade were passing into impotence. The unemployed were everywhere; social conflict was everywhere. Everywhere the rich seemed to be in conspiracy against the poor. In More's own words: 'The rich are ever striving to pare away something further from the daily wages of the poor by private fraud and even by public law, so that the wrong already existing (for it is a wrong that those from whom the State derives most benefit should receive least reward) is made much greater by means of the law of the State.' The poor, in consequence, were leading 'a life so wretched that even a beast's life seemed enviable'. Everything, even Christendom itself, was powerless to avert all this wrong-doing, he moaned.

This indictment is wonderfully modern, wonderfully like the last Socialist speech one has heard, wonderfully like the present-day expressions of reformers who try to view honestly the facts of life.* And yet More, the New Learning, Christendom, did little and could do little to avert or shorten the calamities. The iron law of social evolution grinds out its results with magnificent callousness.

Why? Why did More write as a modern? Why did his criticisms fall like seed by the wayside? The position of Robert Owen may as well be examined before an answer is attempted.

Owen's Utopias were products of the Industrial Revolution. He lived in a system designed exclusively for the production of wealth, devouring both the physique and the character of children, men and women. Human beings were the raw material upon which the growing industry of his time fed. Revolting from the spectacle, Owen began to condemn it on account of its moral deficiencies, began to address protesting appeals to the public intelligence and the public conscience. At first, his schemes were aimed at modifying the structure of the social organism. He proposed to limit by law the labour of children, to provide them with a suitable education, to humanize the environment of the people and, by alluring them to walk in more

* cf. for instance these sentences of John Stuart Mill: 'If, therefore, the choice were to be made between Communism with all its chances, and the present state of society with all its sufferings and injustices; if the institution of private property necessarily carried with it as a consequence that the produce of labour should be apportioned as we now see it, almost in an inverse ratio to the labour – the largest portions to those who have never worked at all, the next largest to those whose work is almost nominal, and so in a descending scale, the remuneration dwindling as the work grows harder and more disagreeable, until the most fatiguing and exhausting bodily labour cannot count with certainty on being able to earn even the necessaries of life – if this or Communism were the alternative, all the difficulties great or small of Communism would be but as dust in the balance.'
Political Economy, Book 2, ch. 1.

pleasant ways, draw them away from the paths of destruction they were treading. His work of that time afterwards earned for him the title of 'the father of factory legislation' and 'the founder of infant schools'. There was, then, little Utopianism about his proposals. They were the constructive schemes of a man of penetrating thought and ripe experience who attempted to modify social environment without creating an ideal society from the material of his own intelligence; and they remain his chief contribution to the social changes of last century.

But as time went on, Owen felt more and more the discouragement of the idealist who lives some generations before society is in a position to listen whole-heartedly to him. Cobbett was unknown in 1800 when Owen took over New Lanark: and Cobbett had to re-inaugurate the Radical demands for political enfranchisement, and the Cobbett campaign had to be carried on for two or three generations, before Owen's social ideas could be pushed to the forefront of public interests. When Owen started his first community (1823) capitalism was but beginning its triumphs. The State had only just given up its attempts to fix wages, having been baffled in its benevolent intentions by the vigorous and extensive changes in industrial conditions which the new economic order was bringing about. Even in industries like the woollen, which had been controlled by capitalists for over two centuries, the employers were but moderately rich. The same was true of cotton.* The Peels were separated by but one generation from their yeoman origin. In Scotland, the first cotton mill had been erected only twenty-two years before Owen acquired New Lanark.† A subscription list opened in Liverpool in 1798 in aid of the funds required to carry on the war with France, contained only two amounts of £500 and one of £400, and these were the largest sums subscribed.‡ As late

---

* 'The cotton industry had not in the fifties sufficiently developed for the notions current today to emerge.' Chapman, *Lancashire Cotton Industry*, Manchester, 1903, p. 250.

† *Industries of Glasgow and the West of Scotland*, British Association Handbook, Glasgow, 1901, p. 141.

‡ Baines' *History of Liverpool*, pp. 503–4. In 1801, £80,000 was sub-

as 1841, according to the report of the Assistant Commissioner for Scotland, presented to the Committee appointed to inquire into the condition of the unemployed Handloom Weavers, out of 51,000 weavers south of the Firth of Clyde, not more than 3500 were employed in factories,* whilst it was quite common until the middle of the nineteenth century for agriculture and weaving to be carried on by the same person.† As late as 1834, it was stated before the Committee on Handloom Weavers that 'if a man can purchase a winding machine and a warping mill and get credit for a skep of yarn he can get into motion as a master'.‡ Powerlooms had not seriously menaced handlooms, and were so imperfect that their use was not clearly economical. Spinning machinery was equally imperfect. Great as had been the strides of invention, and though the 'Industrial Revolution' had been accomplished, the industrial organization of the country was still but rudimentary. The factory system, characterized by specialization and sub-division of labour together with centralized town industry, was but beginning; the means of transport and locomotion were nothing better than the new canal system, which had been the subject of such feverish speculation in 1792, and the stage coach; international trade was insignificant. But the characteristics of the industrial epoch were developing. The economic and political conditions of feudalism were passing away. The national existence of the country had been finally secured, and its economic development decisively begun. The first stage of that development had to solve the problems of how to produce wealth and create markets and marketing facilities. Therefore, the form of the social organism had to respond to those needs of the social life, and all the organs and cells in society had to be subordinated to the organization best fitted for satisfying them.

scribed in three hours for building an Exchange with a Square in front (ibid., pp. 506–7). Even that would not have been considered a great feat a generation afterwards, and the great fuss made about it is significant.
* Quoted by Chapman in *Lancashire Cotton Industry*, Manchester, 1903, p. 24.
† ibid., pp. 10, 11 ff.   ‡ ibid., p. 25.

This subordination entailed suffering and misery. The towns became pestilential, children were done to death in the mills, pauperism increased, the people threw up to heaven angry protests, Utopias were built from the mental stuff of the just and the generous, Owen agitated. But protest as the organs and the cells might, society continued to organize itself so that it could produce wealth abundantly; and all the fine ideas that were scattered abroad made no difference except in so far as they could modify the social structure within the limits of the economic function imposed upon it by the character of the social need which had in due course arisen as an expression of the developing social life.

Processes of readjustment and experiments in amelioration were begun early. It was found by experience, for instance, that, in spite of the opposition of the capitalists, who were chiefly fulfilling the social functions of the epoch (labour, however necessary, being functionally subordinate), certain limitations imposed by Factory Legislation did not retard the development of the Factory System as the most efficient method of wealth production, but in reality aided it. We must not therefore commit the error of assuming that Factory Legislation is in principle opposed to the spirit embodied in the Factory System. Factory legislation, so long as its effect is tested by its compatibility with the efficiency of private capitalism to produce wealth and exploit labour, is an essential part of the capitalist system. It is an essential influence upon the social organism at a time when the form of the organism is determined *solely* by its efficiency in producing wealth. Hence it was that Owen's proposals for the state regulation of factories were effective, and fructified in society, whilst his Utopian experiments were valuable mainly as warnings to future reformers. This was not because the legislative proposals were moral or right in the abstract, but because society was ripe for them; they were 'natural' in the sense that they were produced by the circumstances of the time, and advantageous to the vital purpose of the generation. And, above all, they were modifications of the social structure.

This contention is strongly reinforced if we consider what at first seems to militate against it, the development of Co-operation from Owen's Utopian schemes. Co-operation in Owen's mind was as much a *tour de force* as his New Harmony. It was a new organization of society bringing the workers into a new relation with each other and altering fundamentally the conditions under which production and exchange were carried on. Logically it was an excellent idea. If it were possible for the individual – the cell – to create at any time a new social organization, Owen's scheme of integral co-operation might have worked. But the individual lives in an organism – society, his will expresses itself in accordance with the life of the organism, his morality is able to act effectively only in so far as it can modify the social organism and is guided by the vital activity of the organism, and his confidence is given only to systems similar to, or but an easy stage removed from, the organism of which he is a part. Therefore, when Owen's idea of co-operation was adopted, its Utopian characteristics were gradually dropped, and, as its success became possible, the features it held in common with existing society became more marked.

When the Rochdale Pioneers began their experiment in 1844, the Utopian features of Owenite Co-operation were becoming subordinate. True, the Pioneers threw out foreshadowings of a new earth. The unemployed were to be absorbed, and an identity of interest between producer and consumer was to be established – in the long run. But the organization of the movement was modelled on the organization of existing society. The rest was ornament, and that ornament has had but the slightest influence in the development of the experiment.

There was an opposition in society between the functions of production and exchange, between the wage-earner and the person who sold him his food and clothing; and the latter was drifting more and more completely under the control of the capitalist employers. The question was: Could that tendency be stopped without hindering the efficiency of the social organism to produce wealth, and without having to create an organization different in form and idea to society as it existed?

Ramsay MacDonald's Political Writings

Obviously, dear and adulterated food, the credit system, an alliance between shopkeepers and employers were not only not essential, but might be harmful, to the efficient production of wealth, and the idea of the workmen being their own shop-keepers militated against no principle upon which production depended. So these things were alterable. But the private ownership of capital, capitalist control of the workshop and competition in production, together with the existence of the unemployed, were essential to the epoch of production, and these could not be altered.

The question upon which all the success of the Rochdale experiment depended was: Was there a sufficiently strong sense of solidarity amongst the workers to secure for the stores such a determined patronage as to protect them against outside competition? As it turned out, there was. The Co-operative Store was patronized, not because it was more efficient or cheaper than the shop of the private trader, but because it was the Co-operative Store. The movement, in the main, did nothing to alter the organization of society.* Some of the leaders of the movement, inspired by an antiquated conception of what they call 'self-help', and masses of its ordinary members whose visions are narrowed by dividends and who regard Co-operation as being merely a venture in profitable shopkeeping, have actually turned the movement into a defence of the present industrial system, on the ground that if distribution today is faulty, the reason lies in the defects of human character and not in social organization.

One ought not to blame the Co-operative movement for 'falling away from the faith': one ought not to call its short-comings failings. The line of development which the movement took only illustrates in a very conclusive way how the chief function which an epoch is called upon to perform, postpones

---

* Society is now, however, becoming fitted for an application of principles which underlie the Co-operative movement, and so co-operation, so far as it is intelligently aware of its own interests, is beginning to move in the direction of constructive State action, and society is responding to the co-operative impulse.

the successful application of moral notions of social relationships, until the circumstances arise for such a change as will
allow them to be grafted upon the social stem. That the Co-
operative Congress should be the last resting place of the inadequate theories of the economic period is exactly what one
would expect. The law of parasitism described elsewhere*
provides that in movements like Co-operation, the theories and
assumptions held by the generation which made it a success
should become embodied in the tissue of the movement, and
resist change long after less well organized movements have
responded to new ideas.

II

Now we can see why Utopias of all ages reveal as their foundations practically the same clearness and firmness of moral vision.
They all assert the right of man to life and to human consideration against the operations of social evolution which every now
and again, owing to functional changes, sacrifice the personal
interests of individuals and sections of individuals. They all
demand moral results from society. Men, thinking and writing
at those times of rapid change, make claims and utter criticisms
from an ideally moral point of view. Hence, at every time of
social change and of activity in social speculation, men dead
for centuries are described as being 'modern men'.

The moral standards of the builders of Utopias are the result
of the experience of well-coordinated organisms, such as man
is. But the organization of society has been loose and partial, its
will has been weak, its functioning imperfect, its morality,
therefore, rudimentary. The individual is therefore in moral
possibilities far in advance of society. Society, slowly and by
organic adaptation, becomes more and more capable of expressing the moral consciousness of man, its lack of organic
coherence resulting in a lack of moral impulse. So, before the
co-operative movement could 'go back' to Owenism, it had to
wait for a more complete sub-division of the various functions of
the workman, a more thorough application of mechanical

* pp. 63–6 [of the original edition. *Ed.*].

contrivances to production, and also for the coordinating movement which proceeds alongside the disintegrating one, and which forms into a new social unity of functions the various divided classes which are rendering service to the whole.

But before this advance in social organization has been reached, sociology has passed from its architectural or mechanical stage to its organic stage, and men have left behind the standpoint from which it appeared to be possible to build a New Jerusalem by Utopian methods. Reforming effort is seen to be impotent unless it effects variations in the social structure, because it is seen that the defect giving rise to all the miseries which set Utopists dreaming, is, that every function in society has not been completely organized so that each co-operates with each and all with the whole.

Moral criticisms on social organization are useful only in so far as the critics bear in mind that the organization hitherto has been necessarily unable to respond to them, and that the chief concern of moralists should be to improve the organization of society so as to make every function contribute to and share in the benefits of the whole organic life. This is the aim of socialism.

III

An accurate view of the meaning and the method of social progress could not precede the success of biology in explaining the meaning and method of organic evolution. But biological science is not much more than a century old, and for fully half its lifetime it has had to grope its way through tangled masses of ignorance and prejudice. Being the study of change in the organs and forms of life, biology had to remain dwarfed, whilst the miraculous views of creation, in accordance with which the world was supposed to be but in its youth, man almost as old as it, species the work of the hand of God, prevailed.

The first movement towards the final success of bold inquiry and speculation came from the geologists towards the end of the eighteenth century, and within fifty years this new science had thrown into the dusty lumber room of ancient beliefs the literal interpretation of the Biblical narrative of creation and everything it implies. The geological attack proceeded shoulder to shoulder with speculations regarding the origin of the species, and these cut even more deeply at the roots of cosmological views. Erasmus Darwin in 1794, and Lamarck from 1801, challenged the assumption that species were fixed, argued that differences of function altered organisms, and regarded these alterations as the cause of organic variation. From 1806 researches in embryology discovered the remarkable fact that in his embryonic history man goes through stages of life which are a summary of his species evolution from the protoplasmic cell to the human being. Science was occupying every position, and when in 1858 Darwin's *Origin of Species* appeared, the revolution was complete. There were still gaps in the evidence, there was still a possibility of alternative explanations, but evolution, the dynamic of life, was carried in triumph into the company of accepted beliefs.

IV

The philosophers, however, since philosophy was, had been exploring this same problem of evolutionary processes in its world significance. In the seventeenth century, that part of those processes which is concerned with man in community, began to receive special attention. In the eighteenth century, national circumstances gave these speculations a political character. A contest was raging throughout Europe between the people and their rulers. The people were asserting their rights to political freedom, and such an agitation necessarily brought into prominence the separate individual endowed with natural rights. The view of society which gave most sympathetic countenance to these demands was that of a collection of individuals bound together by some mythical social contract. Only from some such assumption could the advocates of political natural rights find historical roots for their agitation. The questions which were studied in an evolutionary frame of mind were, by political necessity, not the forms of social organization itself, but the changes which had taken place in the political relationships between the parties to the contract, as, for instance, the growth of the kingly power, the deterioration of the status of the people in the government, the constitution of representative assemblies, the character of parliaments. Thus, social science and philosophy were, for the time being, pushed aside to await the closing of this individualistic chapter in politics, and the liberating effect of science upon thought in general.

In Germany, however, the political problems which influenced intellectual speculation upon the nature of the social unity were different from those of France and England. In the German's heart the idea of a national unity lay directing his thoughts to the life of communities as well as to the liberty of individuals. Thus, Herder stated (1767) that 'there is the same law of change in all mankind and in every individual nation and tribe', and later on (1784–91) he developed the idea that each nationality 'lived out its own spirit'. Kant followed and amplified the same idea, and Fichte, smarting as a Nationalist under the heel of Napoleon, and employing his intellect to awaken Germany to a sense of national pride, proclaimed that the perfect individual life could only be found immersed in the common life. Hegel developed the idea. To him all things and all processes were but the manifestation of Spirit or Idea, which evolved itself by a peculiar method. The acorn becomes the oak through self-destruction: the animal continues to live only so long as the tissues which compose it continue to be destroyed: death is life: life is death. Hence, the universe exists by a constant change in its elements. But what is the nature of this change? Not, says Hegel, a change of growth in the things themselves, not a natural succession of one condition from another as youth insensibly matures to manhood. The change is really in the Idea, of which the changing phenomena are the manifestations.*
This, which has been called one of Hegel's 'most unfortunate blunders', is the error of the metaphysician, of the logician, untrained in the methods of science. It is naturally followed by a pronouncement that the issue of the more highly developed organisms from the lower is 'a nebulous idea which thinking men of speculation must renounce'. Hegel's philosophical

* *Encyclopädie*, § 249.

conception of evolution included a defence of fixed species, and was being shattered by science at the time it was absorbing the attention of metaphysicians.

Its interest to us is that, modified and applied to history, it was made the basis of the first grand attempt to give scientific precision to the Socialist idea by Karl Marx.

v

Marx was born in 1818, and attended the universities of Bonn and Berlin at a time when the chairs of philosophy were held by Hegelians, and when Hegelianism was unchallenged in its sway over German thought. He responded to the liberal spirit of hope which the accession of Frederick William IV to the Prussian throne in 1840 quickened in Prussia, and threw himself into politics and journalism. These pursuits required some knowledge of economics; and a study of the French economists, and of Proudhon in particular, directed him towards Socialism. In 1844, he met Engels in Paris, and from that time onwards he was engaged in completing the fabric of his Socialist theories and in creating the organizations which were to give them practical effect.

When Marx became a Socialist, he entered a movement distracted by many leaders each with different views, and ineffective by reason of loose organization. No strong penetrating mind had welded the dreamers into a united and aggressive organization or blended their dreams into a comprehensive social faith.

In France, where Marx then was, several schools of Socialist thought and propaganda flourished, each bearing the name of one or other of the distinguished Frenchmen who paved the way for the modern movement.

First amongst these was Saint-Simon, whose views, indicated by his last work *Nouveau Christianisme*, sought the establishment of a moral order of international peace and co-operative industry, and gave birth to a movement which hoped to bring about the reign of fraternity by destroying all the privileges of birth, of which inheritance of property was considered to be

71

the chief – 'the effect of which is to leave to chance the apportionment of social advantages and condemn the largest class in number to vice, ignorance and poverty' – and by bringing into 'one social fund' all the instruments of production and regulating their use by a hierarchy who should apportion work according to a man's capacity and assign wealth to him according to his work.*

Then came Fourier, the fantastical speculator upon the wonderful cycles of our earth's evolution and the architect of the phalanstery where men, working in groups according as desire prompted them and sharing by certain rules in the wealth produced, would be led by their circumstances to live harmonious lives.

Louis Blanc was the first of those prescientific Socialists to hold that if the basis of Socialism was moral, its method, nevertheless, should be political. He gave up the editorship of a newspaper because his proprietors objected to his opinions in favour of railway nationalization. But he had not discovered that an idea which is not supported by an organization of electors is politically impotent; and his belief that a member of a ministry could, all by himself, effect radical social change by persuasion or permeation, tended to misdirect the energies of his followers from building up an independent organization to taking part as an unorganized party in current political issues. Round him centred the demand for national workshops by which alone the characteristic tenet of his creed, the right to work, could be maintained, and the absorption of the means of production by the community be effected gradually and with certainty.†

* Letter addressed by the Saint-Simonians to the President of the Chamber of Deputies, quoted in Palgrave's *Dictionary of Political Economy*, London, 1904, iii, p. 346.
† Perhaps no social experiment has been more misunderstood and misrepresented than the Paris National Workshops of 1848. Louis Blanc, who is supposed to be their originator, wrote of them: 'As the kind of labour in these workshops was utterly unproductive and

Socialism and Society

But it was Proudhon who was in the ascendant when Marx sought refuge and opportunity for study in Paris; and he stood on the border line between Socialism and Anarchism.

Finally, in intimate touch with the Socialist movement proper were groups of revolutionary and reformist parties aiming at social reconstruction – from Blanquists to Comtists.

Here then was a floating mass of humanitarian feeling, of Utopian dreaming, of fanciful speculation and of sound economic criticism having in common a condemnation of the existing industrial system on the ground that it failed to feed, clothe and protect the producer of wealth, and also a belief that only by the organized people controlling the instruments of production could labour secure its due reward and the workman be able to command the comforts which he had earned.

But this mass of dreaming and discontent could have no great social value until it was pruned of the offshoots which were dissipating its vitality, until it was taught its own real meaning, until a definite statement of what was floating vaguely in its mind had been made, until its feelings were translated into a dogma, until its genesis was discovered. To do this was Marx's task. His Hegelian outlook presented to him a clear-cut view of the process of progress, and showed him the historical place of the whole movement; and he chose words to express its meaning designed to draw together the floating elements of the Socialism of his time by giving simple and clear definitions of the Socialist purpose, and by sifting out from the movement every vestige of vagueness and Utopianism and every trace of bourgeois

absurd, besides being such as the greater part of them were unaccustomed to, the action of the State was simply squandering the public funds; its money, a premium upon idleness; its wages, alms in disguise.' After describing the sort of workshops he wanted to establish, he proceeded: 'The *National Workshops* as managed by M. Marie were nothing more than a rabble of paupers.' Then he goes on to show 'that these workshops were organized in hostility to me, as the official representative of socialism'. Louis Blanc, *1848 Historical Revelations*, London, 1848, ch. 9.

Socialism which would not assimilate with the economic basis of history, surplus value and the class war.

The Communist manifesto was the first result. Issued when France was on the point of bursting out into revolution in 1848, the proletarian defeat in 'the first great battle between Proletarian and Bourgeoisie',* stifled for a time the movement of which the manifesto was the mouthpiece, but it was called upon sixteen years later to perform almost the same service as Marx originally designed for it, when the proletarian movement, divided into 'the English Trades' Unions, the followers of Proudhon in France, Belgium, Italy and Spain and the Lasalleans in Germany',† had to be brought together and its aspirations expressed in a common set of phrases.

Marx rejected the Utopian constructive proposals of his time, and fixed his attention on the evolution of society. He turned away from the creation of phalansteries, and sought to change the social fabric. He also brushed aside, as being of secondary importance in social change, in his day at any rate, moral notions of right and wrong. The broad outlines of the Socialist state were laid down by him, the passing character of existing social conditions was emphasized by him, the democratic control of capital was established for ever by him as the distinguishing mark of Socialist opinion. But his conception of the method of social change misled him as to how the socialist forces were to act. Darwin had to contribute the work of his life to human knowledge before Socialism could be placed on a definitely scientific foundation.‡

The influence of Darwinianism upon Socialism does not depend upon whether Darwin's special theories of evolution do or do not lead to Socialism. Virchow has said they do, Haeckel has said they do not; and the controversy will not be settled until

* Engel's introduction to *Communist Manifesto*, London, 1888, p. 3.
† ibid., p. 4.
‡ This subject is discussed in the first volume of this Library, *Socialism and Positive Science*, by Enrico Ferri, London, 1905.

74

the evolution of the state and society deprives it of reality. Socialism as a conception of a desirable organization of society is an idea which scientific investigations have illuminated and aided, but not created. The plan upon which the reconstruction was to be made, the justification offered for it, the way to attain to it, have depended very largely upon the state of scientific knowledge, and particularly upon the nature of the science which happened to be predominant – e.g., mathematical, chemical, biological or psychological. What Darwin, then, did, was not to lay down biological laws which, to use Virchow's expression, 'lead directly to Socialism', but to present a view of biological evolution which fundamentally affected our view of social evolution, and which, in consequence, indicated to us a more commanding standpoint from which to judge our Socialist proposals, a more accurate way for carrying them into effect, and a more scientific phraseology in which to express them. Darwinism applied to sociology is as far in advance of Hegelianism as Hegelianism was in advance of Kantian individualism. Marxianism, however, is a product of German thought during the second and third decades of the nineteenth century. It reflects the method of that thought; it reveals the imperfections of that thought.* 'Scientific socialism, once for all,' wrote Engels, 'is an essentially German product.'

Marx rejected Hegel's Idealism, but he retained the Hegelian notion of how the Idea evolved itself. Hegel's great contribution to thought was that he once more brought us back to consider all being as in reality a becoming. The metaphysician is ever prone to lose himself in a maze of unreal oppositions and contradictions because he microscopically examines phenomena at a given moment, and refuses to consider their growth, their potentialities, their origin. Thus is created an unreal world of

---

* cf. Engels. 'Readers will be surprised to stumble on the cosmogony of Kant and Laplace, on Darwin and modern physics, on Hegel and Classical German philosophy in a sketch of the growth of Socialism.' Introduction to *Socialism: Utopian and Scientific*, dated 1882. One is surprised to find Darwin, but not the others.

problems, absolutely insoluble because they are not part of the world at all. But so soon as we regard phenomena in their movements, in their evolution, in their potentialities, we are dealing with realities and not abstractions. Hegel brought us back to those realities.

Hegel's idea of growth, however, was mistaken. It is contained in the oft-used expression 'the negation of negation'. A process starts by a certain condition – e.g., the individualized production of primitive times; it then develops an opposite condition – e.g., the communal production of to-day, organized, however, for private profit; it finally reaches equilibrium, and spends itself in a third condition which harmonizes in itself the two opposites of the previous conditions – e.g., the coming Socialist State, which will combine communal production and individual advantage through collectivist organization.

Marx and Engels seized upon the common radical view of the eighteenth century – the view which lay at the root of Saint-Simonian politics – the class struggle, fructified it by bringing it in contact with the Hegelian dialectic and by substituting economic class motives for idealism as the moving power, and constructed, by a remarkable effort, both a philosophy of history and a political method. Change presented itself to Marx not as a process of functional adaptation, but as a result of conflicting economic interests seeking equilibrium. Hence, to this day, the metaphysical and logical faults of the Hegelian dialectic are vitiating the theories and dogmas of one Socialist school – the Marxian.

The Hegelian dialectic is unfitted to describe biological evolution. It describes superficial appearances rather than explains deep seated causes.* It would, for instance, explain what goes on in the hedgerows in spring as an opposition between the bud and the enveloping sheath: it would be blind to the great stirring up of life from deepest root to highest branch tip, of which the opposition between bud and sheath is but a small – if dramatic and easily seen – incident. For this reason,

* This is particularly true when it is used apart from Idealism, as Marx and Engels used it.

it cannot be dissociated from the idea of catastrophe and revolution, of accumulated energy bursting through opposition, of a simplicity of opposing forces which is never found in the actual world.

Marx himself, in his preface to the second edition of *Capital*,* illustrates this in the words he has chosen to express his indebtedness to Hegel. The rational Hegelian dialectic, he says, 'is a scandal and an abomination to bourgeoisdom and its doctrinaire professors, because it includes in its comprehension an affirmative recognition of the existing state of things, at the same time also the recognition of the negation of that state, of its inevitable breaking up: because it regards every historically developed social form as in fluid movement, and therefore takes into account its transient nature not less than its momentary existence; because it lets nothing impose upon it and is in its essence critical and revolutionary'.

One holding modern biological views would have expressed himself differently. Biologically, 'the negation of the existing state of things', its 'inevitable breaking up', 'its momentary existence', is impossible. Here we find, as we find everywhere in the Marxian method, a lack of a real guarantee (although there are many verbal guarantees) that change is progress. The biological view emphasizes the possibilities of existing society as the mother of future societies, and regards idea and circumstance as the pair from which the new societies are to spring. It gives not only an explanation of the existing state of things, but of its death – but certainly not its negation – in giving birth to a future state of things. It also views every form of existence in its actual process of movement and therefore on its perishing – very different from 'perishable' – side. It lays the very slightest emphasis on its 'critical and revolutionary' side, because it is mainly constructive, and the idea of 'clearing before building' is alien to its nature. Street improvements are not biological processes.

There is a very great difference between the constructive dynamic, the perfecting organization, the more coherent cooperation of the organs of society, which is the biological view,

* Dated London, 24 January 1873.

77

and the logical movements, the superficial oppositions, the cataclysmic changes which social progress appears to be when seen through the contorting spectacles of the Hegelian dialectic. The phenomena which need studying in a biological frame of mind, are the growing strength of the life-currents in society, their deflections owing to their strength, and the modifications in functions and organisms which are necessitated in consequence. In short, the biologist as social reformer deals with social life as a whole, studies its evolution as a whole, and in terms of the underlying whole regards the surface things which his eyes see and his ears hear – the oppositions of classes, the brooding revolutions, the perishing social tissues, the 'negations' of what exists.

Biology alone was competent to give the clue to the proper understanding of the process of evolution, because it was the science which dealt with the modes of change followed by organisms, and biology was as yet but stuttering its wonderful tale. Biology alone deals with the processes of vital change, the growth of the unlike from the like, the appearance of new qualities and characteristics, the gradual absorption and modification of parts, the development of new organs to fulfil new functions and respond to new circumstances. Taking on the one hand, the well-marked forms of new species, and, on the other, the forms of old species, biology had to study the growth of the first from the second, and from the very nature of its subject matter it had to reject explanations which assumed revolutionary changes or special creative fiats;* and it held it to

---

* Dr Bastian, Professor Hugo De Vries, Mr Bateson and others have pointed to certain facts and experiments which appear to show that organic transformation takes place rapidly or by leaps. Recently, this view has been brought before us particularly in De Vries's book on *Species and Varieties: Their Origin and Mutation.* If this view should succeed in receiving the support of investigators it will still only partly explain the origin and variation of species and would be very far from affording a biological analogy to the revolutionary conceptions of the *Communist Manifesto* and parts of *Capital.* It would go no further than emphasizing the method of epochal political progress by the formation of independent political parties which I discuss in chapter 6.

be axiomatic that whatever change it was studying issued from the total life of the organism and expressed the needs of that total life. If, for instance, it is a stomach that is being modified, the modification is owing to a change of food which nature has imposed upon the organism, or to the readjustment of the organs and functions of the organism. But Hegel was no biologist, and Hegel, not Darwin, was intellectual father to Marx.

Therefore it is that the expressions 'revolution' and 'revolutionary', which are so frequently met with in the writings and speeches of Marxians today, and upon which they insist as a mark distinguishing them from mere reformers, do not only indicate, as is sometimes supposed, and as Social Democrats when hard pushed try to make us believe, that emphasis must be placed upon fundamental change so as to make it clear that Socialism is not merely a proposal for engrafting upon existing society reformist shoots.* The words mean more than that. They indicate what Marx borrowed from Hegel. From his master in philosophy he acquired the habit of regarding social progress as moving from one epochal characteristic to its opposite over an intervening short revolutionary period. His mind dwelt on a 'periodic cycle, through which modern industry runs, and whose crowning point is the universal crisis'.† He never fully recognized the character of those intervening stages. To the biologist the old disappears by renewing itself, and whilst the transformation is taking place there is perhaps a rest, an apparent reaction, but no revolutionary chaos, nothing 'short and sharp'. But to Marx all that was meaningless. It was a view which was reactionary. Revolution was to him a real social fact when the old idea, crumbling by reason of its

* cf. Ferri's definition of revolution: 'The critical and decisive moment, more or less prolonged, of an evolution which has reached its climax.' What this means exactly is not very clear, and the biological examples which might be produced to throw light upon it cannot be used as sociological analogies. The critical stages through which a butterfly evolves, for instance, are the reminiscences of a racial past summarized in each individual: but there is no analogy for that in society.

† *Capital* I., xxxi. London, 1896.

age, was being swept away by its own antithesis. Our own epoch of production, amongst others, was to pass when* 'the integument [of capitalism] is burst asunder. The knell of capitalist private property sounds. The expropriators are expropriated.'

And again, 'Communists disdain to conceal their vows and their purposes. They openly declare that their ends can only be attained by the forcible destruction of all existing social order.'†

These sentences are typical of the deficiency of a sense of continuity which one finds in Marxian methods. The condition of England when Marx knew it (1840-70) supported him in his error. Economic considerations as the spring of conduct were preached from the most respectable housetops, and the state of society, absorbed as it was in production, and hopelessly confused when higher and more permanent ends were thrust upon it, gave ample justification for the most materialistic conception of the economic basis of history, class war and revolutionary methods. The country seemed to be flushed with incipient revolution. The 'antithetical' stage of production was at its height. The truth of the Hegelian 'movement' of three stages appeared to be about to show itself amidst the glow of flames and clouds of dust. Engels wrote his *Working Classes in England in 1844* as a last chapter in the history of the pre-Socialist state. 'The England of 1840-70 has therefore become to the Social Democrats what the Land of Canaan was to the Covenanters – the land from which all illustrations are drawn, on which all theories of what is and what ought to be are based.'‡

But the England of 1844 did not break out into revolt: Chartism did not develop into Socialism. The logical conclusion was not the line of advance. The class war created trade unionism; the working classes became citizens; law, morality, the force of combination lifted to some extent the pall of darkness which hung over the land. The Marxian today still wonders why England fell from grace. England did not fall from grace. Neither Marx nor Engels saw deep enough to discover the possibilities

* *Capital* I, 789.   † *Communist Manifesto*, p. 31.
‡ Hon. Bertrand Russell, *German Social Democracy*, London, 1896, p. 9.

of peaceful advance which lay hidden beneath the surface. Their analogies misled them.

Only when we understand the mind and the historical circumstances of Marx can we understand the phrases and key words that pass as current coin amongst Marxians all the world over. His philosophy belonged to an old generation; his logical view of the state was unreal; the words which he used, together with the conceptions which they expressed so accurately, are inadequate in relation to modern thought, and misleading for practical conduct; in short, whilst fully accepting the collectivist and Socialist conclusions of Marx, we must explain and defend them with a different conception of society in our minds, different formulae on our lips, and different guiding ideas for our activities.

The place which Marx occupies is on the threshold of scientific sociology, but not altogether over it.

Chapter V

Towards Socialism

What, then, are the forces in present-day society which Socialists should regard as making for Socialism?

I

The Marxian answer is that a war of classes is going on which one's eyes can see and one's ears hear. On the one hand is the exploiter, the person who accumulates surplus value, on the other, the exploited, the person who sells his labour power for a price which tends to sink to a bare subsistence level.* The opposition between those two classes grows in intensity. It will continue to grow until the workers, become class conscious, seize political power, and establish the Socialist state. In the words of the *Communist Manifesto*: 'The proletariat will use its political supremacy to wrest by degrees all capital from the bourgeoisie, to centralize all instruments of production in the hands of the state, i.e., of the proletariat organized as the ruling class.'†

Such a view is both inaccurate as to facts and misleading as a guide for action.

In the first place, it is not true that there are only two great economic classes in the community.‡ Marx was so anxious to

* 'The serf, in the period of serfdom, raised himself to membership in the commune, just as the petty bourgeois, under the yoke of feudal absolutism, managed to develop into a bourgeois. The modern labourer, on the contrary, instead of rising with the progress of industry, sinks deeper and deeper below the conditions of existence of his own class.' *Communist Manifesto*, pp. 15–16.   † p. 21.
‡ The *Communist Manifesto*, even in its day, admitted as much, but made no place for the fact in its theories.

separate himself from 'bourgeoisie' economists that he determined on no account to recognize the conflicting interests of
the receivers of rent and of profits.* Some of his followers
without allowing for the admission in their systems, concede the
antagonism, as for instances when Mr Hyndman describes the
trinity of labourers, farmers and landlords as being 'as compact
a little set of antagonisms as any in our society',† and later on
when he states that 'the only results of the confiscation of
competitive rents or royalties by the State ... would ... be
the strengthening of the hands of the capitalist class'.‡ This
is true only on condition that there is an economic antagonism
between landlords and capitalists as well as between capitalists
and workmen, and that the 'class war' is carried on not between
two but three armies, between any two of which there may be
treaties of peace and offensive alliances.§

But further, any idea which assumes that the interests of the
proletariat are so simply opposed to those of the bourgeoisie
as to make the proletariat feel a oneness of economic interest is
purely formal and artificial.‖ It is a unification arrived at only

* Rodbertus made the same mistake.
† *Economics of Socialism*, London, 1896, p. 194.   ‡ p. 209.
§ e.g., when the landed interests joined with labour to secure factory
laws, or when the capitalist interests join with labour to agitate for
land nationalization or for nationalization of mining rents, etc.
‖ An attempt has been made (cf. E. Ferri: *Socialism and Positive
Science*, Socialist Library, vol. I, pp. 75, 145, etc.) to give the class war
a biological meaning. In industrial society, it is said, the struggle for
life is carried on not so much between individuals as between classes,
the bourgeoisie and the proletariat, the exploiter and the exploited.
This does not correspond to the facts, for the more clearly economic
lines are drawn between classes, the more intense becomes the struggle
for life within these classes. What is in reality the most significant
change in the struggle for life as seen in society is, that the individual
struggle is no longer against nature, but against a social organization.
In pre-civilized days man struggled with man and nature for subsistence which was scanty because nature was niggardly or unwooed
by human toil; today man struggles with man and society for subsistence which is scanty because the organization of society prevents
the plenty which exists from finding its way into the possession of
industrious men. The class struggle is not a biological idea at all.

by overlooking many differences and oppositions, which have been growing for some time rather than diminishing. For although, in the earlier years of the Factory System, the line between workman and employer was not clearly drawn, and men could reasonably hope that by saving and by procuring credit they could become masters, today there is still a goodly number of workmen who cross the line and become employers or employing managers, whilst the great thrift movements, the Friendly Societies, the Building Societies, the Co-operative Societies, connect working class interests to the existing state of things. In addition, there are considerable classes of workers in the community whose immediate interests are bound up with the present distribution of wealth, and who, obedient to class interests, would range themselves on the side of the *status quo*.

Of course it may be said that all these sections, in refusing to help on the change towards Socialism, are making a mistake from the point of view of their own interests, and that if they were properly enlightened they would see that they belong to an exploited class, one and indivisible. That may be true, but a mode of action which is ineffective until men are 'fully enlightened' is a chimera. Moreover, it is equally true that if the capitalist were fully enlightened, he too would embrace Socialism on account of the great blessings which it would bring to him. Thus all that the class war, when used to indicate the opposing armies whose combat is to usher in the reign of Socialism, means, is that an enlightened proletariat, not blinded by its immediate interests but guided by its permanent ones, will be Socialist. But so also will a similarly enlightened bourgeoisie; hence the value of the class war as an uncompromising statement of hard economic fact becomes a mere semblance. It is nothing but a grandiloquent and aggressive figure of speech.

It is an indisputable fact that the wage-earner and the wage-payer have interests which are antagonistic, and in the nature of things cannot be reconciled. The supposed identity of interest between capital and labour, which is assumed to be proved by the discovery that unless capital pays high wages it will not be able to command efficient labour, is no identity of interest at all. The efficient labour which high wages produce is still bought and sold by capital, is still employed or rejected as it suits the convenience of capital, is still underpaid to enable capital to accumulate high dividends, is still treated not as something possessing rights of its own but as something which ministers to the interests of others. This opposition may be expressed as a class war. But it is only one of the many oppositions tending to modify social organization, and it is by no means the [most active or most certain in improving that organization.

There is, for instance, the opposition between consumer and producer. This opposition is peculiarly complex, because a man is a producer one hour and a consumer the next.* The most valid objection that can be taken to Trade Unionism (if it can be substantiated) is that it sacrifices the interests of the consumer to those of the producer. This has been illustrated in agreements between capitalists themselves and also between capital and labour. Combinations of capital to raise prices or to monopolize the market, and agreements with workpeople to share in the benefits of artificially high prices on condition that they support the pool by refusing to work for any firm outside it, are examples of this rivalry between the consumer and the producer. Sometimes the rivalry takes the form of a war between capitalists, as when the German producers of pig iron damage the interests of the German steel manufacturers by dumping the rawer material in England. In other words, trade rivalry is as real and more forceful as an impulse of the day than class rivalry. Sometimes capital and labour in combination fight against a class consuming certain commodities, as in the late bedstead combination; sometimes labour alone fights against the

* Tariff as it affects the wage earning class is the best illustration of this conflict of function in the same person, and the tug-of-war between the Protectionist and the Free Trader largely consists in the efforts of the one to induce the electors to think in the frame of mind of producers, and of the other to induce them to think as consumers.

consumer, as in the building trades where the increased price of labour has influenced costs of building, and consequently of housing accommodation.* The conflict of economic interest between the consumer demanding cheapness and the producer desiring to sell the use of his labour or the use of his capital at the highest rates, is also an economic conflict which must not be overlooked or smoothed away in a formal generalization. And it must be emphasized that the opposition is not one whit more unreal because the same man may belong at the same time to both the opposing classes.

Certain modern developments are tending to break up into well defined economic sections this 'uniform' proletariat class. Of these the Co-operative and Building Societies are the most important. In the first of those movements, the wage earner becomes an employer – or, as it presents itself more familarly to him, he is a receiver of dividends which, in part, are profits from other people's labour. All day, at his work in the factory or mine, he thinks of himself as the victim of the exploiter, as the loyal trade unionist, as the wage earner. But he comes home in the evening, washes himself, puts a better coat on his back, goes to his Co-operative Committee and immediately undergoes a fundamental change. Psychologically, he is a different man. He is no longer a wage earner and a trade unionist, but a capitalist employer, who has been known to join in the anathema against labour combinations.

This does not mean that wealth is being better distributed, but rather that the psychological basis of class is being undermined. The boast of a control of 'millions of money' which is made at every Co-operative Congress and the threat that capital and trade will leave the Stores if this or that departure in policy is decided upon, inculcates the capitalist frame of mind in the

* I desire to guard myself against misrepresentation here. Whilst I believe that the above statement is true, I impute no blame to the building trades' unions. If we have in the community a class so poor that they cannot afford to dwell in a house made under proper conditions of labour, that proves the existence of social evils which are not cured but intensified by keeping wages in the building trades at a low level.

worker, and though his sovereigns may be few, it is not the actual possession of riches which determines with what class a man associates himself. Imitation, as well as identity of economic interest, determines for practical purposes the class to which a man belongs. When a Primrose League dame shakes hands with an elector on polling day, she may or may not leave behind the shake a £5 note. But she certainly removes for the time being the psychological props upon which class feeling has been resting. Down it tumbles, and the elector goes and votes for his 'class enemy'. Patronage and charity have the same effect.

But the point is best illustrated by certain recent developments of co-partnership, which as an industrial theory is admirable, but as a sociological influence may be most reprehensible. The South Metropolitan Gas Company a few years ago determined to put an end to the organization of its men, and considered expedients for doing so. It decided to try co-partnership, and it succeeded. It bound its men to itself in precisely the same way as the proverbial man bound his donkey to his will by hanging a carrot in front of the animal's nose. Hoping ever to reach the carrot, the donkey romped home, and the driver's end was cheaply accomplished.

It is interesting to work out the financial equivalent of the class solidarity of the proletariat, and this gas company's experiment throws some light on the question. The co-partnership scheme has been in operation for fourteen years, 4,000 men are affected, and their total holdings are £170,000.* Hence, in fourteen years under the scheme a man can save a little over £40, or about £3 per annum; and as his active working life does not average thirty years, this scheme allows the average man to save altogether something under £100. For this the men have given up their right to combine and their freedom of action, and have consented to place themselves absolutely at the disposal of the employing company. The result has been that, whilst

* Paper by G. Livesey on the scheme, in *Methods of Social Advance*, ed. C. S. Loch, London, 1904.

nominally they are receiving specially good treatment, in reality specially good profits are being made out of them.*

By the second of those organizations – Building Societies – the interests of the working classes become identified with those of the landowning classes, and are opposed to every attempt of the community to enter into possession of the value which it imparts to land.

There is also another aspect to this. The interests injured by our present social state are not merely those of the wage earners. Considerable classes of people depend on the wage-earners, and of these the small shopkeeper is a type. His social grade sympathy, however, unites him with the *petite bourgeoisie* and divorces him from his economic supporters – the working classes – and thus rebukes the theorists who see in social motive little more than economic motive. Then there are those whose comfort and success under existing conditions are but precarious – the bankrupts, the struggling business people, those engaged in industries which are passing under the control of trusts. All those are in economic positions which expose them to the allurement of the Socialist ideal. But they are possessed by a pathetic desire to attach themselves to the classes which rest in economic calm and bask in a blaze of social sunshine above the tempests and the shadows in which the lower strata live, and from the depths to which they sink they cast an adoring eye upon the villas of suburbia, and from the midst of their ruin they bow the knee to whatever bears the approving stamp of respectability.

At this point we are able to strike at a vital defect in the 'class war' conception of progress. When we appeal to class interests

* This is admitted by the manager, who, in the paper referred to above, stated that the bonus given to the men is first of all earned by them. 'This,' he says, 'is proved by a comparison with the wages accounts of companies where the system is not in force, the rates of wages being the same, but the cost per ton of coal handled is considerably less.'

what do we do in reality? A man's class interests surely appear to him to be only his personal interests, – not his interests as a member of the wage earning class, not his interests as a citizen, not his interests as a member of a community, but his individual interests from day to day. There is no principle of social reconstruction in this feeling. There is the motive of a scramble or of class defence and preservation, the motive to secure big wages, short hours and favourable conditions of work. But that is all. The tug of the class war is across, not upwards. There is no constructive value in a class war.

The best expression of the class war is Trade Unionism. It is created on the assumption and experience that capital will do its utmost to exploit labour, and that labour ought to do its best to prevent capital from succeeding. The position is a simple and frank recognition of existing industrial fact. It concerns itself with no opposition except that between capital and labour, no union of interests except the interests of wage earning. It leads nowhere because it has no ideal goal; its only result can be the bondage of one side or the other. Here is a pure example of the class war. Nay, more, it is *the* class war.

The Trade Unionism, moreover, which is the purest expression of this simple antagonism between capital and labour, is what is known in this country as the Old Unionism, the Unionism which was opposed to labour politics, to Socialism, to everything except conferences with employers and strikes as a last resort. It was sceptical of any reconstruction, and decided in its opinion that if such reconstruction were to be tried, Trade Unionism was far too wise to have anything to do with it. This state of mind was also characterized by a narrow conception of trade interest as opposed to general interest. It is only the emptiest flattery to tell the old Trade Union Movement that its various sections ever have, or ever could have, considered anything but their own immediate interests when settling their policy from time to time. Each of the wings of an army for carrying on the class war is bound in the nature of things to fight its battles mainly for its own hand. Trade solidarity rather than proletarian solidarity is the real outcome of a class war in practice, and trade interest is ultimately individual interest.

Convey it in what spirit we may, an appeal to class interest is an appeal to personal interest. Socialist propaganda carried on as a class war suggests none of those ideals of moral citizenship with which Socialist literature abounds – 'each for all, and all for each', 'service to the community is the sole right of property', and so on. It is an appeal to individualism, and results in getting men to accept Socialist formulae without becoming Socialists. It springs from a time in the evolution of the Labour Movement when the narrow creed of the old Trade Unionism was the widest revelation that nature had yet made to men striving to protect themselves against the encroachment of capitalist power. In other words, the 'class war' idea belongs to the pre-socialist and pre-scientific phase of the Labour Movement.

I am aware that the Marxian argues that this class struggle is the last, and that when the proletariat have been emancipated, the epochs of struggle end. The argument is absurd. The emancipation of the proletariat will of itself be the signal for new struggles of economic sections with apparently opposing interests, and so long as these oppositions are made the main reason for social change, each triumph only leads to other battles, again and again renewed. It is not the emancipation of the numerical majority, or of a class so big as to be 'no class but the nation', which matters. What matters is the character of the motive power which effected the emancipation. If that power is the conflict of interests, it will reappear in the new regime, and if it finds no complete class to infuriate, it will enter herds of sections which will then be prepared to fly at each others' throats. The assumption that by a class triumph society is to emerge from the epoch of class conflict and sail gaily away upon the calm waters of fraternity, can be held only by those who have not ceased to believe in the magical and the irrational.

II

The antagonisms in society which result in organic change of a progressive nature are not merely economic. They are also intellectual and moral. Man is moved by his head as well as by his pocket, by the growth of social instinct as well as by cupidity. The richest possession of any man is an approving conscience. People who themselves have no quarrel with existing economic arrangements, must be sure the achievements of existing society by standards of right and wrong, must enter its dark corners and sojourn amongst its waste places, it wrecks and its ruins, and must turn in horror and weariness from the spectacle and begin preparing for a new order of things. Everybody does not pile up riches on his inner lights so as to smother them. Even if we regard economics as the main spring by which history moves, that does not prevent us from recognizing that only by a combination of intellectual guidance and economic needs does historical change become one and the same thing with progress.

The scheme upon which humanity evolves to higher and more humane stages of existence is either rational or it is not. If it is not, all organized attempts to hasten reform and make it effective – Socialism included – are waste effort. If it is rational, then progress becomes a matter of intellectual conviction, and man, seeking intellectual peace as well as economic security, will have to choose which he is to pursue. Even supposing he is a wage-earner and his pursuit of the means of life brings him into conflict with the existing state of society, his success will not depend upon his richness of experience in poverty, but upon the meaning he places upon his experience and the methods he adopts to place himself in different conditions. Economic needs may give volume and weight to the demand for change, but reason and intelligence, the maturing of the social mind, ideals of social justice grasped so firmly that they have become real existences for those who hold them, give that demand a shape, a policy, a direction. Socialism must, therefore, recognize the intellectual as well as the economic movement. And if it over emphasizes either side, let it be the former. For the pressure of economic need may exert itself in several conceivable directions, not every one of which opens the gateway to progressive advance. A consciousness of class disabilities may be either a motive for reactionary sycophancy or for revolutionary indignation. A man's poverty may make him a Socialist, but it is as likely to induce him to sell his birthright for a mess of pottage. The slum life may blossom into revolution, but it is as likely to flourish into imperialism. The rich are led away from the light by their great possessions, but the pressure of poverty also induces the poor to be content with the immediate satisfaction of appetite, and incapacitates them from patient and strenuous striving.

Not only, therefore, is it incumbent upon Socialism to recognize the existence of an intellectual motive, it must place that motive above the economic, because without it the economic struggle would be devoid of any constructive value; it would be a mere tug-of-war; it would never bring us to Socialism.

This line of thought appears to overlook the article in the Marxian creed that Socialism is inevitable. But the industrial and economic inevitability of Socialism is a mere fancy. It is inevitable only if intelligence makes it so. It is inevitable only if we are to develop on rational lines; it is inevitable, not because men are exploited or because the fabric of capitalism must collapse under its own weight, but because men are rational. It is the action of reason alone which makes our evils a sure cause of progress and not the possible beginning of final deterioration. Intelligence and morality set out the goal which makes struggles to escape the existing purgatory effective. Human evolution is a stretching out, not a being pushed forward. Acorns produce oaks, grubs grow into beetles, tadpoles into frogs, but slums, industrial crises, poverty, trusts, do not in the same way grow into Socialism. Man was 'inevitable' so soon as the amoeba appeared, but in the struggle for life which has taken place in the world of nature since life began, many species have been exterminated, many evolutions have never been completed. Arrested development is as conspicuous as finished processes.

The workmen who vote Liberal and Unionist today are perfectly conscious of the drawbacks of a life of wage-earning; they are also quite conscious that they belong to a separate economic and social class – and a great many of them would like to belong to another. In short, in any natural meaning of the words, they *are* class conscious. But they are not Socialists, because they are not convinced that the intellectual proposals of Socialism should receive their support.

In order, therefore, that the social organism may perfect tself, there must be the will for perfection and the definite idea as to what changes are required. The life of the organism is continued through change, and the organism itself is ever in a state of reorganization. Nation after nation has risen and fallen, others have risen, have attained to a certain civilization and there have stuck. But stagnation is impossible for our own Western peoples. They may fall; political combinations may crush them; the canker of poverty may make them degenerate. But if they are to continue to grow and to adapt themselves to new circum-stances, if they are to continue to improve, it must be by the organization of opinion and the operations of a constructive genius which sees the stage ahead and teaches the people how to attain to it. The Socialist appeal, therefore, is to all who believe in social evolution, who agree that the problem which Society has now to solve is that of the distribution of wealth, who trust in democracy, who regard the State not as antagonistic to, but as an aspect of individuality, and who are groping on-wards with the co-operative faith guiding them. That appeal may find some people in poverty, and they may follow because it offers them economic security; but it will find others in wealth, and they will follow because it brings order where there is now chaos, organization where there is now confusion, law where there is now anarchy, justice where there is now injustice.

Socialism marks the growth of society, not the uprising of a class. The consciousness which it seeks to quicken is not one of economic class solidarity, but one of social unity and growth towards organic wholeness.

III

We can now see to what combination of interests and convic-tions we must appeal, and how we must direct that appeal, in order to create the organic order of the Socialist State out of the atomic chaos of the present day.

I reject what seems to me to be the crude notion of a class war, because class consciousness leads nowhere, and a class struggle may or may not be intelligent. But still, we turn our hopes first of all to the wage-earners. They are the most certainly doomed victims of the present chaos; they suffer most from the inability of the present system to provide employment, wages, life; they are least buoyed up by elusive hopes that a lucky turn of the wheel of fortune will pitch them up on the backs of others; they are the helpless spills tossing on the troubled waters of present day strife; their attempts to share in the benefits of an efficient method of production result in little but turmoil, hunger and poverty; and above all, their needs have now become the chief concern of society, because in fulness of time social organization is being tested by its human results, and because the economic enfranchisement of the people naturally treads upon the heels of their political emancipation.

And it is of special note for the moment, that they have been subject recently to rebuffs and attacks in the press, the Courts of Law and Parliament, and thus have been taught the necessity of political unity and independent organization. The politics of an enlightened industrial democracy is of necessity social, and is aimed at ending experiences of unemployment, old age pauperism, and so on. Hence, as one of the laws of evolution is that need creates organs, redistributes and organizes functions and changes biological types, working class policy must be directed towards the organization and the development of the organs and function of mutual aid in society. So soon as a serious attempt has been made to frame a policy directed to such ends, it will be found that monopoly in land and the use of industrial capital for individual profit, are the sources of the experiences which society now seeks to shun, and they must consequently be supplanted by public ownership and production for use before labour can enter into enjoyment of the blessings which an efficient method of wealth production makes possible. Labour has but one intelligent road of advance – that of economic and industrial reconstruction – that of Socialism.

Amongst the wage-earners, therefore, we must expect to find in fullest development, and in forms most political and effective for organic change, those vital and vitalizing disturbances which indicate active life pushing out to higher forms of organization. But those disturbances, as has been shown, are not purely economic, and are not therefore confined to wage-earners, and consequently in order to gather together the forces making for Socialism, the basis of the movement must be such that everyone sharing in the disturbed promptings may be included.

All barrier phrases and sectional dogmas must be removed from Socialism. The experiments in factory legislation, in public health regulations, in education, in municipalization, are pointing out to men of all classes the desirability of going yet further along the road which leads to Socialism, and are forming in the minds of men of all classes a conception of society, of the community and the individual, formed on Socialist principles. When we think systematically of the scattered fragments of reform promised by the political parties, we see that they are but the foreshadowing of Socialism; when the tendencies begun by scores of experiments – factory laws, public health laws, municipalization – are followed out, joined together, systematized, Socialism is the result. This completeness of organization, this idea of national and communal growth, this state of business efficiency, nothing short of it and nothing which is sectional in it, should be laid down as the basis of Socialism. And the political movement which is to express, and ultimately satisfy, this need for the organic unity of Society, must be a movement of the whole of society and not of one of its functions – the working classes. As the brain moves obedient to the grossest as well as the purest prompting of the needs of the living thing, so must the political organ in society be subject to the purest prompting of moral intelligence as well as the grosser prompting of economic need, but both must be united if a more perfect form of society is to be created.

Ramsay MacDonald's Political Writings

Economic hardships are the flints on the road, but these flints may develop on us the hoofs of the beast, or may compel us to use our intelligence to find smoother paths. Socialism is the latter alternative.

SOCIALISM

Chapter I

The Man and the System

To the ordinary man, not of the street but of the suburb, Socialism covers a multitude of sins. He does not understand what Socialism means – and probably does not want to understand. It occupies in the vocabulary of his intelligence a place with those abracadabra and mystic pass words which, when uttered, raise the seven devils. It is nothing but a waste of time to explain new ideas to such people. They are the despair of everyone who tries to bring commonsense into politics, and the victims of those who appeal to popular ignorance and fear.

Socialism and Social Change

But there are others to whom our existing social relationships are an unhappy puzzle, who are not convinced that the distribution of riches in the State is fair, or that either wealth or poverty is any indication of merit or demerit. Moreover, from the distressing nature of our social problems, these people take an intellectual interest in the present as the transition from the past to the future. At no given moment is society to them a rigid organization. It came from one form: it is passing to another form. This is particularly so in industrial organization. Within the memory of a still virile man, the Limited Liability Company has arisen; within the memory of most, the Trust has been born; and the fundamental and revolutionary change which these events imply in the relations between employer and employed, of capital and labour, in the way in which capital is to be used, and in the considerations which act as restraints upon the too excessive subordination of the human creature to the invested capital, has been seen in its beginnings by this generation. As the organization of capital has proceeded in an increasingly large scale, and as the relationship between employer and employed has become, in consequence, more impersonal, more economic and less human, the State, as such, has passed a series of laws asserting its right to protect the weak and to adjust the admitted inequality established by modern capitalism between employers and employed.

Minds aware of this constant readjustment of industrial functions and of the growing invasion of the modern workshop by law, regard with impatience and contempt the attempts made to present Socialism as the gospel of the envious, the wastrel, the scoundrel. The Socialist doctrine systematizes these industrial changes. It lays down a law of capitalist evolution. It describes the natural history of society. It is not, therefore, only a popular creed for the market-place but a scientific inquiry for the study. Like every theory in sociology it has a political bearing, but it can be studied as much detached from politics as is Darwinism.

Socialism is a theory of social organization, which reconciles the individual to society. It has discovered how the individual in society can attain to a state of complete development. For the foundation of such a theory one of three assumptions must be made. We may assume that a moral relationship can be established between individuals, as the Comtists and some of the anarchists do, and that this will counterbalance the advantages which a superior economic position gives to some men to exploit others unjustly. This, however, gives no guarantee of stability. The son is not as the father was. Or we may assume, as the Individualists do, that economic advantages always tend to pass out of unworthy hands – a pleasure-loving son dissipates the fortune inherited from a hard-working father – so that, on the whole, a state of unregulated competition for economic power allows the maximum expression of individual liberty. This is the present system. Or we may assume that economic sovereignty cannot be safely given to individuals but should belong to society organized, so that by a system of co-operative industrial effort the individual may be freed from the possibility of economic slavery, and may share in the benefits which increasing economic advantage brings.

This last is the Socialist view. We have to experiment with intricate relationships between capital, land and labour; between the interests of those who possess and of those who can only use by permission; between those who live by work day by day and those who live from incomes drawn from profits; and the end at which we aim is such a relationship between the industrial community of men and the tools and the raw material which they use as will completely subordinate production to human well-being. The existence of the slum and the waste field side by side; of the unemployed bootmaker without a decent pair of shoes on his feet and yet unable to translate his natural need for shoes into an economic demand for his own labour as a shoemaker; of dilapidated rural houses and an intense depression in the building trade; prove as conclusively, it seems to me, that our industrial mechanism is out of gear, as a full cistern but a dry tap proves that there is an obstruction somewhere in the pipe. How to make natural need – the shoeless carpenter – the occasion of work for the furnitureless shoemaker – is the problem which Socialists believe they can solve, and the system by which they would solve it is Socialism.

The Human Sacrifice

Most people are unwilling to admit that the grand effect of modern industry has been to subordinate moral and human riches to material gains; but it is true nevertheless.

In a senseless and mechanical way, we reel off our tongues truisms about the responsibilities of property. We mean nothing by these truisms, and they only darken our vision. It is not the responsibility of property which we need to emphasize, but the subordination of property to human ends. Today we have people driven off the land. We regret it, but the land being private property we do not see our way to stop the sacrifice of State and human interests incurred by the use to which private owners put land. We have periods of overwork alternating with periods of unemployment, but industrial capital being held by private individuals 'who are not in business for philanthropic reasons', we regret the circumstances but do not see how we can alter them. We have low paid women's labour being substituted for more highly paid men's labour, and children's labour taking the place of women's; we have heads of families no longer able to secure wages high enough to be a family income; we have children offered the inducement of comparatively high wages for temporary unskilled work which is to doom them to be casuals for ever on the industrial market – we admit with much regret the evil, but commerce must be carried on, competition is severe, and, though we do not like to say so to the world, we whisper up our sleeves that men must be sacrificed to trade. No employer employs a man because he happens to have married a wife and is anxious to do his duty as a husband by her, because he is a citizen and wants the leisure necessary to prepare himself to exercise the franchise intelligently, because he has a soul and needs relief from the worry of bread-and-butter problems in order to prepare himself for heaven. A man is employed because his employer can make a paying percentage on his labour. There are a few exceptions, but that is the rule of commercialism, and the poor employer who breaks the rule breaks himself.

There is a mechanism of commerce. It has no soul and no sentiment. It is economic only. It is built up upon the exchange of commodities. It relates to demand and supply on markets. Theoretically our economists tell us – and tell us truly – the shoemaker makes shoes in order that he may exchange them for a table which the carpenter is making, and for coal which the miner is blasting. But this exchange is carried on by a system of transfers, at every point of which there is a group of personal controlling interests which play their part in exchange only if they can make profit, and the exchange between the original producers is only effected if the whole system is in working order, e.g., makes profit at every point. The simplicity of exchange does not exist. Human interests are subject to the necessities of the commercialist system.

Living as we do in the midst of this system, moving and having our being in it, it is difficult to think of any other order. So unfamiliar to us is anything new that we are completely tripped up by considerations of how wages could be paid, foremen appointed, and roads scraped under any other social organization but that of which we are now part. It is almost impossible for us to settle down to the thought that society grows, that the relations of its functions change, that age slips into age not by mechanical but by organic methods, that we make beginnings here and there, that small experiments proclaim great principles, and that limited experiences show the way to epochal changes. Such a frame of mind comes only after much thought. Meanwhile we are unshakeable in our belief that however little we may like it, humanity *must* be subordinated to our system of profit-making.

The Human Struggle

No *must* was ever more rickety than this. Matter, property, economic systems have always been trying to dominate men, and men have always resisted. They have never fully succeeded in their resistance, but the fact that they have continued to carry it on, points to some state of society awaiting us in which man will dominate economic systems and other purely material things.

Hitherto social history has been the record of conditions under which the individual has been subordinated to social needs. The race and the community have been preserved, the individual has been sacrificed. Intensely dramatic as has been the struggle between individuals for existence, even more dramatic has been that between the community and the individual for a common life. Feudalism subordinated the villein to the social conditions necessary for the continued existence of a political community in the Middle Age; in times earlier than those a more absolute subordination – amounting to slavery – was the common condition of the ordinary man, because the storm and stress then suffered by his community necessitated absolute subjection and unquestionable obedience. If in still earlier times, as tradition has it, a golden age of liberty existed, the necessities of social evolution destroyed it. It disappeared in a 'dark unfathomable sea of cloud' – to emerge some day.

But in the times when obedience was most necessary the *I am I* of the human intelligence was an unwilling bondsman. The slaves and the villeins revolted; the labourers haggled over their hire. Moreover, if individuality in some of its aspects which we profess to cherish today was held upon a low valuation, certain primitive personal rights were generally recognized. Women and slaves, the beasts of burden occupying the lowest status in most primitive states, were as a rule protected by some more or less elementary code of custom or law; and the poor were saved from the direst consequences of poverty.

Our Bible makes us familiar with a method of protecting the poor from the exactions of those in a more advantageous economic position, which was a consciously definite acknowledgment that without such protection the possession of economic power would lead to enslavement. The Jubilee of the Israelites was instituted for the purpose of preventing the few in straitened circumstances from being alienated for ever from the land, the source of their life, even when they had been compelled to part with it temporarily; and other laws and customs kept the usurer in his place, secured some measure of equity for the labourer, regulated the transfer of house property; and, generally, the people were exhorted and compelled to show by their social actions that they remembered the days when they were bondsmen in Egypt, 'to the end that there be no poor amongst you'.* The days came when Israel forgot the bondage of Egypt, when house was added to house and field to field; but when the prophets rose to their grandest heights of vision or sunk to their lowest regions of despair, the Messianic days when a king was to rule righteously and when the widow and the orphan would be no more oppressed, made their joy thrill with lyrical welcomes and their lamentations moan with the sorrow

* Deuteronomy 15 iv.

of the sinful, exiled far from the land of righteous dealings and human relationships.

In the history of every community some such attempts as we see in the history of Israel have been made to protect the individual against the anti-social use of property held by a class.

What is the position of the individual under modern commercialism?

Modern Conditions

A man is not now dragged into a market to be bought and sold, he walks into the market and sells himself. He cannot live without labour, and the earth being private property and production of commodities being carried on under a system which can be worked only by the employment of much capital, he has no free access to the raw materials provided by nature upon which he has to expend his labour, and he cannot enter the ordinary produce markets because they are organized in such a way as to shut out the individual. The necessity is, therefore, imposed upon him of selling his power and ability as a worker to someone who is in a position to use it. He enters into a contract for service. The contract may range from a day to a period of years, but whilst he is working under it, he is as much bound to his employer as the peasant was who had to give labour to his overlord.

I am not urging the essential likeness in this respect between the workman of the twentieth century and the peasant of the twelfth in order to depreciate the position of the former. I am doing so only because I want to point out the absurdity of claiming, as some people do, that the wage-earner, as such, is now free. Society has become more fluid in its class relationships, and that is an enormous gain to the individual, but the condition of the landless and the propertyless man today is still one which compels him to sell himself to another in order that he may command the physical necessities of life. A man will always have to do service in order to be able to command these necessities, and such service Socialists demand. But that which has to be given today is given under certain circumstances which make it impossible for Socialists to regard it as the final economic relationship between a man and his society.

What are these circumstances?

1. *Service today carries with it an inadequate payment.* John Stuart Mill pointed out that in his time reward was great as labour was little, and that reward was little as labour was arduous. Nothing more strikingly shows with how little critical intelligence we approach the common experiences of life than the assumption nearly always made that if we put an end to property-owning no one would be found to work. No one seeks to destroy property, but if he did he would use the existing state of things as an argument in his favour. Poverty rather than property is the reward of labour today. The great mass of the workers own no property – even their most successful attempts to accumulate, such as Trade Union benefit funds and Co-operative Society deposits, are insignificant when divided out per head amongst those entitled to have them.

2. *The bargain between labour and capital stops at a point which shows that it is a contract which uses the needs of the one to add to the profits of the other.* One of the claims which the modern individualist makes with most assurance is that when a man leaves a factory he is free – when he has completed his toil under his contract, he is free. That is true only to a limited extent, as we shall see; but in so far as it is true it is only partly a gain. It means that the person or the class who has been benefiting by the labour of the other person or class, has managed to throw off many of its ancient obligations to the labourers. It has no responsibilities for them so soon as they cease to make profits. It can in busy and profitable years accumulate vast possessions off their labours; so soon as trade slackens it brings its contracts to an end, and its workers have no claims for further consideration. The labourer is no longer a charge upon property in seasons of scarcity. The possessor gets his labour without incurring any responsibility beyond that of paying the wages stipulated in the bond. The free labourer is thus much more a means of serving other people's ends than he

was when he was a bondsman. The movements now on foot to make the rich districts aid the poorer ones in matters of rating, to establish Old Age Pensions from the National Income, to ease the pressure of unemployment upon the industrial classes, are all attempts to get the community to assume responsibilities which are complementary to the labour contracts of our modern 'free' society; and the demand that these obligations should be met by taxes upon property can be defended ultimately only upon the ground that we are exacting from the class which benefits from the contracts the obligations which it eludes in 'free' society, but which it had to bear in more primitive times and under conditions of chattel slavery.

3. *The contracts nominally economic and industrial only, influence thought and conduct.* The slave was not allowed to act contrary to the interests of his master; the free workman who is a heretic in respect to any accepted thought or action is victimized. Putting the most sympathetic explanation upon this, the employer can plead that the opinions and actions of the men are elements in their industrial value to him. This in some cases is perfectly true, but it only proves that the conditions which imposed limits on the action of bondsmen still exist. The trade unionist, the anti-vaccinator, the chapel-goer, the radical, the Socialist are marked for destruction; free thought and free expression of opinion are suppressed.

4. *The contracts tend more and more to absorb the whole active life of the labourers; that active life tends to become concentrated within the years of youth; a ripening skill tends to become of less value, and industrial old age comes sooner and is more and more a state of chronic unemployment.* The English peasant was free from this; slavery was very often free from it. The speeding up of machinery and the increase in the rapidity of work compel the labourer to give more and more of himself in the service for which he receives wages; the liberties which he theoretically enjoys when he is not in the factory or at the bench, become, in consequence, of diminishing value and reality; the absence of the slave's claim upon his master for shelter becomes a greater and more pressing grievance. His *life* is spent in servitude.

And in this stunning whirl the capitalist is equally involved. He, too, is the slave of his system, as the steady increase of insanity and minor nervous disorders shows.

Against such servitude man is still in revolt. These are not the conditions of liberty. Service will always be required, but its reward should be full and adequate, and not merely temporary and inadequate. The man who labours to maintain his community will continue to ask as wages an adequate share in the life and property of his community. Possession in men was bound to decay, and equally so will possession in the fruits of other men's labour disappear. The one was an early chapter in the history of slavery, the other is a late chapter in the same story.

The following reasons may be assigned as the cause of the modern Socialist movement. The existence of poverty, unemployment, slums; an inability to see why the rich are rich particularly when they are idle; the glaring effects of landlordism; the anti-social results of capitalism at its worst, e.g., sweating, Penrhynism, etc.; the systematization of certain modern tendencies like municipalization, industrial laws, etc.; the consciousness of Trade Unionism that it cannot advance the interest of the worker much farther upon present lines; the tendency to relate morals to conditions of life; the reaction against Manchesterism and the worship of the vulgar and uncultivated wealthy; the increased interest taken in historical and sociological science, and the neo-Darwinism which emphasizes mutual aid as well as competition as a factor in human progress; the rationality of the Socialist proposals; the effect of the evolution of industrial organization upon the human intelligence; the lack of philosophical principle in the aims of other political parties.

Chapter II

The Socialist Movement

Industrial Evolution

The Socialist traces in the history of labour a steady consistent impulse. Primitive organization was personal and local. Its economics were those of a people who consumed their own products. But as the bounds of the family and the tribe widened, as means of communication were established and exchange of commodities created a system of commerce, two things happened. The community became subdivided into workers and merchants or traders, and the class of workers was subdivided into specialized trades. At first this industrial organization was subordinated to military necessities. The workman was to all intents and purposes the property of his military superior. This, in the abstract, was the spirit of the Middle Age – particularly of the early Middle Age. But the industrial organization and needs of the community asserted themselves. They grew lustily, obedient to the laws of their own being. They came into conflict with the military organization. They imposed a new necessity upon the State. The social organization of feudalism ceased to be able to express the life of the community. Trade routes were established. South and west the sea rovers went. The Indies were found out; America was discovered.

Here was a new world. Every sea and shore cried out to the West to come and exploit it. Pirates became national heroes. The individual rose up in his rank primitive majesty and literally became a law unto himself. The rules of guilds and the restrictions of ancient municipalities then also ceased to fit the new developments of trade and became hampering restrictions which the newer formed centres of industry would not countenance. The life of the new era refused to obey the rule of the old, and men began to believe that anarchy was the law of nature.

The end of the Middle Age came with the rise of capitalist industry, the industrial predominance of the towns and the beginning of the factory system. It went down into the past in the midst of a bright glare of democratic hope. There was heresy in the Church; there were visions of a new earth in the minds of men; there was revolution in the State. The new age was to be one of rare triumph for the common people. True, a new and threatening kind of poverty was spreading like a foul canker throughout Europe. The ancient aristocracy were becoming commercially minded, agriculture was beginning to be carried on on business principles, commons were enclosed, the ancient peasant rights to the use of the soil were being denied, the heroes of the wars were tramping on every road and begging in every shire. These, however, were but incentives to the democratic evangelists. Utopias, theocracies, democracies were dreamt of, and the French and American Revolutions appeared as angels in the air summoning the chosen ones of the people to smite the Canaanite and enter into possession of his lands. In these times, the roots of the modern Socialist movement are embedded.

It sprung into being almost simultaneously in England and France, and was an offshoot of the radical movements which passed over these countries in the last quarter of the eighteenth century.

France

In the bosom of France lay the terrible diseases from which sprung the French Revolution, and which worked themselves out on the Place de la Concorde. But until the wars of the Empire had ended, France had no time to consider what had really been the effect of her Revolution. Personal liberty had been greatly amplified, but the economic positions of authority from which the aristocracy and the clergy had been evicted had fallen into the hands of the middle classes. By the beginning of the nineteenth century factory industry on a modern scale had fairly begun in France, and the town workmen suffering from the immigration from the country and from those economic tendencies, which were then almost unbridled, to reduce wages to a bare subsistence level, commenced to think politically in terms of class conflict. Rousseau, Mirabeau, Condorcet, Mably had taught the people to hold property, as it was then known, in light esteem. 'I know of only three ways to exist in society,' said Mirabeau in 1789; 'one can be a beggar, a thief, a worker. . . . The property owners are but the agents, the economists of the body social.' 'To each his field' was a shibboleth of the Jacobins. The economic conditions of France gave rise on one hand to the physiocratic school of economists – the school which gave the world the watchword of unscientific individualism, *laissez-faire*, *laissez-passer*; and, on the other hand, it gave birth to a Socialist school of thinkers who laid down some of the most important foundation-stones of the Socialist fabric of thought. Commercialist individualism and Socialist proletarianism sprang into existence simultaneously.

Saint-Simon (1760–1825)

The sociological and economic speculations blended with a generous humanitarianism, which marked the intellectual revival of France after the exhaustion of the Napoleonic wars had worn off, focused themselves, first of all in Claude-Henri de Rouvroy, Count de Saint-Simon, a scion of a noble house devoted to absolute government, a volunteer with La Fayette to the War of American Independence, a rare soul who, largely under the influence of that queer customer, Benjamin Franklin, came to understand that civil life and the workman were quite as honourable as the military calling and the soldier. Made a prisoner by the British, he was sent to Jamaica, where he spent his time speculating upon such questions as how to make a canal through Central America. Natural Science was still in its infancy. Imagination and enthusiasm were its companions, and a fellowship of worthy but pottering investigators and speculators were sponsors to the infant. Saint-Simon was one of these. Endowed with extraordinary prophetic foresight in some respects, and in others devoid of practical capacity, Saint-Simon passed from abstract Natural Science, and, in 1817, appeared his first volume on social matters entitled *l'Industrie*, its sub-title being – *Political, Moral and Philosophical Discussions in the Interest of all Free Men, and of useful and independent Work*. He died on 19 May 1825.

His system at its best and fullest development is moral, or, to use a more recently adopted phrase, it is 'economic chivalry'. 'Men ought to conduct themselves as brothers one to another.' He translates the formula of Benthamism into terms of his own creed thus: 'Men ought to place before themselves as the purpose of their work and actions, the most prompt and complete possible amelioration of the moral and physical existence of the most numerous class.' The Revolution has come far short of doing this. The middle class has reaped all its benefits. This class has been content to establish the English parliamentary system in order to exploit twenty-four twenty-fifths of the nation. The industrial nation should be organized so as to secure for each member the maximum of comfort and well-being. In working out his scheme of reorganization, he seeks to base it on the intellectual and moral elements in the State. His system does not rest upon its own foundation; his machine does not work by its own mechanism. A good will and a pure motive in certain classes are essential to the success of Saint-Simonism. A council of scientists, thinkers, artists, industrials is to be the active functioning authority in Saint-Simon's Utopia, and later on when the moral and philanthropic emotions of Saint-Simon take a more definite place in his intellectual scheme, his council undergoes a corresponding modification, and, at the same time, he somewhat surprisingly increases his trust in the State as the condition of industrial liberty, and restates his belief that the right to individual property is a matter of utility.

Saint-Simon was, therefore, not so much a Socialist as an originator of Socialist thought. He suggested systematic thinking rather than presented it himself. He held up an ideal of society which men approved; he proposed to create it by ways which men rejected, but in rejecting them they built up Socialism. Above all he taught men that the control of a system of property-owning was more vital to a people than the control of a legislative machine.

Saint-Simon's disciples carried on his work after his death, systematized his opinions and imparted propagandist force to them. Chief among these as Socialist pioneer was Bazard, the severe practical logician, who thought his way from the Is to the Is-to-be, unified and completed his master's creed, and took his stand upon political revolutionary Saint-Simonism, rather than upon the Saint-Simonism of vague moral phrasing and ecclesiastical tone. The law of association is developed by Bazard, and becomes a definite creed in the philosophy of history. As slave, as serf, as proletariat, the worker has been exploited. Every stage is an advance upon the preceding one, and now comes the next stage when by association the workers are to exploit the globe. At present, under pressure of the necessity to do something in order to live, the workman has to submit to be exploited by employers, and the landlords exact rent to which they are not entitled. The social system by which that is done is perpetuated by the laws of inheritance. That all the instruments of production should be held by industrial associations of workers is the only remedy for this state of things, and Saint-Simonism thus drifts into economic Socialism.

Fourier (1772–1837)

Charles Fourier, born in 1772, is another type of those times when science awoke men's curiosity, and enticed them to the fantastic. Fourier was destined by his parents to be a draper, but was devoted to musical harmony and mathematics of an occult kind. At an early age he was punished for telling the truth when a falsehood would have been commercially profitable, and a further experience in business led him to the belief that commercial art consisted in buying sixpence worth for threepence and in selling threepence worth for sixpence. A quaint, gentle, simple-minded character, he hoped to cure all social evils by giving free play to the human passions. He was, therefore, essentially a Utopist and social architect. The phalanstery which he built up in his imagination as the perfect community, with its three square leagues of land, its three hundred families, its ingenious rules of economic housekeeping, its repulsive innovations, could not succeed in practice. But it was an attempt to show how co-operation and association in industry could succeed in abolishing poverty without the coercion of a central State, and without the collective property in the means of production which the Saint-Simonians had come to regard as essential. Fourierism was, indeed, anarchism in one aspect, individualistic co-operation, as developed by Godin, in another aspect, and municipal Socialism in yet another aspect. His system was one of co-operation in production and in the arrangements of life, but with individual rights always in the background to fall back upon should the community – the phalange – prove tyrannical or otherwise obnoxious.

Fourier's essential anarchism balanced the State authority of the Saint-Simon school, and his mechanical arrangements were at the opposite extreme from Saint-Simon's ecclesiastical moralities. Although Fourier's first published work appeared in 1805, his system received little notice until after the school of Saint-Simon had passed under a cloud.

Louis Blanc (1811–82)
The Industrial Revolution proceeded apace in France, and the propertyless worker became a larger and larger class separated from the propertied land and capital owner by a widening gulf. Saint-Simonism and Fourierism were mainly intellectual in their appeals. They did not at first reach the working classes. But the democratic movement was at hand. France, after the regime of autocracy which followed the wars of the Empire, was governed from 1830 by a Liberal monarch. Free discussion

was allowed. Political economy was moulded in scientific moulds. Reason knocked at the closed doors of religious tradition. Beranger, Victor Hugo, Balzac, George Sand brought romance into touch with the life of the common people. Cabet reverted to the ancient methods of building Utopias from dream stuff. Responsive to this outburst of life, Buchez tried to found a progressive Catholicism; Villeneuve-Bargemont and others advocated various modes of association based upon doctrines akin to Christian Socialism; but, above all, Louis Blanc established a connection between these social theories of equality and political action.

If anyone is entitled to be called the Father of modern Socialist methods, Louis Blanc has claims almost as good as any rival. He drew men's attention away from revolution: he felt that the liberal epoch had made revolution unnecessary and therefore misleading. His two chief ideas were that under the stage of individualism, labour was disorganized; that there was unemployment and over-production; and that the State should bring cosmos out of this chaos. In a sentence, his Socialism was a system under which the 'Right to Work' could be recognized. He saw that fundamental social change was to be brought about by reform – not reform of the liberal kind, but reform which meant the systematic approach by stages, each one of which led up to the next, to some well-defined end. Capital and the large workshop were accepted by him as necessary, but he argued that the State, and not a private individual, should be the capitalist – 'the banker of the poor'. He therefore devised his scheme of 'social workshops' which were to be subsidized by the State and were gradually to take the place of individually owned workshops which competed with each other. He also claimed that his schemes could be worked more economically in every way than those of private capitalists, and that, therefore, they would become general by reason of their own merit.

When he became a member of the Provisional Government in 1848, he had an opportunity of subsidizing some social workshops. Although in time – one lasted for about thirty years – they were all closed, their large measure of success and their capacity to struggle against most adverse circumstances showed the practicability of the scheme. Unfortunately these experiments are almost forgotten, and people remember only the Paris National Workshops, which in no way tested Louis Blanc's proposals, and which were opposed by him as being started on wrong lines.*

Louis Blanc had the misfortune to arouse the enmity of the communist revolutionaries and the dogmatic school of collectivists, the revolutionary political impossibilists, who have added heroic chapters to the sad history of the collectivist movement, but who have done little to 'make their dreams come true'. Whilst lacking in force of will and definiteness of purpose, he could not face the attacks made upon him and use the splendid political opportunities which he had more than once. Driven into exile during reaction, blamed for not siding with the revolution of 31 October, and again for taking no part in the rising of 18 March, and sinking finally into impotence in the National Assembly, he is held up as being a mere reformist politician. His opponents – some of them moved merely by personal dislike – who ought to have been his friends, drove him from the Left towards the Right in politics, and the Socialist movement continued to be an agitation rather than a transforming fermentation. Louis Blanc never entered into his inheritance.

Proudhon (1809–65)

Finally, so far as this stage of the movement goes, came Proudhon, a kind of French Cobbett, an educated workman, a genius enlightened by flashes of wisdom which in their detached gleams were illuminating but intermittent. His political creed

* 'It is perfectly clear that the *national workshops* were simply a travesty of the proposals of Louis Blanc established expressly to discredit them. . . . The history of the whole matter fully justifies the exclamation of Lassalle that "lying is a European power". It has been the subject of endless misrepresentation by writers who have taken no pains to verify the facts.' – Kirkup's *History of Socialism*, 3rd edn, pp. 49–50.

is a distrust of the State. The individual alone is sovereign; his realm is himself only. But Proudhon is best known as the author of the economic dictum, 'Property is robbery', by which he means that property which is accumulated by rents and profits, never having been worked for, ought not to be held. The exploitation of labour under existing economic circumstances is the central problem which he desires to solve. He rejects communism* on the ground that it is a system for the exploitation of the strong by the weak; he concludes that 'possession' must remain, but that it should be recognized only as the reward for labour. The only organization which, in his opinion, can secure this, is one of free associations of workpeople holding industrial capital, land, and the means of production. The doctrines of Proudhon, enunciated with such violence, amount, when pushed to their conclusion, to nothing more than autonomous self-help workshops and peasant proprietorship, operating to maintain equality by nothing more reliable than a spirit of mutualism.

These pioneers of the Socialist movement, in spite of their diverging opinions on many points, occupied to a great extent precisely the same ground. They agreed that individualism had broken down, that it had resulted in industrial chaos, that property was used for the exploitation of labour, that wage labourer was a phase of slavery not of liberty. They further agreed that the association of labour was the way to end the chaos, and that this association in some way or other should be the owner of the means of production. They hoped, as a whole, for the quickening of the spirit of morality, which would sharpen the desire of the people for equality and the sentiment of solidarity and fraternity. Living at a time when the political organization of Europe had not been settled, political change through Parliamentary methods did not figure very prominently in their proposals. The democratic State was only being formed,

---

* Communism at that time was the name under which Socialism under its more modern form passed: e.g., *The Communist Manifesto* – Socialism being then applied to the disorganized socialistic utopian proposals like Saint-Simonism.

and they could not be expected to see that it was an essential part of their Socialist system. When they were not practically absolutists, like the Saint-Simonians, they were generally to be found in the camp of the Revolutionists. At this point, the dominating dogmas of Marxism appeared, and the International movement was established.

Great Britain

Whilst this first phase of the Socialist movement was being worked out in France, in Great Britain a movement on somewhat similar lines was evolving.

The Socialist movement in England* has a history quite as distinguished as it has in France. Robert Owen is generally regarded as its founder; but before Owen's time there was a considerable economic literature showing the groping of men's minds towards a Socialist system of production and exchange. In the seventeenth century, before the science of economics was divorced from the practice of politics, as it was in the eighteenth and nineteenth,† attempts were made, as in Harrington's *Oceana*, to establish an essential relationship between wealth and power, and in consequence to plan a state on the firm economic basis of an equitable distribution of property. In England, political unrest and economic speculation about the ownership of wealth and its effect upon the community, went hand in hand.

Godwin (1756–1836)

Godwin published his humane thoughts and opinions after the fury of the Revolution had spent itself, and when reaction

* This period of English Socialism is dealt with fully in Menger's *Right to the Whole Produce of Labour*, and particularly in the Introduction by Professor Foxwell to the English edition.

† The fact that the Free Trade doctrine was an application of the economic needs of manufacturers, certainly does not contradict this statement. The economic needs of a class influencing politics is totally different from a scientific economic relationship with politics, which was what seventeenth-century economic writers tried to maintain.

shadowed every respectable household in the land. He followed the light of pure reason. What men can dream, men can do. 'Our only true felicity consists in the expansion of our intellectual powers, the knowledge of truth and the practice of virtue.' But barring our way to the attainment of this true felicity is the present method of owning and holding property. Control of sufficient 'means of consumption' is to Godwin an essential condition of human happiness. This one point in his creed distinguishes him from the group of reformers who surrounded him. Dr Ogilvy, the Aberdeen professor of Latin, had preceded Godwin in pointing out the fatal consequences to the community of private ownership of land and its rent, but if Dr Ogilvy was the precursor of Henry George, Godwin was the precursor of Karl Marx. Godwin went to the root of things. English capitalism, unbridled by legislation, and unrestrained by any influence but the impetus of its own immediate requirements, had begun to make those inroads upon human felicity which mark the times when the Industrial Revolution was re-creating industrial processes and changing our social relationships. From such conditions, Socialism was born. Godwin's insistence that society had ultimately to reconsider both the economics and the ethics of property-holding was the first attempt to comprehend and express the state which was to grow from the anarchy of capitalist production.

Charles Hall (1745?–1825?)

Next in the line of Socialist pioneers comes Charles Hall, a doctor whose contact with human misery made him turn his attention to constructive sociology. Hall's great distinction was that he saw how little difference political forms make in economic facts. Under the American Republic, without titles or nobility, he predicts that every economic problem which oppressed Europe would grow up. The distribution of wealth, determined primarily by the private ownership of the land, settles the amount of misery there is in 'civilization'. 'The labourer', observed Hall in his reply to Malthus, 'produces eight times the amount which it is necessary for him to consume, but he starves because those who produce nothing rob him of the fruits of seven-eighths of his labour.' The spirit of these products of what they called 'civilization' – meaning by the term, an elaborate system of artificiality which on its economic side destroys the natural right of man to gain access to the land and consume his products. 'Civilization,' wrote Paine in his *Agrarian Justice*, 'has operated two ways, to make one part of society more affluent, and the other part more wretched, than could have been the lot of either in a natural state.'

William Thompson (1783?–1833)

Then, we reach the summit of English Socialist theory prior to the modern movement. William Thompson, an Irish landlord of the county of Clare, was the first of the Socialists to apply the Ricardian formula, that all wealth is produced by labour, to social theory. His Socialism was an economic system, approaching anarchism in the voluntaryism of its politics. The combination of politics and economics, which characterizes modern Socialism, could hardly have been anticipated even by such seers as those pioneers were, but Thompson saw that moral voluntaryism, as a guarantee that an industrial system would work justly, was too weak. The economics of Ricardo displayed the problem of poverty in an exceedingly simple way. Wealth was created by labour but distributed in accordance with a system of ownership which secured to rent and profits a lion's share.

Patrick Colquhoun (1745–1820)

Patrick Colquhoun carried the logic of Ricardianism very far in his *Treatise on the Wealth, Power and Resources of the British Empire*, published in 1814. In this study, Colquhoun published a 'Map of Civil Society' which showed the distribution of wealth, and which drew in the most striking way the difference between producer and non-producer, between him who works much and possesses little and him who does no work and possesses much.

Thomas Hodgskin (1795?–?)

This school of Socialist pioneers found its most popular champion in Thomas Hodgskin, a member of the staff of the *Morning Chronicle*, a friend of the Mill and Bentham group, and one of the most acute of the Socialist economists before Marx. His central contention was that capital was in a position to exact too large a share of the national product. 'The exactions of the capitalist cause the poverty of the labourer', is a corollary he approvingly draws from Ricardian economics.

A crowd of minor agitators, pamphleteers, politicians – amongst whom Thomas Spence deserves mention – kept the ferment working, until the time was ripe for a comprehensive and scientific analysis and treatment of the problem.

On all these pioneers the same criticism can be passed. Their criticism was admirable; the logic of their analysis was accurate. But they failed in their constructive proposals. Bray, who came nearer to the modern Socialist conception than any of them, when he proposed the organization of the workers by trades into great co-operative companies, still labours under the difficulties of a time when the State as a great co-operative concern had not as yet been discovered. Economic analysis and criticism had gone as far as they could in preparing the complete Socialist theory; they had to end with some futile proposal to moralize society, or to found voluntary communities, or to recast the medium of exchange. Socialist theory could not then be dissociated from anarchist practice.

Robert Owen (1771–1858)

At the threshold of the nineteenth century these theories and theorizings suddenly found a powerful expression in the experiments of Robert Owen. Working, first of all, as a philanthropist who cared for his employees, he proved that by nurturing the best that is in human nature, you produce improved types. His New Lanark acquired world fame. But, by and by, fundamental questions of the relationships between capitalism and the worker were forced upon him by the extreme poverty which followed the closing of the Napoleonic wars, and in 1817 he addressed a communication to the committee appointed to consider the working of the Poor Law, in which he pointed out that the distress was caused because machines were supplanting men, and because the increase in productive capacity was being turned into a means of making men more subordinate to wealth. The communication also contained the first hints of the utopian settlements, built from the idea stuff of Owen's mind, in which social relationships were to be adjusted as though a new social organization could be built up by kindly men as children build castles with wooden bricks. These experiments were destined to failure by the laws of historical growth.

But if Louis Blanc in France united Socialist theories with democratic politics, Robert Owen in England united them with political social experiments like factory laws, democratic education, co-operation, trade unionism, and brought the absolute theories of economic Socialism into touch with the evolutionary processes in English industrial life. His method, not the many mistakes he made in applying his method, remained to determine the course of our industrial movement.

Liberalism

Meanwhile, political evolution was proceeding apace. The struggle for political liberty, begun by the middle class and reaching the end of its first stage in 1832, had awakened the working class to the fact that political power is the arm of social progress. The law-maker is the sovereign. The Chartist movement had beaten the foundations of the existing order like a mighty storm; it had died away, but the disturbance it had created remained to agitate the waters of democracy. Futile as a storm, it had given rise to agitating currents which in time were to wear away old political foundations. Part of the people were enfranchised in 1868. Society was impregnated with democracy; aristocracy and plutocracy existed only on condition that they made peace with the democracy; they became modified in order to enable them to make that peace; they faced the task of 'squaring up' democracy by feasts, Primrose League dances, social programmes, imperialist escapades.

At the same time, the vital forces of a democratic society made themselves manifest. Factory Acts, sanitary laws, expanding markets, enormous increases in the volume of production removed for a generation the critical nature of poverty. Poverty lost its revolutionary power. Owenism, failing in its Utopian aspects, led democratic effort by chance into a wide field of voluntary ameliorative experiment which withdrew it for a time from more revolutionary broodings. The difference between the classes became the reason for political rather than for economic and industrial conflict. Thus the liberal epoch went by. The Socialist pioneers were forgotten. They ceased to influence our economists. Mill did not think it worth his while to know them, believing that when he referred to Fourier and Saint-Simon, he was dealing with everything and everybody of importance to Socialism.

But the stream of Socialist evolution had never been altogether absorbed in the sands of the liberal epoch. A section of the working class had never been liberal, because liberal stood in its eyes for the triumph of the capitalist employer, or for the destruction of inter-class personal relationships which marked the old order at its best, or for some other aspect of the dominance of wealth over everything else. This section grew more numerous as liberalism developed. The success of the 'squaring up' process coupled with these more rational feelings, organized anti-liberal political forces until most of the great industrial centres had either gone over to the other side or were tending in that direction. This tendency was rather anti-liberal than pro-conservative. It was negative rather than positive. It was no indication that the English workers were reactionary, but that they had no confidence in the Party that stood for progress.

Parallel with this political drift was one of humanism and sentiment. Christian Socialism raised its emphatic protest against the crucifixion of humanity on many a factory town Calvary; the literary and artistic humanists, of whom Carlyle and Ruskin were the chief, proclaimed that there is no wealth except the life which commercialism was sacrificing. Moreover, on the left fringe of the Liberal Party were camps more hostile to the Whig centre than to Toryism itself. There were Democratic Associations, Land Leagues, Republican groups, Home Rule Committees and similar things; and when through the seventies and eighties liberalism capitulated to the Whigs and made itself responsible for such excursions from Radicalism as the bombardment of Alexandria and Irish coercion, these sections of the Left were brought to the point of secession.

Socialism

Meanwhile Socialism as a definite theory had been revived. The political epoch with its trade unionism and co-operation, and its liberal labourism had starved Socialism as a thickly leaved tree kills all vegetation beneath it. But the life of the tree was not to be eternal, and the leaves began to thin. Socialism had gone to the continent, where a livelier imagination, a keener interest in purely intellectual topics, more despotic and rigid forms of government, and a greater proneness to resort to revolutionary methods owing to the political unsettlement of the nations, gave it an opportunity to grow which it had not here.

The violent efforts of 1848 exhausted for a time the vitality of this Socialist movement, and, in addition, its revolutionary programme and expectations received a stunning shock. Perfunctory associations formed round Weitling's doctrines, and Cabet's *Voyage in Icaria* had multitudes of disciples. But the movement as a definite propagandist organization had to wait for the three remarkable Germans whose names will ever be associated with the fortunes of Socialism – Lassalle, Marx and

Engels. They were of middle-class origin, and the first two were Jews.

Lassalle (1825–64)

Lassalle led off. German liberalism, in the constitutional struggle with the monarchy which began in 1861, was weak. Lassalle revived the democratic feelings of '48, and in his *Working Men's Programme* energetically contended for the establishment of a social democracy as the next phase in the evolution of Germany. This brought him into conflict with the authorities, and this again made him the hero of the people. In 1863, he addressed to the working men of Leipzig the *Open Letter* which started the definite working-class movement as an independent factor in politics aiming at economic adjustment by political means, and which categorically laid down the Iron Law of Wages as an explanation of human destitution. The Universal German Working Men's Association was formed, and it agitated for universal suffrage as a means to Socialist ends. A miraculous upstirring ensued. Lassalle declared that the enthusiasm with which he was met was like that which accompanies the founding of new religions. But Lassalle had not the temperament to enable him to take advantage of his opportunities. His intelligence began the Social Democratic movement; his temperament bedecked his career with tawdry tinsel and led him to his fatal duel.

Marx (1818–83)

All this time, Marx, if not with greater insight or a more brilliant imagination, certainly with a sounder judgement and a more scientific intellect, was writing, studying and agitating from London, where he had gone in 1849. Marx made Socialism scientific by approaching it in a scientific attitude of mind.

The working classes of Europe drew together again, and in 1864 the international movement was reorganized, the International Association of Working Men founded, and *The*

Communist Manifesto, which had been issued in 1847 but had lain dormant during the reaction, again became the handbook of an active agitation.

The *Manifesto* opens on a high note. Communism is everywhere in Europe. The powers, liberal and reactionary, are alarmed. What is this movement? Its foundation is a belief in the class struggle. 'The history of all hitherto existing society is the history of class struggles.' At present we are in the midst of a struggle with the bourgeoisie, which has risen to power by a successful struggle with the feudal aristocracy. To retain its power it has to exploit every market in the world, and constantly to revolutionize the instruments and modes of production. Its instrument is the organization of capital, its method of warfare free competition. It has no sentiment, no culture. It brings man face to face with the hard material facts of the struggle for life. But the victory of the bourgeoisie proceeds alongside the growing power of the proletariat. The small capitalist is crushed out and joins the working class; the working class herded into towns becomes conscious of its mass and power and organizes itself; political and industrial collisions take place which become more and more bare class conflicts; a time is reached when part of the bourgeoisie, moved by intellectual motives, go over from their own class to that of the proletariat; and, finally, to this new class movement, becoming conscious of itself and its meaning, victory is inevitable. Being the whole nation, its triumph will not be a class triumph, however. It is the last of the class struggles.

The second section of the *Manifesto* deals with the relations between the proletarians and the communists. The communists declare that the proletarian struggle is international, and that the conflict in the various nations must not be split up into sectional demands, but must be organized into a united proletarian movement. The practical proposal of the communists is that the working classes should possess themselves of supreme political power; their theoretical proposals are not the result of idealistic imagination, but of a study of history and of the movement of contemporary events. The communists do not intend to abolish private property. Whose private property is supposed to be in danger? Bourgeois property is not earned. It is the accumulated result of proletarian labour. The workman does not earn property for himself; he produces capital which the bourgeoisie use for his further exploitation. Under communism capital will not be destroyed. It will only lose its class-exploiting character. 'Communism deprives no man of the power to appropriate the products of society: all that it does is to deprive him of the power to subjugate the labour of others by means of such appropriation.' In scathing terms the *Manifesto* replies to the base attacks which had already begun that Communism means to destroy family life, religion and 'eternal truths' like justice, morality, freedom. This part closes with a programme demanding abolition of private property in land, a progressive income tax, certain changes in property-holding, like the concentration of credit in the State, nationalization of the means of transport, further extensions of State activity in production, the making of work compulsory upon all, an organization of industry which will fuse town and country into an industrial unit, free education, the abolition of child labour.

Another section criticizes the Socialist* movements of the time. There is 'Feudal' Socialism – the Socialism of the patron; 'Petty Bourgeois' Socialism – the Socialism which seeks to go back on old methods of production, and which does not admit that the economic relations of modern society must be fundamentally altered; German or 'True' Socialism – the Socialism of vague humanitarian phrases which cannot be crystallized into economic doctrine; 'conservative or bourgeois' Socialism – the social reform Socialism; 'critical-Utopian' Socialism – the Socialism of the transition, when the problem of the proletariat is understood as to its facts but not as to its communist remedy.

The *Manifesto* ends with a statement of the relations between

* I must again remind my readers of the distinction between Communism and Socialism which existed when the *Manifesto* was published. See p. 117.

the communists and the other political parties. 'In all these movements they bring to the front, as the leading question in each, the property question, no matter what its degree of development at the time.' The final sentences ascend in a crescendo of force to that appeal which is thundered today from platforms all over the world, and is inscribed in every tongue on the banners of the working-class movement: 'The proletarians have nothing to lose but their chains. They have a world to win. Workers of all countries unite!'

Engels tells us that after the Commune and the other changes which took place in the last thirty years of the nineteenth century, Marx felt that the *Manifesto* should be redrafted. But that was never done, and the original document still remains as the most prominent landmark in the history of the political labour movement.

The 'International' was a premature birth. Vigorous national Socialist parties had first to be created. This was done in the last three decades of the nineteenth century, and in 1889 it was again revived. Congresses at which representatives from all parts of the world have attended, have been held in Paris (1889 and 1900), in Brussels (1891), in Zurich (1893), in London (1896), in Amsterdam (1904) and in Stuttgart (1907).

Great Britain – Recent Developments

But I must return to the British movement.

A nucleus of Socialists always remained through the generation of liberalism – a few Chartists, a few Owenites, a few exiles from foreign countries. In addition to that, one section of the Socialist creed, land nationalization in some form or other, had always had the support of a reputable number of British public men, and the denial of an ultimate and incontrovertible right to ownership of the soil had always been an axiom with British publicists. George's *Progress and Poverty* came in 1881 as a revolutionary force. It familiarized people with the idea of common use of property, of common creation of values, of common claims to share in aggregate wealth. It led them to discuss the problem of poverty, not as the result of personal shortcoming, but as an aspect of a certain form of social organization.

By this time the problem of poverty and the share of the worker in the produce of his wealth had again come to the surface of public concern. We were prepared to take up the thread of the Socialist controversy at the point where Thompson, Hodgskin and Bray left it. The expedient of nationalization as applied to land suggested the expedient of nationalization as applied to other things. Chapters from Marx were published and read as sequels to *Progress and Poverty*. There were unemployed agitations and controversies. The historical Industrial Remuneration Conference met in London in 1885 and received much attention, and whilst this marshalling of the forces making for a new birth in British politics was going on, a Socialist organization had been formed in 1884 under the title of the Social Democratic Federation; Christian Socialism lifted up its head again and gave life to the Guild of St Matthew, which had been started in 1876 as a democratic Church society; whilst in 1884 the Fabian Society was founded for propaganda purposes.

By this time, criticism of existing conditions could be supplemented by an adequate theory of reconstruction. The democratic franchise had given rise to a positive theory of the State. The voluntary communities of Owenism had become the national and the civic communities. The whole people, willing and acting through town councils, Parliament, administrative departments, were to control the means of production, were to establish a machinery of distribution which would not result in giving an unjust share of the national wealth to rent and interest. I must emphasize this change in political thought which took place between the time of Owen and the founding of the Social Democratic Federation, and which was the result of the work of the liberal epoch, because it alone made it possible for Socialism to advance beyond its utopian stage. The experiences and the conception of the State which enabled it to take the place of the voluntary associations to which the

Ramsay MacDonald's Political Writings

pioneer Socialists were always driven, is of major importance in the history of the evolution of Socialism.

But even then that evolution in Great Britain was not complete. The organizations created thus far failed to penetrate into the mass of the British workers. The foreign outlook, phrases and criticisms of the Social Democratic Federation never quite fitted themselves into British conditions; whilst the Fabian Society, much more successful in adapting Socialism to British evolution, never succeeded in applying it to the movements of contemporary politics, and never faced the problem of how to organize the masses so that they might be available for the advancement of Socialist legislation.

The great trade union movement had been neglected. Then it held a unique position, for it was to be found in no other country. It was class-conscious with a vengeance. It was organized to protect the wage-earner from the capitalist. It was separated into trade sections – engineers, cotton operatives, miners, etc. – and that was its great weakness whenever it attempted to formulate a national policy. It had its annual Congress which discussed politics and passed resolutions relating to the working class as a whole. But the Congress only passed resolutions to lay them at the feet of Cabinet Ministers. It was liberal and its leaders were liberal, whilst some of the ablest of the younger trade unionists were Socialists. None of the existing Socialist organizations appeared to be competent to handle this situation, and until it was handled, Socialism had to remain obscurantist, academic, foreign, critical and impotent in England.

This last chapter in the preliminaries to the placing of the Socialist movement on a national foundation in this country, consists of a series of interesting events, all of which deserve detailed study. Local Labour Parties arose in industrial centres like Bradford and Manchester; the London Dock Strike gave rise to the new unionism; at the Trade Union Congresses between Dundee in 1889 and Norwich in 1894, a small handful of men challenged the rule of the liberal officials; during the Congress at Glasgow in 1892, a private conference was held, and this resulted in the formation of the Independent Labour Party at Bradford in the following year.

With the formation of the Independent Labour Party, Socialism in Great Britain entered upon a new phase. Continental shibboleths and phrases were discarded. The propaganda became British. The history which it used, the modes of thought which it adopted, the political methods which it pursued, the allies which it sought for, were all determined by British conditions. One thing in particular did the new Party see – in fact, it was created to see this thing. Socialism as a political force and as a creative agency in Great Britain would remain feeble until it gained the confidence and the co-operation of the industrial organization of the workers. The struggle between the old school and the new in Congress calmed down, but it took place every year. At Cardiff, in 1895, the old school fired its last effective shot when it altered the constitution of Congress so that only paid officials and those actually working at their trades could be recognized as delegates. The shot did not take effect. In 1899, at Plymouth, the new school won decisively, and a resolution was passed instructing the Parliamentary Committee to convene a conference, to which the Socialist organizations were to be invited, to consider if the various sections of the working-class and Socialist movements could co-operate for political purposes and create some organization to that end. The Conference met in the Memorial Hall, London, on 27 February 1900. One hundred and seventeen delegates were present representing sixty-seven trade unions, seven representing the Independent Labour Party, four the Social Democratic Federation, one the Fabian Society. A private consultation between the leaders of the various sections had taken place some days before, at which an agreement had been arrived at, and this agreement, somewhat weakened by the Parliamentary Committee of the Trade Union Congress, became the agenda of the Conference. The result was the formation of the Labour Representation Committee. Before the Committee had been properly formed, the elections of 1900 were sprung upon it, but the first test of its strength came when, in

1906, it ran fifty candidates for Parliament and returned thirty. That year its name was changed to the Labour Party.

When I come to deal with the approach to the Socialist State I shall discuss the relations between the Socialist organizations and the Labour Party a little more fully, but in order to complete this rapid survey of the growth of Socialism in this country, I need only indicate how these movements are now related to each other, and the following table enables readers to see this relationship at a glance:

LABOUR PARTY

Trade Unions	Independent Labour Party	Fabian Society	Social Democratic Federation

SOCIALISM

This is how the Socialist and Labour forces are marshalled today for their further advance.

Chapter III

The Industrial Argument

Economists tell us that wealth is produced by the co-operation of three primary factors – land, labour and capital. Sometimes it is denied that capital is a primary factor because it is merely the stored results of past labour; sometimes it is said, with Adam Smith, that labour is the source of all wealth because without labour both capital and land are inert and dead.

We need not quarrel about these technical points, provided we know what we mean when we use the words.

Socialism, however, has become most intimately attached to the proposition of Adam Smith, which, coming through Ricardo, was made the foundation of Socialist economics by Marx, that labour is the source of all wealth and the basis of value; and Socialist economic aims have become identified with the demand that the worker has a right to the whole produce of labour.*

A criticism of these economic dogmas is generally held to be a reply to Socialism. But this is a mistake. The Ricardo–Marx economics can be knocked on the head at any time, and Socialism would not suffer in the least. These dogmas are explanations of Socialism, not its foundations. Their discredit would no more destroy the rationality of the Socialist structure than the discrediting of a biological working hypothesis like evolution would destroy biological science.

* 'The produce of labour constitutes the natural recompense or wages of labour.'—*Wealth of Nations*, i. 8. 'It is the comparative quantity of commodities which labour will produce that determines their past or present relative values.' – *Principles of Political Economy and Taxation*, ch. i.

Production and Distribution

An accurate economic definition of the creation of values does not, in my opinion, assign them to labour solely without so greatly stretching the meaning of labour as to do serious violence to the ordinary use of language. Capital is an invaluable tool in the hands of labour, and the efficiency of labour varies directly with the efficiency of the organization of capital. Labour's quarrel with capitalism is not in the sphere of production but in that of distribution. Moreover, an accurate theory of distribution would not assign to labour the whole value of its production, because there are certain communal charges upon national wealth which must be met if the civic and political conditions of labour's well-being are to be maintained.*

Capitalism has been created to develop the machinery of production, and it has done its work very well. A hundred years ago our national annual income was £270,000,000; today it is £1,700,000,000. The desire for profits has led the industrial nations – which for this purpose pride themselves in applying the term 'civilized' to themselves exclusively – to enter into relationships with the most remote and obscure corners of the earth. They have covered the world with a network of lines of communication. They have turned the globe into one great market. Exchange, hampered here and there by artificial barriers raised by nationalism expressing itself as economic policy, proceeds between the most primitive of peoples little removed from the brutes and the most cultured and advanced. The Manchester cotton prince relies on the Boxer for part of

* It may be argued, and I do argue so, that the values taken by the community in the shape of rates and taxes should be levied so that they are those values created by the community as a whole. The Socialist theory of taxation and rating is based upon the assumption, somewhat inconsistent with earlier Socialist economics, that value is created otherwise than by labour. The 'total produce of labour' is thus less than the total national production of value. But if these socially created values were not sufficient to meet the costs of government, claims would legitimately lie against individual incomes.

his income, and the Boxer becomes a revolutionary because the profits he pays to Lancashire enable and necessitate the building of railways in China. Further, in order to keep up an uninterrupted exchange between Lancashire and China, Uganda must be made a cotton-growing country, and the Southern States of America be deprived of their monopoly in cotton cultivation. The romance of capitalism is quite as marvellous as any tale of the Crusades, quite as gorgeous as any of the Arabian Nights, quite as magnificent in its demonstration of the power of human will as any story of the great conquering epochs of the world's history.

But eventually the triumph of production will be judged by the equity of distribution. The Lancashire cotton operative spins and weaves, not that railways may be built in China, but that his cupboard may be full, his back clothed, and his head sheltered under a decent house. And if you tell him that in these respects he is better off than his grandfather – far better off – he will reply to the effect that he himself and not his grandfather is his standard of content and measure of discontent, and that he knows nothing about his grandfather's comforts or discomforts but a great deal about his own; or, if he goes a little deeper in searching for a reply, he will say that the relationship which is the motive force in his life is not that between his grandfather and himself, but between himself as he is and himself as he desires to be. The future is not created by contemplating the achievements of yesterday, but by contemplating the promises of tomorrow. The potential of progress is derived not from the past that has been, but from the future that is still to be. Therefore, capitalism will not be judged by this generation according to what it has done as an agent in production, but according to what it is doing as an agent in distribution.

Capitalism, described from the point of view of distribution, presents a spectacle almost as extraordinary as it does from that of production. Under it, land, capital and labour, the three essentials to production, have been separated in their immediate interests, and upon them have been created three classes which divide the national product between them, not on any basis of equity, or of the value of the services they respectively render, but in accordance with the economic power they possess under any given circumstances. At one time – a rising market – labour can exact its demands from capital, at another – a falling market – capital can exact its demands from labour; and the only meaning attached to the identity of the interests of both is, that capital occasionally discovers that starved labour is inefficient labour, and that labour occasionally experiences that capitalist losses mean a diminished demand for labour. Meanwhile, the land interest manages to prey upon both, and rising rents in towns, equally with rural depopulation and depression in agricultural values, show the triumph of the landed classes.* These three factors, therefore, instead of being co-operative are antagonistic and agree to work together only after settling, like footpads, what their individual shares are to be.

Thus we get our land passing from the control of those who use it and becoming vested in those who abuse it for their own pleasure. It is controlled so as to suit the wishes and convenience of the landlords rather than the wishes and convenience of the whole of the community. We have, for instance, landlords like the Sutherlands burning their tenants' houses about their heads when it was convenient to put estates under sheep farms, and then, when circumstances have changed, asking the town dwellers to submit to a dearer loaf in order to repopulate the places made waste by sheep farms and deer forests. Landlordism has meant everywhere a depopulated country and overcrowded towns, or, as an alternative, artificially high rents paid for from the high prices which a fiscal policy allows the landed interest to impose upon food.

* Therefore, although private ownership in land as a matter of historical fact appears in the capitalist period, it is not economically essential to it. Its persistence is owing to the fact that capitalism trembles to challenge the right and utility of any kind of property. Capitalism defends all property in order to preserve its own.

The Organization of Production

Nor has capitalism, in its own sphere, ever given the least hope that it was creating an organization which would equitably distribute wealth. It has two stages in its development: the first when it is subject to free internal competition; the second when it is controlled either by regular Trusts or by widely spread agreements which reduce competition to a minimum.

The first stage was antecedent to the universal world market and to persistent international competition on that market. During it, there were many opportunities presented to labour to become economically independent, because local industry for a local market was still important in national economy, and there was also a close personal touch between employer and employed. Production and exchange had not become so organized as to have ceased to be personal. Competition between producers was, on the whole, carried on on terms of equality because capitalist machinery was not much developed, and for this same reason the workman was still a craftsman and could produce the articles of his trade in all their parts. The distribution which followed on that state of things was tolerable, but it could not last. It was only a beginning.

The second stage is marked by the organization of production on a large scale. Village needs are supplied from factories hundreds of miles away. Local habits and styles disappear and conform to general habits and styles. The Joint-Stock Company takes the place of personal undertakings, industries amalgamate, a corporation grows until it covers the main transactions in a given trade, it comes to agreements with its rivals, it acquires interests in businesses which either supply it with raw materials or sell its finished products, until at length it is not an industry but an economic group of industries controlled by one capitalist combination.

This process may be illustrated in the development of a few of our great iron and steel working businesses. I may instance the firm of the Bells, the famous ironmasters.* The firm

* For the particulars given, I am indebted to that laborious study in

was established in 1844, and began with furnaces and coal and iron mines and limestone quarries. In 1873, it became a private limited liability company, and in 1899 its shares were put upon the market. In 1898, it started new steel works, and Dorman, Long & Co. took half of the new shares then issued. This firm also had a history. Started in 1876, it became a limited liability company in 1889. In 1879, it assimilated a rival firm, the Britannia Works; in 1899, it swallowed up the sheet works of Messrs Jones Bros., and the wire works of the Bedson Wire Co. In 1902, the interests of the Bell and the Dorman, Long firms were more closely united by a rearrangement of capital holdings. To strengthen the position of the firm, the North-Eastern Steel Co., manufacturing a different kind of product, was acquired in 1903, the latter company explaining to its shareholders that the amalgamation was largely owing to the fact that the Dorman and the Bell firms were in a superior position owing to their possessing mines and quarries of coal and iron. The original Bell capital was only a few thousand pounds; the capital of the amalgamated firms now stands at £3,059,594.

The evolution of the firm of Sir W. G. Armstrong, Whitworth & Co. is an even more interesting study. The original firm gained a name as makers of ordnance. In 1882, it amalgamated with ship-builders; in 1897, with engineers; in 1899, with locomotive and marine engineers; in 1906, with torpedo makers. The capital manipulated is now £5,710,000.

Equally interesting is the evolution of firms like John Brown & Co. of Sheffield. This firm originally made steel rails and armour plates. In 1870, it bought coal mines and ore fields and erected furnaces. In 1899, it assimilated the Clydebank Engineering and Shipbuilding Co., with an enormous annual output of ships, battleships, marine engines. In 1902, it acquired seven-eighths of the shares of a rival Sheffield firm. The capital is now £2,200,000.

The United States Census of 1905 enables one to see at a

Trusts and Combinations, *The Trust Movement in British Industry*, by Henry W. Macrosty, and to it I refer those who wish to study the matter more fully.

glance the general effect of such movements. According to that Census, out of 216,262 factories in the United States, 162,000, or 75 per cent, were owned by individuals separately or in partnership, and 51,000, or 23 per cent, by corporations; but whereas the 75 per cent worked a capital of only $2,150,000,000, the 23 per cent worked a capital of $10,510,000,000, or 83 per cent of the capital shown to be invested in industrial concerns in the country. 1,600,000 wage-earners were employed by the former, 3,800,000 by the latter.

Germany tells the same tale.* In 1886, there were 1337 Joint-Stock Companies with 1,904,000 Marks capital; in 1896, there were 2307, and their capital was 3,512,000 Marks. Many of these in the latter year were federated for competitive purposes. In 1882, 123 businesses employed over 1000 persons each; by 1895 there were 248 such businesses.

These instances make the movement of amalgamation and coordination clear. Separate industrial processes that are inter-dependent tend to be amalgamated. Labour is obedient to the law of subdivision; capital to the law of concentration.

Industrial organization obeys a law of economy. When capital has to be supplied by a class that takes no further part in production, that class becomes a burden upon the community, and the vitality of the community bends itself to get rid of that class. When an organism is bearing useless organs, or organs which do their work badly, its vitality tries to effect economies, because the condition of its existence is that it can work economically. Hence these industrial phenomena which I have been describing. Hence also the Socialist movement.†

* Howard's *Industrial Progress of Germany*, pp. 70 *et passim*.
† During the summer of 1905, James T. Hill, the American railroad magnate, wrote to the *New York Herald* pointing out how inefficiently the natural wealth of America was being used. The *New York Times*, commenting upon Mr Hill's statement, said: 'It is perfectly true, as Mr Hill says, that "what is needed the country over is a great awakening, a sort of revival in its business methods, in domestic and foreign trade". We want to rid ourselves of "the hampering influences".' That is just what Socialists say. A study of 'the hampering influence' is an introduction to Socialism.

The Organization of Distribution

Under this system, distribution becomes markedly inequitable. The good and worthy man rising to success is now almost an old wife's tale. As the economic machine becomes more and more perfect and the personal relationship in it disappears, considerations of personal worth are of less importance in success, and the law of the survival of the most adaptable selects men specialized as economic machines for the control of industries. This change must be apparent to everybody. The value placed upon bare riches rises rather than falls in spite of our education and our culture, and the pressure which vast economic interests now bring to bear upon every outlet of public life from the House of Commons to the Church of God increases. The economic machine gets more important; its drivers get more powerful and wield greater influence; social classes become stereotyped.* Capital swells in volume every year. Sometimes it is so easily available – either because there is plenty of it or because there is not much demand for it – that it is cheap; sometimes it is dear. But in spite of fluctuations it mounts up upon the back of labour. There is hardly a public company in the country that has been anything like successful at one time or another of its life, but is carrying a load of capital which is too heavy for it. Its stock has either been watered or has been bought at premium rates on the market, and it has now to provide profits for capital which it never spent and never put to any use.

Thus the aggregate of profits rises in every prosperous country, and so does the aggregate of rent. Wages of management and labour may also increase, but part of their increase is purely nominal, and substantial improvements, amounting to any considerable portion of that extra reward of labour which is available owing to new machinery and the more efficient

* That a few men pass from one class to another is no disproof of this statement. The classes remain, and they change less as a whole than they did before our present vast accumulations of wealth.

organization of labour and of markets, are made impossible owing to the industrial mechanism which allows unearned increments in rent to pass into private pockets, and the advantages of industrial improvements to be capitalized and sold on the market, and thus be burdened by the weight of exploiting investments.*

Thus it came about that the portion of the national income which went in rents in 1890 was about £230,000,000, whilst it amounted to £290,000,000 in 1900; the portion which went in interest (not including wages of managing capitalists) in 1890 was about £280,000,000, whilst in 1900 it was about £360,000,000; whilst that paid in wages in 1890 was about £530,000,000 for 13,500,000 workers, and in 1904, £690,000,000 was handed over to 15,000,000 workers.†

The further proposition that distribution is, on the whole, regulated by merit, and is as good as possible for the purpose of keeping the machine of production and exchange going, is little removed from the ridiculous. Who will seriously state that the enormous wealth of the ground landlords of London is due to their merits or value? Who will say that the great mining landlords of the north-east of England, of Yorkshire, of the Midlands, have 'earned' in any way whatever their huge incomes from mining rents? And yet the system of landlordism which enables both of these classes to flourish at the expense of the community, is one of the great determining factors in how wealth once created is to be distributed. Quite apart from landlordism, the organization of capitalism determines the method of distribution. Some services are absurdly overpaid,

* On page 96 of *Riches and Poverty*, Mr Money gives a table of gas companies, showing the difference between the real and the market value of shares. From this table it appears that, for instance, the Harrogate Gas Company has to pay interest on £340 for every £100 capital it has used. The chapter in which this appears is well worth studying in connection with my argument.

† These figures are taken from Fabian Pamphlet No. 5, various editions. This pamphlet gives interesting information about wealth distribution, about which limited space prevents me from giving further details.

others as absurdly underpaid. The reason is that the mechanism of competition cannot be applied to a considerable part of social service. Our present economic constitution has been built up mainly to enable wealth to be created and to allow the capitalist competitors to fight each other; and this constitution decides the shares into which national wealth is divided. We are working in a system which makes an equitable distribution impossible, and the labourer will not get his proper hire until the system is changed. Until the machinery of production is controlled by the community, the volume of production will be divided in accordance with the relative strength of the economic classes which own the elements necessary to production, and the distribution secured by such an arrangement will never materially alter from the present position when, out of an annual income of £1,170,000,000, 1,250,000 rich persons own £585,000,000, 3,750,000 comfortably-off persons own £245,000,000, and 38,000,000 poor persons own £880,000,000.*

Labour and Industrial Organization

Statistics of material distribution only reflect many other forms of inequality. The organization of capitalist production could only have proceeded by subdividing to the minutest degree the process done by any one man in complete productive operations. The striking figures published in 1898 in a report on *Hand and Machine Labour* by the Labour Department at Washington, have already been much quoted, and I need only illustrate my point by citing one industry here. I take that of watchmaking. In 1862, watch movements were made by hand; in 1896, they were made by machinery, and a comparison has been made between those two years. It was found that to produce a certain watch in 1862, 347 operations were required; in 1896, 881. The 347 operations were done by 13 persons, most of whom were styled watchmakers, and could do practically every process needed; the 881 operations were done by a some-

* *Riches and Poverty*, by Chiozza Money.

what indefinite number of men and women – very much greater than 13 – most of whom were called 'machine hands' or 'bench hands', but apparently only two small sections, still working by hand, called themselves watchmakers. None of these could make a watch.

The effect of this is to make labour more subordinate to the capitalist machine of production. The amount of practically unskilled labour is increased as skill goes into the machinery used, whilst on the top grades the demand for skill is perhaps greater than ever. The industrial population is thus divided by a deep gap, the lower having little training for the skill required at the top. This threatens society with serious consequences. Labour tends to be divided into two grades diametrically opposed in quality, and yet the recruiting for the higher grade ought to be done in the lower – unless we are to again create a class economically more subject than any class of hewers of wood and drawers of water ever has been. Production organized for individual profit actually flourishes for a time on the very conditions which create the unskilled workman, the casual labourer, the improvident jack-of-all-trades, the unemployed and employable. The stream of labour under the old apprentice-ship and craftsman era was from below upwards – apprentice, journeyman, foreman, master; now, it is right across, the youth being put to some mechanical process which leads to nothing else, and when he asks for more wages, or when more skill is required of him, he is passed out on to the street and has to pick up a new job, which, in the nature of things, will have little relation to his earlier employment.

The upward stream is maintained in a somewhat enfeebled way by technical schools and colleges, and as these are always liable to become preserves of the well-to-do, or are opened only to the children of the poor who at an early age, before their inclinations and tastes are really fixed, can pass competitive examinations, this method of supplying the higher branches of industry will tend to stereotype industrial classes and to supply an anaemic management for our industrial organization.* The

* 'Here [America] men enter business in a subordinate position with

individuality, the energy, the concentration of attention, which was secured under the first stage of industrial organization must become enfeebled under the second. The first stage could not be made permanent because it was subject to a law of growth, and, therefore, one of the most pressing problems of the second stage is how to maintain its organization and yet preserve skill and initiative amongst the workers throughout. The feeble and querulous complaints against 'ca' canny' policies, against the thumb-like skill, against the industrial habits of the workers made by middle-class critics of our present industrial state, are hopeful, inasmuch as they indicate that by and by with more information and a good deal more reflection, these critics may grasp the real nature of the problem revealed by one or two surface manifestations about which they are uttering wails of class prejudice and ignorance.*

If society suffers by the subordination of skill to individual profit, the workman is put in a still more parlous position. The man who is only a workman in one department of a factory is exceedingly helpless. He builds his house on an alarmingly narrow basis. He is bound to a place almost as rigidly as though Parliament had enacted a new Law of Settlement. Under the machine production of boots and shoes, for instance, a man is not a shoemaker and is quite useless away from his machine. Outside Leicester, or Northampton or Norwich, he is an unskilled labourer. He cannot bring himself into direct touch with the consumer as his grandfathers did when they were shoemakers. This means a serious limitation of liberty, a serious increase of precariousness. It means that the difference between

the hope of learning it with their daily duties, and they expect to be promoted according to the cleverness and ability with which they learn the business. In Germany, a man could not hope to rise to the higher administrative positions unless he received special training therefor, in most cases training in a school outside the business itself. . . . Consequently we have in Germany a special class of schools for each grade of worker.' – Howard's *Industrial Progress of Germany*, p. 98.
* cf. Professor Flinders Petrie's *Janus in Modern Life*.

144

unemployed and unemployable is very narrow, because it makes a man's ability to earn a living depend upon his being able to fit himself into such a limited and definite set of circumstances; it means that when a man can no longer work in a factory, he can hardly work at all. The machine of production brought to perfection under individualism involves a serious limitation on a man's freedom and chances of being able always to earn a livelihood. Individualistic production needs as a supplement charity, pauperism, public relief works, old age pensions, assistance to keep family life in existence. The individual, under it, not being allowed to provide for himself, claims assistance from others, and suffers the moral degradation which accompanies such assistance. Family life deteriorates, family instincts – paternal affection, the art of housewifery – disappear. Industrial exigencies disintegrate all spiritual social organization.

And the possession of wealth forms no defence against this disintegration. The people do not suffer because they are poor; all men are subject to the same disease – the blight of profit-making and of commercialism on life. Thus industrial perfection in production involves the deterioration of human qualities.

In summary, the effect of our present development of industry is to organize capital and create interests which threaten to dominate our political and civic existence by putting the life of the State under the control of a few commercial syndicates;* to subordinate human interests to capitalist profit which, to an increasing extent, can be made off a deteriorating people, and which, as it must be made at once, cannot afford to take long

* This pure evolution of capitalism has not been manifested so much here as in America, mainly because we have a social history which mingles with and colours the pure industrial stream of tendency. But we must be watchful even here. Mr Macrosty in his work on Trusts quotes from the *Economist* of 12 August 1899: 'It is undeniable that during the session just ended, there has been an atmosphere of money in the lobby and precincts of the House of Commons, scarcely known before. All manner of interests have gathered there as they gather in Washington and in the various State Legislatures of America.'

views and subordinate immediate and apparent gains to permanent and real ones; to create a machinery of production which does not secure equitable distribution; to give rise to ethical demands which it cannot satisfy, and hence to compass its own destruction.

Socialism and Production

Lest, however, it should be assumed that the emphasis which Socialists place upon distribution as the final test of whether an industrial system is or is not satisfactory, indicates that they neglect the conditions of effective production, I must point out that under Socialism the efficiency of production developed by capitalism will not only be preserved but improved. Mechanical invention will be encouraged and utilized to the utmost. Today we observe a feeling of resentment on the part of labour against machinery, but that is due to the undeniable fact that every readjustment of industry caused by discoveries of more efficient means of production involves suffering to the workers, displacement of labour, further exploitation. This may not be the case when the whole of society is taken into account, but at the points affected it is the case, and the workman, just like the capitalist, takes short views. The failure of the present system is that under it, it is difficult for either capitalists or workmen to see that the well-being of the whole involves the well-being of every individual. Under Socialism, however, all that will be changed. More efficient production will then mean more efficient distribution. The man in the workshop will not be an economic alien to the owner of the machines with which he works, and, consequently, machinery which today is labour-substituting will then be in reality what it is now only nominally, labour-saving.

Moreover, the present system is both wasteful from a business point of view and unjust from an ethical point of view. The Trust and syndicate develop largely owing to the necessity of securing economy in working. That this is so is somewhat obscured as yet by the fact that so many Trusts have been

promoted by speculating capitalists. But it is notorious that the
Steel Corporation found it most economical to close down
plants. The whisky Trust closed sixty-eight out of eighty dis-
tilleries, and then kept up production to its old level. Mr
Edgerton* quotes with approval the opinion of an expert that
'there is nail machinery enough in this country [America] to
produce four times as many nails as can be sold'. Professor
J. W. Jenks,† reporting on an inquiry made by the United
States Government, says under the heading of 'Closing of
Plants': 'Seventeen of the combinations reported that some of
the plants that had been taken into the organization have been
closed. . . . The proportion of the capacity of the plants closed
to the total manufacturing capacity of the combinations has
varied from 1 per cent to as high as 25 per cent.' It is true that
this closing process goes on without Trust organization, but
it is by bankruptcy and ruin – surely the very worst of all
methods.

But these organizations can go much farther in these directions than has hitherto been the case, and, meanwhile, a recital
of such facts makes it evident that fabulous waste is involved
every year in carrying on competition in those industries which
have not been organized into Trusts, and in the anarchistic
method of distribution which fills whole streets with rival shops
and warehouses and keeps bankruptcy officials busy. If everything that is said in praise of competition were true it would be
dearly bought.

The figures of bankruptcies alone are most eloquent. The
Inland Revenue benefits every year by about £50,000 for
stamps issued in connection with industrial wreckage;‡
£110,000 is spent in paying salaries to officers, and £22,000
goes for remuneration to County Court Registrars. The losses
to creditors by settlement under the Bankruptcy Acts each
year on the average in England and Wales alone, since 1900,
have been £5,000,000, and under deeds of arrangement

* *Trusts, Tools, and Corporations*, ed. Professor Ripley, p. 70.
† *Bulletin of the Department of Labour*, 1900, p. 674 ff.
‡ *Accounts of Bankruptcy*, Parliamentary Paper 130, 1907.

£2,800,000. This is, of course, not all economic loss, as part of these sums represent the cost of experiments in industrial methods – costs, however, which ought not to be borne by individual but by national income. The lack of any attempt to estimate what needs are, and to regulate the use of productive power accordingly, not only means terrible extravagance in manufacture, but unsettlement in industry, because it leads to overproduction, to glutted markets, to loss of capital, to unemployment, and contributes to those psychological panics, when the public will risk nothing and invest nothing, which cause financial and commercial crises. The individualistic, anarchistic, happy-go-lucky, devil-take-the-hindmost way in which production is conducted and markets scrambled for today, is a negation of law and order, and a cynical challenge to the human intelligence to charm chaos into cosmos.

The apologists of this disorder find consolation in telling us that it enables the consumer to pick out what he likes, to award those who please him and send into bankruptcy those who cannot gauge public needs. This, of course, is mainly fancy with a tinge of truth in it. A man who genuinely tries to manufacture soap bubbles will come to grief, but if he can do a little swindle at the same time by lying advertisements or judicious manipulation on the Stock Exchange, he will be able to purchase a peerage.

On the other hand, there is little margin for variation on the ordinary markets. The arts employed in the production of clothing, for example – the texture, colours, make-up – are now not the subject of 'trade secrets'. They are common possessions. The artistic taste and the scientific skill are developed and moulded by schools, colleges, technical classes, art galleries, craft exhibitions. The individualistic exploitation of a happy idea is, therefore, not only less justifiable as a matter of economic equity than it used to be, but it is also less necessary as a reward encouraging others to show initiative and inventiveness.

When we carefully consider the reasons why this waste of competition is tolerated, why a great standing army of travellers, advertising agents, bill-posters, printers are maintained at an enormous charge upon national income, and expense upon national consumption, involving terrible waste of service that otherwise would be available for other purposes, we see that it is necessary simply because the law of competition is in the main that one man's business must be built up at the cost of another man's business. The volume and the quality of consumption are not increased thereby; the apportionment of trade and profits between individual competitors is the main thing affected. But all this army is a dead weight upon the producing community. A writer has estimated that in 1890 between 50 and 60 per cent of the total production of the United States was dissipated in maintaining this competition between individual businesses.*

When we consider the great savings in the cost of production which will be effected by Socialist organization – the elimination of the useless classes, the absorption of sections which are necessary only as armies in the wars of commercialist competition, the diversion of wealth which now only maintains individual luxury into channels which will maintain State efficiency, – we can see how far from the truth is the fear that under Socialism it will be impossible for us to carry on foreign trade, or that a Socialist State could be wiped out of existence by an industrial competitor. In fact, in foreign trade, a Socialist State would be paramount because it would have carried farthest the Law of Economy. We can also understand how mistaken is the argument that Socialism will require protection to preserve itself. These and similar views are held only by those who have not made themselves familiar with the Socialist organization of industry. If the further consideration, that under Socialism the captains of industry will be managers, seems to point to inefficiency, it must not be forgotten that the best of them and those bearing the greatest responsibilities are only managers now.

The rise of the Trusts necessitates some modification of the above criticisms. For the Trust reduces waste and is also always striving to estimate demand so that it may thereby regulate

* Reeve's *Cost of Competition*, p. 283.

production. When the Trust becomes more of a legitimate business concern than it is as yet, it will do more in these directions. But the solution of these problems by Trust only creates further difficulties. A committee of directors, responsible, not to the community whose interest is the main thing involved in their transactions, but to the owners of the capital which they are using, must always threaten to become a public menace. They hold the gateway to life. They are like the occupants of the ancient castles on the Rhine. Their conduct depends upon the question: Will pillage or law and order pay us better? Now the sociologist and politician will say: 'Law and order', and they are right. But the peculiarity of the business method is that it must have profits now – maximum profits; it cannot take long views; it is feverish, not cool; its ends are not sociological values which show themselves in a generation, but ledger balances which are struck twice a year. Its answer would be that of the barons – pillage – though not too much pillage.

Further, it must be noted that this development in industrial control assigns to capital a new position. It creates a pure form of capitalism* – a special class taking no part in production, and having no responsibilities in industry. Interest thus becomes sharply divided from profits in the ordinary sense and also from wages of management. It becomes nothing more than income derived from the loan of capital required by a class which has no capital, or by a social function – production – which is as yet depending on a specialized class of investors for the sustenance of capital which the community itself ought to have the means of supplying. We are thus creating a capitalist class as different from the old employing classes which received the title of 'captains of industry' as the modern factory hand is different from the old craftsman.

Here we reach the bedrock of our criticism. Trade and

* Criticisms upon capitalism must not be confused, as some opponents of socialism are always doing, with criticisms on capital. Capital, capitalist, capitalism are three absolutely distinct things. The socialist objects to capitalism.

150

commerce tend more and more to become widely organized functions and to depart from being a series of independent transactions carried on by separate capitalists. The exercise of this function of trade should be conducive to communal ends or it may prey upon the communal life, as the appetites may prey upon the general health of the body, or as the landlords by depopulating the soil have preyed upon the national life. When trade and commerce become organized functions, their communal and sociological purpose must be definitely set up and guarded by making the control of the function communal and sociological, a control which can never be supplied by capitalism. As the supply of gas, of water, of trams, of milk that is milk, has been shown by experience to be most safely placed in the hands of the community, so will it be found that the community will be forced to control and manage other supplies beginning with monopolies, Trusts, and prime necessities for communal life.

This development is natural and necessary. It is an attempt to bring order out of chaos, reason out of chance. It is progress. Production under competition for the personal profit of the individual master responsible for his own capital, is a state of unstable equilibrium. It is youth; it is not fully developed manhood. Production ever tends to be an organized function of the State, carried on not as a personal matter but by salaried managers responsible, not for their own capital, but for capital provided from many sources. Thus the Joint-Stock Company and the Trusts are not the final forms of production. They are the first stage of impersonal production. They appear contemporaneously with municipalization. They are far removed from Socialism, but they are still farther from the individual capitalist employer, and they have developed in the direction of Socialism. They are not a modification of the old one-man business; they are a fundamental change in it. When Adam Smith wrote of Joint-Stock Companies, his vision was limited by his experience, and we are in the same position today in relation to the public control of industry as he was in 1790 as regards the practicability of Joint-Stock enterprise. He said

Ramsay MacDonald's Political Writings

Banks only can be controlled as Joint-Stock affairs; we say gas and water only can be controlled by public officials.

Today we stand on that indefinite territory where the old is cast off and the new is put on. Capitalism evolves upwards to organic harmony, not downwards towards revolution. If, politically, the first duty of a State is to preserve itself, so economically, the first duty of a people is to protect the mechanism of industry by which their economic powers to consume are secured. So soon as production is organized upon a Trust basis and becomes a social function, it becomes more and more a pressing need that the organization should be controlled by the people and be part of the communal life of the people, just like national education, government, and so on. The nationalization of production is just as necessary to democracy – and just as inevitable if democracy is to mature into fullness – as the nationalization of the sovereign authority by the suppression of the personal right of kings to rule. We must look upon production as a national function, and not as a task assigned to a class of separate individuals pursuing their own ends.

This is the case for Socialism. It is the stage after capitalism; it is capitalism ripened into a higher form of trade organization; it is the organization which includes distribution as well as production within its scope, and which reconciles individual with national prosperity. It is the Law of Economy moulding industrial forms, creating the Trust from competitive industry, and extending the economy of the Trust until it is merged into the greater economy of Socialism.

Chapter V

The Political Future of Socialism

One is often met with the inquiry: How is Socialism going to be brought about? and on such occasions one is expected to produce the architectural features of the Socialist State and defend them to the most minute particular against attacks of 'the practical man' who 'knows that human nature will not budge an inch from where it now stands'. It is as well to remember that the evolution of human conduct and motive is still in process and has not come to an end, and that what satisfies people as aims in life or rewards for effort can be greatly modified by social circumstances and education. We dogmatize about what human beings will or will not do, and about nothing are we less well equipped for dogmatizing. Moreover, the question really does not arise in our Socialist problem at all, because under democratic government we can never have more Socialism at any given time than human nature will stand, and that settles the question.

If, however, we may properly decline to go into a barren discussion as to whether we must change human character before we have Socialism, we must not decline to lay down the general lines of the Socialist programme because that is the path, up to the limit of our present horizon, leading to the Socialism beyond.

Industrial Reconstruction

The Socialist objective is a State wherein labour will meet with an adequate reward and human life be valued above property. Today, property rules life and life is bent and twisted so as to fit into the contorted ethics and other imperatives of this

153

property-worshipping age. The Socialist believes that so long as private property in things essential to human well-being is recognized, so long will property dominate life. An essential feature of the Socialist State will, therefore, be the common ownership of all those forms of property in the use or abuse of which the whole community is more interested than private individuals, and the employment of such property for common ends and not for private profit. Where the line is to be drawn between common interest and individual interest cannot be determined by theoretical considerations of the rights of the State or of the individual, but by practical experiences of the working of Socialistic experiments from time to time. The Socialist, however much he may be inspired by *a priori* reasoning, must always be guided by practical results. The Socialist method is a combination of theory and practice: it is the scientific experimental method.

With these considerations in mind, the principles and major items of the Socialist programme easily can be deduced.

The first task of the Socialist living in these transition times is to make the public familiar with the distinction, on the one hand, between property which enables the holders to exploit the labour of other people – property which means the impoverishment of society – and, on the other hand, property which an individual must possess in order to enable him to live and develop his individuality. Between the two extreme limits of such a classification of property, there is a graded scale with a middle zone where classification is impossible. But the extremes are perfectly clear. On the one side, there is land, the value of which is to the greatest degree dependent upon the community; on the other side, there is food, clothing, a living income. The Socialist policy regarding the first is State ownership; regarding the second it is private ownership.

Experience has shown us that the private ownership of land has led to depopulation, to the waste of national resources, to the diversion of national wealth from public to private uses; and the same experience has proved that an essential to a constructive national policy of race building and the organization of national wealth is the national control of its land. However complete may have been the justification for private ownership of land at a time when an impetus was required for cultivation, that justification rested upon a temporary condition, and has long ceased to exist. 'The common and general utility of the exercise of the right of property,' said Saint-Simon, 'can vary with the times.' 'Landed property in England,' said John Stuart Mill, 'is thus very far from completely fulfilling the conditions which render its existence economically justifiable.'

There can be little improvement in the use to which we put our land and little reconstructive work done in dealing with the overcrowding of towns so long as private ownership of land exists. Electric traction overcomes to a certain extent the tendency of landlordism to herd population together in towns. But every dispersive force can operate only if it makes it worth the while of the landowners to allow it to operate. By the expenditure of public money, great tracts of land adjoining our industrial centres have been brought within the limits of building areas, and suburbs have grown to increase enormously the rent-rolls of landlords who have never lifted a little finger to benefit the communities which are presenting them with such substantial increases to their incomes.

Even in new countries like Australia and New Zealand, the curse of landlordism has already made itself felt, and the first thing which the national reformer had to do was to shatter its power.

It is, therefore, perfectly clear that public utility is no longer served but sacrificed by the private ownership of land.

Monopolies work out in the same way. In its simplest form, a monopoly consists in a service which by its nature cannot be given by competing undertakings. Rival gas or electricity or water or tram companies cannot supply towns. Electricity may compete with gas, buses or underground tubes may compete with trains, but the competition is in reality between two monopolies in lighting or travelling facilities, each being a monopoly in itself, and each representing a different form of convenience, and tending to reduce the competition of other forms to vanishing point. Hansoms no longer compete with four-wheeled cabs, and motor cabs will, by and by, supplant hansoms except for some special services.

The Socialist programme regarding these forms of property is that the community should own them. The nationalization of land, the nationalization of railways; the municipalization of the civic services like gas, water, electricity, trams – that is the first instalment of the programme which is to give effect to the Socialist doctrine that public property is as necessary in a modern State as private property.

Socialism and State Income

Akin to our programme of property-holding are our proposals regarding taxation. The theory of taxation held by the individualist liberal school has remained as Adam Smith defined it. His 'canons' assume that taxes are deductions from private incomes taken by the State because the State has power to take them. 'Taxes,' says Ricardo, 'are a portion of the produce of the country placed at the disposal of the Government.' John Stuart Mill refers to a just system of taxation as one which apportions 'the contribution of each person towards the expenses of government, so that he shall feel neither more nor less inconvenience from his share of the payment than every other person experiences from his'. Thus, the assumption that underlies the 'classical' discussions on taxation is that it is a sacrifice of individual property to Government needs. And the greatest of all the statesmen who translated into political creeds the theories of the individualist economists – Mr Gladstone – rarely touches taxation without reminding the country that the income of the State must necessarily be derived from the income of citizens, and probably no doctrine of a past generation has been less effectually challenged than this, by a new generation thinking out its problems for itself. Today its errors and failings are available for political use by any of those middle-class reactionary sections whose notion of the State is that it should do as little as possible beyond providing policemen to protect their property and a navy to guard their trading ships, and who are trying to get the working classes to pay more of the heavy debts of past national escapades than they now do.

The principle that each should contribute to the State revenues according to his ability is of secondary importance to the Socialist, to whom the fundamental principle of the levying of State income is that the State should secure for its own use the values that are created by the existence and activity of the State.

It is quite possible to classify incomes so that those gained solely by individual energy may be placed on one side, and those obtained by exploiting the community may be placed on the other. Incomes display a gradation of merit, not all merit on one side and all demerit on the other. In a sense, nearly all incomes made in settled society depend upon the existence of the State. But there are extremes which very properly can be classified into those which the individual has earned and those which the community has created. Most of the rent for land, practically the whole of urban rents, are communal in their origin. Most of the dividends paid by undertakings like railways and municipal services, and particularly by most undertakings, the nominal capital of which is in excess of the capital actually absorbed in starting and developing them, should be similarly regarded. To say, for instance, that the private enterprise of railway shareholders and directors made our railways flourish, is a proposition which no one can defend seriously for a moment.

The Socialist programme, therefore, includes a method of obtaining a State revenue adequate to State requirements, by securing for the State an income from its own property. A rough classification of income according to its source, the imposition of an income-tax increasing in heaviness as the source approximates in character to rents from urban land, and all but disappearing when incomes are, for all practical purposes, solely the result of individual effort, is the Socialist programme of taxation.

This proposal must not be mixed up with that for a graduated income tax, because it is totally different. The graduated income tax depends upon the theory that each should pay according to his ability – a theory which has none of the constructive value of that which provides that the State should enjoy the reward of its own efforts and be possessed of property so as to express its own personality.*

If the income from public property and State effort be not enough for State purposes, we must then devise the best means for levying supplementary contributions from individuals. A graduated income tax ought then to be applied – or, better still, graduated death duties.

These are the main roads by which Socialism is to be approached, because when they have been fully traversed, property will be held in such a way that the wealth produced by labour and by all useful service will fructify throughout society, and the State will have an income sufficiently large to enable it to carry out the communal will and so make the community an efficient co-operator with the individual in establishing liberty. Nationalization of monopolies and a system of taxation such as I outline may appear to be devoid of all the heroic remedies which one associates with Socialism, but nevertheless a political policy devised under the guidance of these aims would fundamentally alter economic relations within the State, and when its full consequences would be reaped, Socialism would have come upon us.

Socialism and Reform

But society not being a mechanical relationship merely, but being united by habits, laws, customs and interdependence of interests, the Socialist change must be gradual and must proceed in stages, just as the evolution of an organism does. Society will resist a too violent readjustment. Kings can be removed and a republic established by revolutions, but in

* It is sometimes argued, however, that a graduated income-tax means in reality a specially heavy tax upon unearned incomes. That may be so in practice, but the two principles of taxation which I discuss are quite distinct.

establishing Socialism we change organic relationships, not superficial forms of government. Socialism, therefore, calls for the highest qualities of statesmanship, for that rare faculty of knowing how much change can be assimilated at any given time, how drastically one can readjust without producing reaction. Also the parliamentary work of Socialism must be supplemented by educational propaganda, the chief aim of which is to induce the intellectual portions of the community to adopt new modes of sociological thought. The present organization of society will be impossible, not when it has actually crumbled beneath the weight of its bankruptcy, but when its absurdity, its injustice, its waste are clearly shown up against another system of organization which has been proved to be rational and moral both in idea and experience.

As we approach the Socialist State by the changes in property-holding and in finance which I have indicated, certain things will happen. The weight of economic and social parasitism now preying upon the industrial State will be lightened, prices of commodities will fall, the volume of exchange will swell, and the average standard of life will be materially improved. The industrial efficiency of the country will be vastly increased.

But the saving which will arise from the destruction of parasitism and Dick Turpinism must be fairly distributed. Some of it will, of course, go to cheapen commodities, and this will at once improve the standard of living at home and increase our efficiency as competitors on foreign markets. But that will not absorb the whole advantage. Both a reduction in working hours and an increase in wages will be possible. Sweating will disappear. Women's cheaply paid labour will no longer compete with men's. Industry will be steadied and unemployment as we now know it will cease. The road to the Socialist State will be opened up.

In the meanwhile, a vast network of evils and evil tendencies has to be unravelled. We do not build on vacant ground. We have inherited the failures of the past – the slum, the sweating den, the starved child, the drunkard, the neglectful parent, the ignorant and dehumanized citizen, the pauper young and old, the unemployable, the unemployed. In dealing with these problems which press us with such troublesome insistence and which crowd so closely upon us as to shut out the way ahead, lies our greatest danger. It is so easy to agitate for a palliative, to stump for things which do nothing but harm, and to gain a reputation for human sympathy by flitting from agitation to agitation without troubling to think systematically of the future. Wandering aimlessly in the wilderness is a delightful pastime, and leading a crowd from oasis to oasis gives a man, for the time being, the reputation of being a great leader. If the advance to Socialism is to be retarded as this country grows older, it will be because at the beginning the Socialists made themselves responsible for legislation which was merely palliative, which touched the surface only, and which became assimilated by the old order and gave it a new lease of life – for instance, tinkering with the rates of nominal wages, or playing with fanciful democratic toys like the Referendum. It is perfectly certain that everything which is not in some way a carrying out of the principles of Socialism will have to be undone – or those principles are false. The idea that a lax administration of the Poor Law is Socialistic, that putting an unemployed man on a farm for six weeks at the public expense is Socialistic, that feeding school children is the beginning of the Socialistic State, is absurd. We can deal with our unemployed, our sweated workers, our derelicts, only by attacking the causes of unemployment, of sweating, of human deterioration, and though, at a crisis, our humanitarianism will compel us to resort to palliatives and give temporary relief, our action at such times should not be a willing and proud thing, but one which is hesitating and temporary.

Socialism has also a great part to play immediately in international politics. It alone can banish national jealousies from the Foreign Offices; it alone offers the guarantees of peace which are a necessary preliminary to disarmament. And in addition to that it is formulating a policy defining the relationships between the white and the yellow races, between the civilized and the backward, which offers some promise of averting what would otherwise be the almost inevitable conflict between East and West, and also of preserving the existence of races that seem otherwise to be doomed to disappear from the face of the earth. Socialism has a world policy as well as a national one – a corollary to its belief in the brotherhood of man.

Socialism in Politics

A final word regarding the political relations of Socialism is necessary. Where Parliamentary Government – as in Germany – is only a name, a Socialist Party can exist separately and distinct from other parties; and as under this form of government politics are more theoretical than under a democracy, the existence of such a Party is still easier.*

Under a democratic Parliamentary Government, however, it is practically impossible to maintain a pure and simple Socialist Party – although government by parliamentary groups makes this easier. Even then, as we see in France and Australia, the Socialist Party will have on occasions to co-operate in a *bloc* either refusing or accepting the responsibility of office.†

In Great Britain at present, political parties are in confusion, but the lines of division between two great parties are emerging. The mass of the people are prepared to accept the new doctrines not as absolute ideas, as the fully-fledged Socialists do, but as guiding principles in experimental legislation. That is what the rise of the Labour Party means – that is all that it ever need mean, because that is how society develops from stage to stage of its existence. The Manchester school was never more than a tiny nucleus in the political life of the nineteenth century, but it supplied progressive ideas to that century and consequently led it. Nineteenth-century politics without Manchesterism

* It must be pointed out, however, that even under the political conditions of Germany the rise to power of a trade union organization is compelling the Socialist movement to modify its old position and approximate to that of the British movement, e.g., the Labour Party.
† At the International Socialist Congress at Amsterdam in 1904, it was emphatically laid down and accepted by all the Socialist leaders, that in times of national crisis this should be done. No attempt was made, however, to define a national crisis.

would be a body without a brain. So in the twentieth century, Socialism, which will be infinitely more powerful than Manchesterism was in the nineteenth, will probably fulfil itself by being the creative centre of a much more powerful political movement. This is the position of the Labour Party at present.

The voting strength of this movement will come from the ranks of labour – the organized intelligent workers – the men who have had municipal and trade union experience – the men of self-respect who know the capacity of the people. These men will feel the oppression of the present time, its injustice, its heartlessness. They know their own leaders and have confidence in them. Their concern is that of the man who gives service and who sees his reward disappear like water through a sieve. They are to be the constructive agents of the next stage in our industrial evolution. But they are not to stand alone. Socialism is no class movement. Socialism is a movement of opinion, not an organization of status. It is not the rule of the working class; it is the organization of the community. Therefore, to my mind one of the most significant facts of the times is the conversion of the intellectual middle class to Socialism. Those who think that the middle class is to organize against Socialism are to discover that they are profoundly mistaken. To put it on the lowest ground, only part of the interests of the middle class is opposed to Socialism, and against that must be placed the intellectual attractiveness of the Socialist theory. In determining political effort an active intelligence and an awakened idealism are always more powerful than personal interests. To quote *The Communist Manifesto* once more: 'Just as, therefore, at an earlier period, a section of the nobility went over to the bourgeoisie, so now a portion of the bourgeoisie goes over to the proletariat, and in particular a portion of the bourgeois ideologists, who have raised themselves to the level of comprehending theoretically the historical movement as a whole.'

In the ninth book of *The Republic* Plato discusses the wise man as citizen. ' "He will look at the city which is within him, and take heed that no disorder will occur in it such as might arise from superfluity or want; and upon this principle he will regulate his property and gain and spend according to his means." "Then, if that is his motive", remarks Glauson, "he will not be a statesman." "By the dog of Egypt, he will," ejaculated Socrates.'

So long as Plato's reading of the human heart remains true, men will take up their abode in the city 'which exists in idea', and rich and poor alike will labour for the establishment of the State where life alone will be valued as treasure, and the tyranny of the economic machine will no longer hold spiritual things in subjection. That State I call Socialism.

SOCIALISM:
CRITICAL AND
CONSTRUCTIVE

Preface

In issuing a new edition, a few notes have been added bringing one or two statements up to date. Socialism still remains a bogey to a considerable remnant. The somewhat deteriorated methods of party political controversy have led, especially since the Labour Party came into prominence, to a use of Socialist literature which indicates that in anti-Socialist headquarters it has fallen under the scrutiny of people who are either peculiarly stupid or peculiarly dishonest. When every new and unfamiliar idea is seized upon and broadcasted for the purpose of creating prejudice, and is annotated and commented upon for the purpose of rousing ignorance and fear into activity, ephemeral party gains may be recorded. It is a sorry game to play, however, and its results will have to be paid for dearly.

There are grades in the heinousness of the offence, ranging from the disreputable slanders that Socialism means the nationalization of women, to the muddle-headed attacks that have been made from Front Benches in the House of Commons, on the ground that Socialists believe that the credit power should be held by an organ acting not for private advantage but for general industrial well-being. The reason for the muddle-headedness of the latter is that the Socialist method of transformation is not at all understood by those whose only interest in it is the advantages it gives to political leaders, who are willing to build up majorities on ignorance and fear.

The Socialist transforms by the well-defined processes which a living social organization allows. He does not stop the life of society in order to try new experiments or to put a brand new system into operation. The pledges he gives do not concern his achievements of the morrow so much as the purpose which underlies and impregnates all his continuing action. He has ideals and they guide him, and he rejects everything of the nature of violent breaks and brand-new systems. He is an evolutionist *par excellence*, and even though he knows that the resistance of interests and log-like minds may defeat his methods at times, he remains an evolutionist because he is convinced that when revolutionary methods have done their work, the people whom reaction has victimized, by imposing a revolution upon them, will have to return to evolutionary transformation so soon as they have gained freedom. To him, Russian bolshevism is but an interlude in tsarism, and British toryism an obstructing but moving mass of interest and mind. The revolutionary and materialistic frames of mind created by the war have been a serious menace to the Socialist spirit of common service. Profiteering has become universal and action has shown a deplorable tendency to centre in self. The evil has not been confined to the classes generally designated as 'profiteers', but has infected all sections. That workmen should not tolerate without a struggle to remedy their conditions, which are not only hard but unjust, is good, but in their struggles to secure their ends they are tempted to forget that they are all interdependent members of a social unity, and that consequently they only injure themselves by punishing those against whom they have a grievance to such an extent that they injure the society to which they belong. The trade unionist has the same limitation imposed upon him in this respect as the capitalist – he cannot advance his interests at the expense of his society. No system of thought except Socialism not only makes these limitations of wise action clear, but indicates the method by which labour may obtain justice. It cannot be over-emphasized that public doles, Poplarism, strikes for increased wages, limitation of output, not only are not Socialism, but may mislead the spirit and the policy of the Socialist movement. Socialism calls men to give unstinted service in return for a reasonable reward measured in terms of life, and no one should be more impatient than the Socialist with the fallacy that a man cannot be expected to give the service before he gets the reward. The Socialist, therefore, looks with some misgivings upon some recent developments in the conflicts between capital and labour. They are contrary to his spirit; he believes they are both immoral and uneconomic and will lead to disaster. It is only when the worker by brain or by hand does his best for society that he will create in society that sympathy and support without which the labour movement will never attain its goal.

June 1924   J. Ramsay MacDonald

Chapter IV

Production

The Organization of Production

Products are the economic life blood of society. As the ages have gone past, the organization of production has widened over fields farther and farther away and has become more and more complex. Our ancestors who made flint instruments chipped them from flints found on the spot; when the Iron Age arrived, the forges were blown where the ore was to be found along with the fuel, as in Sussex. The mobilization of raw material in convenient spots came later; now every producing centre draws upon the whole world for what is necessary for its production and uses the whole world as its market. As the massing of the raw material proceeded and production on a large scale became possible, there were so many simple processes to do, that bodies of men did them and nothing else, whilst others brought them together and thus the product was completed. There were both subdivision and coordination. That was a cheap and a quick way of doing things. The effect was to make the individual workman incomplete in himself; his particular product was not immediately fit to be exchanged for commodities; he and the work of his hands or his machine were but little things to be fitted into great things. An enormously complicated system had grown up which embraced the whole earth and every race and colour, which brought every treasure and necessary to its market and workshop, which gave men work and careers, and which, indeed, was the scaffolding, rickety and dangerous as I shall show, upon which the life of communities came to depend with a completeness in proportion to their advance in civilization.

Thus capitalism arose through a process that has been described until it has become tedious. When a producer made things to meet his own needs and found his material in his chalk pit or his forest, he required the economic help of no one whilst he produced. But when his raw material had to be brought to him, or he only did a part of a finished product or produced one thing in great quantities, a market had to be found and exchange began to operate. Someone was then required to organize all these things and so keep all the processes in touch with each other. Some form of accumulated wealth or credit was also required, so that the workers engaged on a job might be able to draw upon the values they were creating before these values were fit to be used. Production and marketing having become a long process, means had to be devised to keep things going until the product was sold and its price realized. So capitalism arose to mobilize material, to conduct long processes of production, to handle the mass material produced, and to supply the instalments of money required by labour for day to day consumption.

This is also the basis of the economic defence of capitalism. It not only does these things as a matter of historical fact, but it alone can do them – so it is argued and still oftener assumed. Production is no longer the result of a man's labour employed to make what he wants to use, but of organization, in which the act of working is divided by many incidents from the complementary act of consuming. The workmen's stores of food and clothing have to be replenished many times before their work can be exchanged and marketed. Therefore, manual labour has to be directed by organizing skill and brought into contact with a reservoir of wealth and credit. The effect of this is to draw the workman away from his product and to put the product in the possession of the organizer and the capitalist. These are sometimes one and the same person, but often they are not, and then the actual organizer of business is a salaried agent of those who supply the capital and entrust it to the care of others. This separation became formalized in law when the Limited Liability Companies Act was passed in 1862. The capital of trading and manufacturing companies is supplied by investors who have no knowledge of the business from which they draw their incomes, directors are appointed to look after the interests of the shareholders with the guarantee that they themselves hold a certain number of shares in the companies they 'direct'; the managerial skill required is hired; the workmen have no concern in the affair but to do a day's work upon a fixed wage, or wage rate. These are the general features of industry today. Finance, management, labour, are distinct functions in production united into an interrelated system by capitalist interests, and the product is the property of capital and those that control it. Labour and management thus become the servants of the owner and controller of capital, are paid wages and salaries, and have no guarantee that their interests as producers and consumers are to be studied. The ledgers of business alone control business.

The effect of this on production is easy to see. The whole process is divided into rival interests each one limited in its view to its own particular part. The dealer in raw material, for instance, has no concern in manufacture except in so far as its success or misfortune may affect his market. Each one manipulates his market, organizes his interest, like a military conqueror tries to make the particular field of his operations the seat of imperial authority. When prices fall, he adopts expedients to keep them up by such resorts as rings, selling agreements, limitations of output, destruction of what, in his interests and in view of his profits, are surplus stocks.* Every controlling

* If labour were as responsible as capitalism for limitation of output there might be some justification for part of the attacks made upon it for that crime. I select at random one or two statements made officially on this subject within the past month or two: The Chairman of the Rubber Plantations Investment Trust (1 September 1920) said that tea production should be limited to keep up the price (the company controlled tea plantations). On 10 October the Dutch Rubber Growers' Association decided almost unanimously that rubber output should be reduced 25 per cent. This was done to grip the market and keep up prices. The Dutch move became international, and *The Times, Economist, Financial News* and other papers, during October, reported the adhesion of British, German, French, Chinese, Japanese

producer runs his little affair in his own interest. That interest may in the long run be conditioned by the communal well-being, but it often is not. And at no point is this well-being considered as a dominating factor in production. Communal advantage has more frequently to accommodate itself to the interests of capitalism than to direct and control those interests.

A study of the way in which raw cotton is handled will show the nature of the system upon which I am commenting. Of the cotton crop raised in the world, America contributes from 50 to 60 per cent. It uses about half in its own mills and exports the rest, Great Britain taking about half of that. Roughly, of every three pounds of raw cotton used by us two are American grown. In this industry about 600,000 people are employed, and they with their dependents account for from three to four millions of our population. Such is the importance of the industry.

The American cotton growers are in a slavish economic position. Some own their own lands, but many rent them (usually at high figures) from plantation owners. The grower, as a rule, is short of capital, and lives from season to season by running up accounts with local storekeepers, who are generally agents of cotton factors. The storekeeper has a lien on the crop by which the grower's debts are guaranteed. Growers on a large scale can finance themselves or deal with banks. The first middleman is the factor who handles a considerable percentage of the total crop, and he in turn is in the hands of banks and cotton syndicates. Thus, the financial transactions involved in cotton sales provide for commissions for local money-lenders, local banks, factors, New York banks, inland bills of lading, bills of exchange – from beginning to end a most wasteful system.*

---

growers. Early in December 1920, it was reported from Cairo that capitalist interests had decided to restrict the cotton-growing area in Egypt. Evidence of the destruction of raw material by capitalist owners in order to keep up price is plentiful.

* The world is full of experiments and the failure of experiments made by producers and consumers to come into direct contact with each other, and so save industrial waste and bondage, and a description of

Ramsay MacDonald's Political Writings

The importance of the cotton trade, the vast sums of money involved in it, and the precariousness of the crops, lead to colossal speculation. Uncertainty and need are used to increase profits and to add to charges. 'Can I make money out of this?' is the question which this system of capitalist operation dins into the ears of everyone in the trade. Risk is the mother of speculation. Thus, in addition to the wastefulness which the poverty and lack of organization on the part of a large section of the growers involves in the marketing of raw cotton, an elaborate network of gambling has also been woven into it. Theoretically, this has its uses. It might result in preventing violent seasonal fluctuations and in stabilizing the market, making rises and drops in prices orderly by averaging them. That is urged when dealing in futures is criticized. It is said that when the price of cotton depends less upon uncertain harvests than upon business speculation, the supply goes through to the mills at prices which are determined not by momentary but by more permanent influences. It is argued that gambling depends upon mathematical laws of chance, and that consequently dealings in cotton futures steadies the market. Though in a given season this would mean that the price of cotton is higher than that season's conditions warrant, still, if it enabled manufacturers to calculate costs ahead with some certainty, it would benefit industry. It fails to do this, however, and does much more than this. It is worked for the manipulation of prices, it introduces reasons of its own for fluctuations, it entails great financial transactions which add to

---

the American cotton market suggests the long struggle that has been carried on by the Nebraska farmers to do their own marketing. The result enforces later arguments which I am to develop. They built their own grain elevators and ran them by a co-operative society of their own. They failed and failed, but they were not discouraged, and in the end they overcame. Today, in wide districts their societies have eliminated the grain middleman, the livestock middleman, the miller manufacturer and middleman; they control their coal supply, lumber yards, creameries, insurance. Nearly two-thirds of the 75,000 Nebraska farmers are members of these co-operative undertakings. The pooling of crops is beginning. At the outset, Nebraska was faced by the opposition of a railroad ring, but that it broke by politics.

the market price of the crop, and it lends itself to frenzied speculation on the uncertainty of demand which is as disturbing to prices as the uncertainty of supply. It promotes rings and monopolies in supply, and transfers to financial operations the control of the industry. On account of it, the cotton crop of an ordinary season may be sold from twenty to forty times over.*

Thus, the needs of industry are lost sight of in the pursuit of wealth. Of course, if the holders of raw material were to stifle industry by their folly, they themselves would be involved in its ruin and would lose their market. But that obvious truth does not primarily control their action. Industry is hard to ruin. Consumption must go on, whatever difficulties are put in its way. Therefore, raw material may be the subject of the fiercest and most costly speculation, its amount may be limited in the interest of its holders, its price may be artificially forced up, its marketing may be the occasion for an elaborate system of commissions and profits secured by financiers and middlemen, and industry will still go on overcoming all obstacles and shifting costs ultimately on to the final consumer. But the community suffers and has to pay the bills of the waste either in high prices or in a low standard of life.

Obviously, if production is to be carried on with some security and efficiency, the supply of raw material ought not to be the subject of an interest organized apart from the users, but should be subordinated and controlled by the users. It should be an organic part of the system of production managed to meet its needs and reduce its costs. This contention is indeed admitted by capitalist production itself, where we observe that the tendency is constantly to coordinate complementary industries and supplies under one management, and to eliminate separate interests in linked processes. The United States Steel Corporation (capital £369,000,000) was created on this idea, and brought coal, iron ore and furnaces under one management. Soapmaking firms find it necessary to be the owners of their own

* I have used for the purpose of this summary statement an article on 'The Selling and Financing of the American Cotton Crop' in the *Economic Journal*, December 1920.

oil-producing estates and acquire islands in the Pacific and tracts in Central Africa. Iron smelting firms, like Dorman, Long and Co., which is the centre of a great group of contributing industries, work coal mines, lime quarries and iron ore deposits both at home and abroad, and treat the whole as one producing unit, with one trade balance, whilst other firms, especially those engaged in armament manufacture, have, by purchases of each others' shares and exchanging directors, become an intricate network of combined interests. Cotton manufacturers have promoted cotton growing enterprises which they could control, and, like the Fine Cotton Spinners' and Doublers' Association, own plantations. Wherever any form of production is being carried on on a large scale, a tendency arises for it to try and command its necessary raw material on the one hand, and its market (as, for instance, in the case of boot and shoe manufacturers who start multiple shops to sell their products) on the other.

But the best example of this inevitable tendency to coordinate the whole process of industry from raw material to the wares passing over the shop counter, is seen in the co-operative movement. This acquired its power as an agency of distribution through separately managed shops. Its first extension was to provide a wholesale organization for itself, and this it built up. Then it proceeded to manufacture so as to supply the more generally used household necessities, like clothing, bread and other foods. From that it went on to acquire land, both at home and abroad, for agricultural produce including such things as tea and coffee.* From that it proceeded to organize its necessary transport, and became possessed of a fleet of ships. Its latest development is a bank by which it finances itself.

Thus we can see that in industry there is a law of concentra-

---

* As an indication of the scale upon which these developments are being made I note on the agenda to be considered by the delegates attending the quarterly meeting of the Co-operative Wholesale Society that approval is asked for the purchase of estates in India, Ceylon and West Africa, and for land in twenty-four different English towns for business extension (January 1921).

tion by which not merely do small businesses of the same kind tend to unite into large ones, but different processes with the same inevitability tend to be coordinated so that they become related parts of one industrial unit.

I must not anticipate the completion of my argument, however. Thus far I have been dealing with the effect upon production of the control and supply of raw materials by profit-making interests, and I have shown that such control must hamper production, must make it costly, and must prevent social wealth and advantage from being the predominating consideration. In modern production, the tropics are a source of essential raw materials like vegetable oil, and mineral oil abounds where government is weak and civil order uncertain. This leads to territorial annexation, to the economic rivalry of great states, to the exclusion of unpopular ones, to armaments and to war. It also leads to politico-moral results almost as disastrous to a healthy state. It puts temptations in the way of civilized states to employ 'natives' as tribute labourers, as has been proposed by our Empire Resource Development Committee, and thus to become demoralized by something akin to slave owning. The next step will be that capitalism, in its own interests, will establish extractive plants in these regions, use forced labour in them, and export the partly finished products to go through the more technical final processes here. When that takes place, we approach the end of states, for wealth created after that fashion and brought in as tribute, is a canker at the heart of peoples. All this happens not because community interests require such developments, but because the interests of capitalists must extend their possessions and their conflicts, and must not only dominate the community by their trade combinations, but drag the political state into these foreign annexations and rivalries as well.

Free Competition

When we follow materials to the next, the manufacturing, stage of production, we find the same evils springing from the same causes. Controlling capital puts itself first. It arranges the markets, if it can, to suit its own interests primarily. In a world of absolutely free competition, public advantage might coincide with capitalist profits. The argument is that too high prices could not be charged, too low wages could not be paid for the necessary skilled labour, adulteration would be difficult, quality in production would carry against inferiority – if we had truly free competition. This is set off, however, by the consideration that, in bargaining on the open market, labour is at a disadvantage against capital owing to the difference of their training and of the pressure of their necessities, that the public has no protection by reason of its knowledge against adulteration and that it will always be imposed upon by low priced bad articles. Absolutely free competition requires these amongst other conditions. The purchasing and consuming public must be intelligent enough not to be imposed upon but to take the trouble to understand and pursue its own advantage; there must be no tendency or opportunity for competing capital to combine and, by agreement or extension of control, relieve the pressure which free competition imposes upon rival manufacturers and salesmen; the workman must be really as free as the capitalist to hold out for a just price, not in relation to immediate needs, but to a normal satisfactory life. These conditions do not exist and in the nature of things hardly can exist. The workman in combination can put up a good fight for equality, but sweating is always possible in a very extensive field which may, however, be substantially narrowed in time by such expedients as wages boards. The public must trust to honest men to supply it with goods of a quality which it desires but cannot test, and therefore the competition between salesmen, whether of drugs or pots, must always produce a rivalry in the arts of 'palming off' and, in a large part, though certainly not all, of its transactions must be concerned not with serving but with victimizing consumers. In fact, it is a complete fallacy to suppose that preying upon the public will be cured by free competition as tuberculosis is by fresh air. The inferior in commerce as in life cannot be stamped out by rivalry or mechanical means. It has to be attacked by the organized reason.

Moreover, there must always be a tendency in capitalism to avoid the troubles of competition whether by tariffs or combines. It is quite true that an economic monopoly, not being a natural monopoly, can never be made complete, and that if it goes too far in its exactions, it raises new rivals. But as is abundantly shown by the history of such ventures as the Standard Oil Company and shipping rings, the power of the combination, by undercutting or by penalizing those who deal with rivals,* makes it difficult for competing enterprises to spring up. It is not outside the bounds of possibility for capital to entrench itself so securely in the major industries of the whole world as to defy effective competition. So, within a pretty extensive margin, economic combination can act as though it was a natural monopoly.

Economic Monopoly

In our own time we have seen two prodigious monopolies of this economic kind created here – the Coates' combination in sewing thread and the Imperial Tobacco Company; in America, these combinations are more common, and one of the latest, the Meat Trust, a combination of the five† most powerful packing firms, has been repeatedly dragged before the public owing to the complaints regarding its transactions, and has finally been the subject of an adverse decision in the Law Courts.

The Sewing Thread combine has been in existence since 1890, when it started with a capital of £5,750,000. In 1895 and 1896, it absorbed important competing firms and increased its capital finally to £10,000,000. In 1897, a rival combine was

* This method was practised by the owners of boot and shoe machinery patents much to the hampering of other patentees and the interests of the trade. Contracts had to be signed binding users to purchase no patents or machinery, but what the monopolist firm held, or could supply, and as the firm held key patents, this was tantamount to the enforcement of a complete monopoly.
† In their foreign business these five have traded under no fewer than thirty-eight different names.

formed against it, and the war between the two was felt in low prices. In the end, the second combine had to surrender with its capital of nearly £3,000,000, and was brought into association with the other.

The Tobacco combine was effected in 1902 owing to the purchase, for $5,000,000, of an English firm by the American Tobacco Company, and the starting of fierce competition on the British market. By the end of the year the two leviathans came to an agreement, and, by the formation of a British American Tobacco Company, covered the whole world and divided it. The issued capital of the Imperial Tobacco Company was, when its books were closed on 30 September 1920, 4,500,000 Preference and 16,002,523 Ordinary £1 Shares, and in 1919–20 its current account with, and loans to, associated companies amounted to £7,200,000, and in these companies it had invested £11,356,000.

Capitalism is Combination not Competition

These are huge outstanding examples towering over business as mountains over a landscape, but they are unique only in size, and it has been estimated that there are now at least 500 effective combinations operating in British trade. The Committee on Trusts appointed by the Ministry of Reconstruction began the report which it presented in 1919 with this statement: 'We find that there is at the present time in every important branch of industry in the United Kingdom an increasing tendency to the formation of trade associations and combinations, having for their purpose the restriction of competition and the control of prices' (p. 2). It names thirty-five combinations (warning us that the list is not 'at all exhaustive') in various sections of the iron and steel industry. These control 'a large proportion of the trade', which makes the Committee remind us that an economic monopoly to be effective need not be complete. The production of chemicals, an industry which now ramifies into a great variety of other industries, 'is almost wholly in the hands of two great consolidations'. The electric, soap, wallpaper, salt, cement and textile industries (spinning, dyeing, printing), as regards output and prices, are 'effectively' controlled. There is a prices and output control in the furniture trades. The building trades are in the clutches of rings formed 'for the monopolization of raw materials or means of production by limitation of output and maintenance or inflation of prices'.* Fifty-nine per cent of building materials are fully or partly controlled.† The Ministry of Munitions supplied the Committee with names of over ninety combinations of one kind or other, formed to restrict competition, with which it had come in contact.‡

* 'Report of Committee on Trusts', p. 36.
† In 1921 (when this was written) the Lockwood Committee made a series of the most astounding revelations regarding building combinations in America, which have resulted in smashing fifteen combinations and a fall in prices of 30 per cent. The American methods were precisely the same as those described in the text, with the exception that they included agreements with Trade Union leaders – one in particular – to aid them. In America, capitalism works with a thoroughness which it hardly dare to employ here, but in view of the reference I make later on to the Bedstead Makers' agreement with labour, this is what is stated of this American case. 'On 17 December 1919, the Building Trades Employers' Association entered into an agreement with Brindell's [the Trade Union official] Building Trades Council, whereby the association members were to use none but Brindell workers and the Brindell men were to work for no one not a member of the association. This eliminated from the building field the few independent contractors remaining.'
‡ I supplement what I have written in the text with a short list of some of these combinations, because readers should be in no doubt as to the fact that combination has secured the great strategical points of advantage in industry. Bedstead Makers' Federation (controlling four-fifths of the output); National Light Castings Association (including about 100 firms); Associated Brass and Copper Manufacturers of Great Britain, which works with several combinations to keep up prices; white lead, sheet lead, lead oxide and spelter are also controlled; carpets, linoleum and floor cloth are under what 'are understood to be definitely price associations'; the output and price of bobbins are controlled; explosives, nitrates, oil and petrol are controlled; dyes are controlled and the Government policy regarding them is to extend the power of the control; glass, especially glass bottles, is controlled. Some of the controlling companies with their

Nor are these operations confined within national boundaries. The International Rail Makers' Association is an international syndicate which, like the Tobacco Trust, covers the whole world, and is controlled by British, American, German, French, Belgian, Spanish, Italian makers. This was before the war. The International Aniline Convention of German and British producers of Aniline oil, controlled prices and output and rigidly fixed conditions of marketing. The International Glass Bottle Association, formed in consequence of an American patent which revolutionized production, combines the interests of makers in Britain, Germany, Austria, Holland, Norway, Sweden and Denmark, and, working with American producers, controls the world supply and its price. I have dealt with tobacco. There are also metal syndicates, like the Aluminium Syndicate, operating in the same way; and from both Germany and America this recital could be considerably extended. Sixty per cent of our imported beef (before the war) came from combines, and steel, drugs, chemicals and the bulk of our trade with Germany passed through the hands of the 500 kartels then in existence in that country.

If I were to compile an exhaustive list of all known syndicates, formidable as it would be, it would be but a fraction of the combinations which limit output and control prices. For this is done to a considerable extent by understanding and agreement never expressed in documents. For instance, when the United States Steel Corporation was being harassed by anti-Trust

---

capital are as follows: Fine Cotton Spinners' and Doublers' Association (capital including debentures £8,450,000); Bradford Dyers (£5,300,000); Calico Printers' Association (£8,227,000); Bleachers' Association (£7,073,000); Associated Portland Cement Manufacturers (£8,734,000) and British Portland Cement (£2,800,000); Salt Union (£2,600,000); Borax Consolidated (£4,252,000); Wallpaper Manufacturers (£4,000,000); United Alkali Company (£6,175,000); Brunner, Mond and Co. (£4,598,000); Lever Bros. (£15,143,000 in 1917; by 1921, £47,000,000 plus £4,000,000 first mortgage debentures); British Oil and Cake Mills (£2,336,428); an association of electrical material producers controls an aggregate capital of £33,000,000. The figures are those given in the Report on Trusts, *q.v.*

legislation, for a period of over three years it transacted its 'illegal' deals without let, hindrance or fear at the famous Gary dinners given by its president to representatives of about 90 per cent of the steel production of the United States. These 'understandings' are common in the British coal trade, both locally and nationally.

A survey of the facts at our disposal compels us to conclude with the report of the Committee on Trusts unanimously signed: 'We are satisfied that Trade Associations and Combines are rapidly increasing in this country and may within no distant period exercise a paramount control over all important branches of British trade.'*

I shall discuss the social effect of combinations presently; all that I wish to establish now is that the free competition of the theoretical text-books does not exist. It is as much an abstraction as the economic man. Its elements are there, but they are in combination with modifying and opposing elements. And I wish to emphasize the fact that so far from the system of private capitalism being one based on competition, its urgent tendency is to limit competition, and confine it to the smaller and less organized transactions on the margin of the trading field – the small booths on the outskirts of the great show. In considering how far the present system works for the communal well-being, we must not make the mistake that that system is one of free competition. Rather it is one of economic monopoly tempered by the fear of a return to free competition. Such is capitalism.

The Power of Capital

When the features of capitalist combination are studied, the first thing that must strike one is the overmastering advantage which it gives to capitalist interests. To begin with, the combinations are generally over-capitalized, and that means that their advantages, if they succeed at all, belong to capital. The process is easy to understand. A business succeeds and can pay a high percentage on its original capital. It then enters a combination

* 'Report of Committee on Trusts', p. 11.

Ramsay MacDonald's Political Writings

where, by the elimination of competition, its dividend-earning value is enhanced, or it is turned into a limited liability company, with the result, in either case, that the burden of capital which it has to carry, and upon which it has to return satisfactory profits to its new owners, is multiplied five-, ten- or twenty-fold. Its original success was due, perhaps, in a small degree to the capital invested in it, and in a great one to the brains and business ability spent upon it. In its new phase it has been turned into a purely profit-making machine – a means of earning incomes for shareholders who bought not the business but the profits, paying for them the market rate of industrial capital. If the combination or company should succeed and earn profits so ample that great reserves have to be accumulated, the reserves may be distributed in the form of shares, and so the burden of capital which has to be borne is again increased without increasing by the fraction of a cent the amount of capital required in production. Capital harnesses to its service all available surpluses, however created. Capital seizes for itself the product of brains, the marginal profits that cannot affect price,* the power of the economic concern to keep prices above cost of production. Capital is often hard squeezed by finance, by rent-owners, by labour and so on, but it is the residuary legatee of production, and were it not dissipated by folly and redistributed at death it would soon be in absolute control of society.

* This takes into account the contention made, particularly by the directors of the thread combine, that though their aggregate profits amount to millions and their dividends to Midas proportions, the number of reels of cotton sold is so great that if these profit balances were used to reduce price the gain would be an infinitesimal portion of a penny per reel. Supposing the contention is sound, and that the colossal fortunes made by the chief capitalists in this industry represent profits that cannot be distributed amongst customers, the question has still to be answered: 'Why do they go to capital?' Why should capital claim the right of residuary legatee, and why should it use that right to fix upon industry obligations to pay for vast sums of capital which it never has used, never will and never can use? On the moral side capital has less right to those surpluses than labour or the community; on the business side their capture and use by capital is a handicap to production and an injury to the body of consumers.

The facts upon which this estimation of the power of capital is based lie plentifully at one's hand and can be drawn from every department of industry. Let me instance what was done in 1918 by the shareholders of the Powell Duffryn Coal Company. This company gave each of its shareholders one share for every three held, and in addition paid them dividends of 20 per cent free of taxation. When it was known that that would happen the £1 shares of the company were quoted at 74s. An apologist for the transaction defended it in these simple words, to which the most avowed enemy of capitalism need ask no addition. 'A distribution of shares in this way is more advantageous to the shareholders than cash, as the bonus shares are themselves dividend earning.' The meaning of the state of things described is not difficult to see, and can be put in this way. The Powell Duffryn Company required £3, as assistance from capital for its development, and upon that capital it was very successful. On account of the dividends it paid, the £3 were sold on the market for something like £7 10s, and the new holders of the bought shares would not, therefore, be content unless they had dividends of an average amount on what they paid for their shares. The management had, therefore, to produce results on a capital which had been multiplied by two and a-half without an extra pound having been sunk in the undertaking. Then by a resolution of a meeting, the three pounds became four,* but on the market, the money articles told us, they became about ten guineas. Thus, capital, by seizing upon all the surpluses, had increased its hold upon the industry three and a-half fold. The Metropolitan Carriage, Wagon and Finance Company, in 1912, gave to its ordinary shareholders one bonus share for every two they held, and in June 1917 one new bonus share

* So far as I have been able to find out, this is literally what happened. If the fourth pound had been used as capital for development or other profitable expenditure, the real capital of the company would have been increased and would have been drawn from reserves, a legitimate proceeding. But there appears to have been no increase of real capital, and the extra shares only represent a power to draw dividends earned by the original capital without appearing to be drawing too much.

for every old one held. On this watered capital it paid dividends of 15 per cent free of income tax, which is equal to 60 per cent on its true capital. In other words, the capital in this company gets six or seven times its economic share. Of the British American Tobacco Company's capital of £8,359,272 (in 1918) the astonishing sum of £5,571,123 was created by the issue of bonus shares. In May 1919 the chairman of this company boasted that whereas the net profits distributed in the first year of its existence were only £148,541, for the year 1918 they were £3,140,174, and 30 per cent free of income tax was to be paid as dividend. This abnormal dividend represents nothing but the exploiting value of combination. That year a further issue of 2,131,733 shares at bonus rates was made, Lord St Davids remarking: 'As nearly as I can reckon, the shares that have been allotted to the shareholders at £1 per share are a bonus to the shareholders of something like £10,000,000 sterling.'* In August 1916, the company which owned the White Star Line increased its capital of £750,000, to one of £3,750,000, by distributing £3,000,000 of reserves not as dividends† but as shares. When the Moor Line was wound up in 1920, £130 was paid on each share (these were issued at £10). This is enough to prove my case, but, did I care to multiply examples, I could cite what has been done by companies like the Birmingham Small Arms, Brunner Mond, Maypole Dairy, Babcock Wilcox and others all engaged in industries of the most vital importance to the general system of national production.‡

* It may be observed that when the British-American section of this combination was declaring a dividend equal to 37½ per cent, it was discharging Liverpool employees and congratulating itself on its charity for giving them a month's wages!

† As I shall not return to this again, I note in passing that this method of dealing with what are really dividends and income incidentally cheats the nation out of income tax.

‡ In some cases these share bonuses are true additions to capital, as when reserves have been used for development and the amounts sunk ultimately distributed amongst the shareholders. Cf. Sir Hugh Bell's statement to the Horden Colliery shareholders; *Common Sense*, 11 December 1920.

These profits are accumulated from prices. They can come from no other source, for even if they are possible only by reason of the economies and efficiencies of combination, they ought, on all theories of the virtue of competition or of the social ends of production, to be used to reduce price, after the proper charges for services have been met. I have just noted that one of the justifications put forward by a possessor of an enormous fortune made possible by combination was, that though the profits were large they were accumulated from such vast numbers of units of purchase that, if distributed in a reduction of prices, they would be dissipated without helping the customer to any appreciable degree. With the implications of this argument I shall deal in a later portion of this section. It comes into my mind at this point so that I may say of it that it is certainly not generally true, whatever may be the case with cotton reels.

Combination and Price

Competition may be carried on till it can be justly described as 'cut-throat', and then the consumer receives privileges in lowness of price to which he is not entitled, and which are made possible by doing injustice and injury to one or other of the factors in production. We can all remember the cut-rate Atlantic fares when the steamship companies fell foul of each other; and most people who follow political controversy will remember the accusations which his political opponents used to make against Mr Chamberlain for having been a party to the ruining of rival screw producers by under-cutting prices. In streets where shops run in unbroken lines, we often see this warfare in window prices. It is only fair and expedient that suicide and murder should be avoided if possible in trade, and combinations seek to put in that plea as a justification for themselves. It does not explain their prospectuses or their working, however. The rule of combination working is that prices shall be kept as high as possible – that is, up to that point when the increase will diminish the total profit derived, or opposition and exposure will lead to unwelcome results. This is true

Ramsay MacDonald's Political Writings

whether the combination is in the form of a trust like that of sewing cotton and tobacco, or of a prices ring like the Bedstead Makers' Federation, or the combinations in building material which received such scathing exposure in the press in connection with the controversy on housing shortage after the war. Nearly every combination confesses in its articles that its main purpose is to keep up prices.

The associations in the iron and steel industry mentioned in the report of the Committee on Trusts to which I have referred, are, in 'a large proportion either permanently or intermittently *price* associations'. Ninety per cent of iron casting production is priced by a ring, so is the product of four-fifths of the metal bedstead firms. It has been stated repeatedly that a combination which controls 80 per cent of the products, can control price. According to one of the appendices to the Report on Trusts, 'it transpires that in innumerable lines of manufacture anything from 80 to 100 per cent of the whole national output of the articles concerned is either in the hands of one dominant consolidation or of manufacturers grouped together for purposes of concerted price and other control in a trade association.*

The facts are beyond dispute. The consumers, and the community as an organic whole, are no longer protected by the levelling influence of competition. The public is at the mercy of combinations of capital controlled by their own interests

* During the war the farming interests made abundant use of the economic advantage which their position gave them. For some time attempts were made to force up milk prices by combination which offered some extra profits to retailers, the wholesale combinations fixing minimum retail prices. If retailers sold below those prices their supply was stopped. I have a letter before me which was sent to a Co-operative Society from a farmers' combination known as the United Dairies (Wholesale), Ltd., and it contains the sentence: 'We understand that you have been selling at ½d per quart less than other dairymen in your town. If so, we shall be glad if you will now fall into line with the others, otherwise we fear we shall be reluctantly compelled to stop your supply.' The Society, I may add, was making a satisfactory profit off the lower price.

primarily, and by their own judgement of the conditions under which these interests are to be promoted. The facts from which my case has been built up are, in the main, pre-war facts, but the experiences and practices of the war have given a great impetus to further combination. The organization of capital has proceeded apace since 1914. It is urged by the spokesmen for the combinations that they are necessary, and that, though in practically every case they are by their own declarations formed to raise and maintain prices, they do not propose to go beyond what will give a fair return on capital and encourage the development of the trade itself. What that is to be, however, the capitalist is himself to judge – a position of privilege and power which is inconsistent with any sense of security or of confidence – a position, moreover, which balance sheets and resolutions of shareholders' meetings show will be grossly abused. A customer of one of the combinations gave evidence to the Committee on Trusts: 'It starves its distributors, its heavy profits are a toll on the wages of the poor, and the necessity of the public becomes its opportunity';* and officers of the Ministry of Munitions referred to 'very exorbitant prices' and the operations of combinations 'which had, in fact, led to a rise of prices to an excessive extent'.† Again, to quote once more from an Appendix to the Report of this Committee, 'although exceptions are not wanting, it may be said generally that the result of combination has been to increase profits'; and, dealing with the plea that combinations can be trusted not to use to the fullest their powers of exploitation, 'little more can be said than that the power conferred by monopoly is *capable* of being used to exact immoderate prices',‡ or, as the Committee itself has said: 'Whilst fully recognizing the honesty with which the great bulk of business in this country is conducted, it is obvious that a system which creates virtual monopolies and controls prices is always in danger of abuse. We are confirmed in this view by a survey of the operations of similar combines and associations in other countries.'§

* 'Report', p. 5.   † ibid., p. 7.
‡ ibid., p. 24.   § ibid., p. 8.

Ramsay MacDonald's Political Writings

That that power is imperial is only too plain from a study of how it is exercised and the machinery available for its exercise. The grip of the combination suits itself to every opportunity. Some combinations bind down their users after the manner of the boot and shoe machine-making company to which I have referred;* some work through special rebates or discounts deferred until customers have in their trade over a period observed conditions, including a promise to handle no goods competing with those of the combine; some work a pooling arrangement by which the combined firms are penalized if they produce more than their quota, and are indemnified if they fall short (this limits production, and, if it were a trade union rule, would be anathematized from every housetop); some bind their retail customers not to sell below a certain price fixed for them, and thus appear to protect them in the enjoyment of specially high profits; some fix the prices at which the products must be sold wholesale by the combined firms; some prevent free tendering for contracts (as in the building trade); some divide the country, some the world, into areas, and assign them to members of the combine; some absorb the combined businesses, whilst some keep them separate but submit their activities to a grand controlling executive which manipulates the total production; some have selling organizations which sometimes handle the goods of other firms. Combination has been long at work meeting its problems in detail and overcoming them. It is perfectly plain that a combination controlling the necessary percentage of the output of certain essential products, or owning a key patent, can hold the whole consuming community at ransom, and fix prices far above economic levels.

The Necessity of Combination

The necessity of combination I admit. In the earlier stages of industry – a hundred years ago in our own country, for instance – when organization is loose and the pressure for raw materials and upon markets is not great, before fierceness has appeared,

* 'Report', pp. 86 and 120.

competition can rule and be accepted as a tolerably satisfactory safeguard. But these times pass, and organization and combination come naturally into the system. Then competition brings new results. It becomes the law of the jungle within production, it preys, and is gradually superseded on account of its destructiveness. It finds a last refuge in the somewhat starved patches where the factory, or shop, or trade is not well equipped with the means of self-protection and not favourable to the formation of unions for mutual protection. In the fiercer times of trade and in these margins where mutual aid does not run, competition becomes something like cannibalism, and while for a time it may secure cheapness to consumers, the apparent advantage is paid for from capital and from the deterioration of the trade. For price is kept uneconomically low by using wealth that ought to be reabsorbed to increase efficiency and promote development, and also by encroaching upon labour standards and so creating a sweated system. A community cannot avoid paying the full price for everything it uses. If it does not pay in one coinage, it pays in another.

Therefore, the Socialist takes a purely historical and not a moral view of combination. It is the inevitable development of capitalism, not the sinister design of the capitalist. Its appearance, though attended with the dangers I have indicated, ought not to give rise merely to moral condemnation; it is a problem in the evolution of economic power. It marks the end of one phase of the function of capitalism in society and the beginning of a new one with problems peculiar to itself. Capitalism grown into the giant that controls monopoly is in a totally different relationship to society from what it was when it was merely a lusty youth increasing its strength by wrestling in competition with others of its own kin. The end of capitalism is monopoly, and when that end is reached, the menace of capitalism, uncontrolled except by its own self-regarding will, is undoubted. It then becomes a State within the State with power that can be used far more effectively than political power. 'Freedom (for capital) from public control will therefore mean not free competition, but concerted or unified control by private interests.' The simple issue then is: Can the community be the combination, or is it doomed to be ruled by the combination?

The Function of Capital

Before proceeding to detail the constructive plans of Socialism to procure abundant production, I must point out how impossible it is under capitalism to procure the most essential condition for such a production, namely, the getting from labour a hearty and a maximum effort. Let me try and make this hard and clear, even if, in order to put the essential facts together here, I may have to repeat some already used for other purposes.

The interest of capitalism is to take to itself all the advantages of improved management, invention, efficient labour, social opportunity, and in its practice, as I have shown, it is often very successful. On the other extreme, labour often puts forth the claim that all wealth belongs to it, basing itself on the generalization of Adam Smith that labour is the source of all wealth, a statement very much in need of analysis and definition. Further, more confusion has arisen in sociological inquiry owing to technical definitions of capital which do not correspond to the common and every-day use of the word. Where the context does not show otherwise I use the word in its every-day meaning. But if we stick to simplicity where that does no serious injury to accuracy, we can say that in the process of production labour has to be aided by accumulation of past products, the consumption of which has not taken place at the time of production but is averaged out so that some prolonged period can divide production and consumption and thus enable long processes of production to be undertaken.* As I have pointed out, this necessity for holding up and averaging consumption was the condition from which the system of capitalism arose. As economic systems become more complex, means are found – characteristically by banking and credit – for handling and systemati-

* This is only a prolonged and organized form of the capitalism of the primitive man who sustained himself by the game which fell to one arrow whilst he was making a new one.

zing the processes of deferred consumption and add to it the equally potent instrument of anticipated production. In the end, we have the capitalist system armed from head to heel with all its resources from workshop ownership to high finance – the humble but useful servant of the community become its controlling and all-powerful master.

Labour under Capitalism

In this system, labour is absolutely subordinate, and its function is as mechanical as though it were a machine driven by power, and begun and stopped by the pulling of a lever. It has its prescribed day; it has its stoppages to prevent deterioration, to enable it to be oiled, adjusted, mended; it has to produce a standard product in quality and amount; its costs are reckoned up, and how to work it most efficiently is studied – whether it should play football at its employer's expense or have 1 per cent of his profits; when producing, it is the property of other people; when it is not required for profit, its power is turned off and it lies idle. The friction shown in that false distinction which has been creeping into our minds of late owing to the claptrap phrases of politicians who are demagogues and can only appeal to passion and enmity – labour *versus* the community – is a proof of the constant injustice in thought and word done to labour when it comes into conflict with capital or capitalist governments. People will not take the trouble to understand that this mechanical and property relation is the actual relation of labour to capital under capitalism. Labour is the property of capital, and when it fights to be free it must damage the community through capitalism, and on such occasions 'the community' imagines itself to be the party attacked. The enemy of the community is in reality capitalism, whose economic system is at war with reason and equity.

The temper shown by classes to each other and the way they regard each other, are products of historical experience.

Labour is no willing or hearty co-operator with capital. Its first position on any matter in dispute is one of opposition. In every trade, at some period or other, the hard and absolute relationship of ownership, the relationship of labour as a seller and capital a buyer driving an exclusively economic bargain on a market where the seller was so weak that his bargaining power was nil, held good.* The personal touch of the employer could modify this to some extent, but with combination that goes, and labour then comes in conflict with a system or a machine, and personal influences are no longer available for reason and amelioration. The most cruel case of all is that of the miners, who, a century ago, were sunk right down to the bottom of the darkest pit of brutish treatment and economic slavery. No social conscience came to their aid. They had to perform the miracle of lifting themselves up by their own belts. Society regarded them purely as outcasts moved by passions and appetites that were sub-human. So, when they began to improve themselves, their very degradation was the cause of prejudice, and to this day the public cannot weed out from its mind the terrors which possessed its forbears a century ago, when the horrid miner was mentioned, or when he stirred ominously in his pit or his hovel. A movement on the part of the miner has always filled the mind of the ordinary member of society with a resentment and fear which lend themselves to an unbridled credulity as to the habits of this poor human being struggling from slavery to self-respect. He meets on the way all the temptations to which his superior brethren joyfully succumb, but to him they come in hobnails and fustian – whippets instead of racehorses, cheap fancy drink (occasionally) instead of dear champagne (habitually), Ford cars (now and then) to go to work in instead of Daimlers (always) to go to pleasures in. (So far as the miner is concerned the last two luxuries are more imaginary than real.) And those whose 'respectability' he would imitate and whose pleasures he would copy with the means at his disposal, find in his efforts nothing but proofs of his degradation! No section in the community has had more injustice done to him by public opinion than the miner. Can it be wondered if he, left to battle

* See Mr and Mrs Hammond's 'The Agricultural Labourer', 'The Town Labourer', 'The Skilled Labourer'.

his own way to self-respect, returns these feelings with interest? In none of its effects has the system of capitalism done more harm to society than in this divisive tendency. Labour eyes capitalism as a traveller on the highway used to eye every gay and well-appointed gallant whom he happened to have to pass. And, again, the experience of the war has added to the suspicion and the enmity. I can speak from my own experience of both sides of the gap. Class antagonism is more bitter, and the gap itself is wider, in 1920 than it was in 1913. Each side fears the other, more than it has ever done, as an enemy seeking to take advantage of it. To capitalism, labour is bolshevik; to labour, capitalism is a White Guard; the Girondins on both sides are being wiped out by the demagogues on both sides.

The effect of this upon production is direct. Labour considers that it produces for capital not for society. It organizes to protect itself against capitalism; it trusts to legislation to secure the human consideration which capitalism will never give of its own free will, or from its own sense of justice, or by a use of its power as a trustee rather than as a Shylock who exacts the uttermost farthing. When the national need is clear as during the war, labour produces heartily and throws away its safeguards against capitalism; only when it finds that capital is less disinterested in its service, when it meets the profiteer at its threshold and sees mountainous fortunes piled up from its needs, does it slacken in well doing. When the nation called, labour responded with alacrity; when through the voice of the nation it heard the Jacob pantings of capitalism hastening to make rich, labour paused in its service and thought of looking after itself. Now we are at peace, the old bad relations return, one side stronger by its gains and the other more embittered because it has been cheated. If the community suffers, who can wonder? But why blame one side?

Labour and Capital in Antagonism

At the time when this is being written every thoughtful person is disturbed by the prospects of continued ill-will at the worst, and lack of confidence at the best, between these two agents in production. The industrial strongholds which we held before the war have gone and, handicapped in every way, we look out into the future. A series of disagreements in our main industries will prevent us from reclimbing the high pinnacles which we held, and our industrial future will then be almost as insignificant as though we had not been victorious on the field of battle. The smallness and tricky resourcefulness of mind which is trying to guide us is appalling. Patchings here and there, insignificant compromises, unprincipled manipulations, may put on the brake, but do not turn the coach from its downward course. The policy of waiting for the most opportune moment to have a spill – for the industrial *der Tag* which many capitalists are now toasting – is madness. Safety lies in views which recognize the depths and the heights of the problems which the country is called upon to solve, views which penetrate into the facts and which reach the causes of the unrest and the reasons of the antagonism, views, moreover, that are not bounded by the conflicts of the moment and the unpleasant ways in which they may show themselves, but which see them in their historical growth and relate them to the problems of expanding individual and social life. In any event, it is not a negative peace that we need but a hearty co-operation in securing communal well-being.

To see where we are, we must take a backward glance, which, however, will be very cursory and summary. Before the war the discords of the system were only too apparent. Labour had combined to protect itself against the working of capitalism and had formed trade unions, the practices of which, just like those of capitalism, could not always be defended from the point of view of society, but could be explained as a natural part of a conflict with capitalism itself. After a generation or so of this, trade unionists were beginning to widen their outlook and were considering the social obligations of labour and the conditions under which those obligations could be fulfilled. Following this quest, they were coming to the conclusion that the whole system of capitalism was unfitted for that peace and whole-heartedness in production which everyone saw was essential for communal prosperity. The fixing of wages as a mere price for labour power and skill sold on a market. The frequent recurrence of unemployment, the poor return for unstinted effort, the baffling of labour's legitimate ambition to secure something better than the poverty-stricken conditions of the vast masses of the workers, the utter irrationality of the purely servile state of the workmen and the deadening effect of a toil that was always mechanical without being lightened by the incentive of responsibility, the irritating hopelessness which came when labour saw every substantial industrial gain grabbed at, and too frequently secured, by capital, and every depression of trade used to thrust the wage earner down again into the ruts of poverty from which he was beginning to rise – these things, combined with the new appreciation of what the position of the workman might be in a well-organized industrial society, were producing a discontent which was challenging the practicability and the justice of the capitalist system.

To this discontent the education of the young workman had contributed largely. For a generation education had concerned itself with little more than teaching how to read, write and count. A few specially favoured, specially lucky or specially clever, children of the working classes had passed through the higher educational institutions and had found places in the professional – especially the teaching – classes. They lost their sense of unity with the people amidst whom they were born, and the process tended to impoverish the mass rather than to enrich and raise it. At the same time, workmen, including not a few of the leaders of organized labour, rising into positions of comparative ease and security, moved in their minds into the lower middle class and yielded to its ideals, its comforts and its attractions. A process of skimming the cream and taking the heart out was going on. By the loss of its best brains and the lack of complete identification between itself and many of its official leaders, the mass seemed to be becoming a reservoir for the recruitment of middle and professional classes, and was not retaining within itself the qualities and forces which alone could transform it by giving it a greater intelligence and spirit. Obviously, however, this was only a transition period, and the process of education proceeded. Secondary schools were multiplied and became filled by the children of workmen. There intelligence was awakened to such a wide extent that it could not all be drafted off into the service of other classes but remained in an increasing volume to guide and enliven the minds of the mass itself.

The first result of this was an educational movement from within the working masses. Socialist and Labour propaganda had aroused interest in social and economic subjects, and indirectly had also created interest in general culture. Whilst the mass was using its ability to read by buying great quantities of the cheapest and most worthless – often degrading – stuff turned out day by day and week by week by the popular press, a movement of a totally different kind was spreading, especially amongst the younger men and women. The young workman was buying good books on science, economics, sociology and politics. Itinerant teachers appeared and considerable numbers of workmen attended their lectures, read the text-books prescribed, and wrote papers on the work done. The teaching was by no means always sound. Much of it was frankly propagandist and dogmatic, but at the very worst, it made the students independent and indocile; it occupied their minds and exercised their intelligence, and its effect was very soon seen in the general Labour movement. No longer was trade union propaganda confined to defensive work against capitalism as regards wages, hours and such superficial things that, when gained, often meant nothing of substance. The structure of the capitalist system was studied and understood, the relationship between capital and labour was grasped, the historical evolution of industry was known, the forces within it working for its transformation were calculated and explored. Labour was retaining its own intelligence, was, in consequence, making new claims to importance, responsibility and respect, was developing a spirit of democratic aristocracy, was declining to accept any further a position of mechanical subordination in industry.

From the point of view of capitalism all that this meant was that labour was becoming more prone to strike, to quarrel with employers, was less tractable and more touchy, and the whole condition was described as 'Labour Unrest'. Capitalism was shocked and injured to find that labour not only understood the ways of capitalism, but imitated them – scamped work for profit, used every opportunity for exploitation, drove hard bargains on wages' markets; and the general public, working on the axioms of capitalist habit, could not detect in the 'errors' and the 'tyrannies' of Labour policy the very methods which capitalism had always practised with impunity both against the public as consumers and users, and against labour itself. The experiences of years of war have accentuated this. What was originally a movement of the intelligence has been augmented by a movement of the passions and emotions on account of the way that capitalism unmasked itself during those years of national sacrifice.

Whoever sees in the Unionist threat of rebellion in 1912–13 opposition to the Home Rule Bill only, sees but the centre front of a stage with far larger issues in the background. The political party that stood in pocket, in mind and in instinct, for the existing order of social and economic relationships, had felt the ground slipping from under its feet. Parliament was being captured and the sky was darkened by ominous clouds. The classes were being driven back upon the last resort of men who find their wills no longer in command of power – force, illegality, unconstitutionalism. They were in exactly the same position as the Bolshevists were in Russia a few years later, and were preparing to adopt exactly the same weapons. As the Bolshevists could not trust the Constituent Assembly and so dissolved it in Cromwellian fashion, so the interests represented by the Unionist party were losing confidence in Parliament elected on Limehouse speeches and beginning to raid henroosts, and declared on an apparently favourable issue that they would maintain their ascendancy by unconstitutional means. The impulse to Unionist illegality came from general political conditions, though it was the Home Rule Bill that, like Moses' rod, enabled it to gush out. The Unionist psychology in 1912 was of precisely the same nature as the Bolshevist psychology in 1918.

The war first of all turned these currents back upon themselves, then its influence slackened, finally the currents returned to their normal flow with an augmented force. The history of the Unionist party in these years is the first chapter in how economic and social antagonism divided our country and ended the Parliamentary regime – if the events of today are to turn out to be incidents in such an unfortunate history, Mr Lloyd George's later speeches will in time be recognized as the first bugle sounds in our class war. [. . .]

Capitalism and Production

Thus far I have been pointing out how the system of capitalist dominance, whatever may have been its justification as an historical period in the evolution of the industrial community, must fail to provide a satisfactory machinery for production, and must be a menace of ever growing potentiality to the life of the people who come more and more under its authority. But, despite this, it has been claimed for the system that it could produce wealth; that, under the pressure of interest, the machine, with all its faults, jerked along with energy and, though often stopped and never worked in full good will by the hired servants of capitalism, still, in the end, gave a satisfactory result. I have given reasons for an opposite view, and I am supported by a mass of germane evidence.

I take first of all the prevalence of strikes and stoppages owing to disputes in industry. To those to whom trade unionism is anathema and the workers always wrong when they do not accept their master's decisions, the figures I am to quote will only prove the terrible perversity of labour and the extent of the victimization to which it subjects the 'community'. To those who know the actual state of the workmen's minds and hearts, the figures will show that the machine of capitalism cannot run smoothly, that disputes belong to its nature, and that it produces strikes and lock-outs just as it does profits. I take pre-war figures because since then all industrial statistics are compiled from abnormal conditions and prove nothing except that war produces chaos. For the five years ending 1908, 20,800,000 days were lost in the aggregate owing to strikes; for the five years ending 1913, 75,500,000 days were thus lost. Even the higher of these figures is but a small proportion of the aggregate working time that was wasted, for they do not reveal the full extent of the damage. Dependent trades are put upon short time or are stopped altogether, and the time thus lost is not included in these totals. A system of production which involves strikes is a wasteful system, and capitalism makes strikes inevitable. Unemployment is another grievous form of waste, for it is not only a temporary cessation of production by willing and capable men, but it slackens demand, lowers standards of consumption and helps to clog the market. At any given moment when trade is at its best three out of every hundred skilled workers are unemployed; when trade is bad, the three sometimes become ten – at the present moment, owing to the war and the foreign policy pursued since the armistice, it is in some trades ninety.

The figures of total production, presented in two different ways, enable us to see what is meant by the inefficiencies and the antagonisms which I have been discussing. I shall deal first with the estimates made of the average value of production per head, and then with the national total of production. The first is a complicated figure to fix, as three things must be taken into account: the national income, prices and the number of the working population. But there is no dispute as to general results. Between 1760 and 1803, when our productive machinery was being rapidly developed, production did not exceed £12 per head; it grew steadily for the next seventy years, when it reached £30; between 1870 and 1895 it went up rapidly to £54; then there was a check, and, up to the outbreak of war in 1914, the increase was not more than £2 5s. Some statisticians indeed believe there was a drop. This period coincides with growing labour discontent with capitalism and a weakening in consequence of incentive to work. I regard these figures as showing the moral breakdown of capitalism amongst other things. It is true that the parasitism of wealth had increased and had drawn more and more people from the ranks of productive workers, that our national output was meeting with strenuous foreign competition, that the Boer War had had an adverse effect upon our industry; but over and above those things is the fact that the man at work was a discontented man.

The Census of Production taken in 1907 was, in consequence, a revelation to many complacently minded people. The net output of all the mines, quarries, factories, workshops in the United Kingdom was estimated to be not more than £762,000,000. No indictment has been made against the system of production in this country so strong as these official figures. A population of 11,000,000 people returned as workers, of whom a very large percentage are highly skilled, a country specially situated for export trade and possessed of many advantages arising from historical, geographical and geological reasons, the centre of an empire – and a total net product of £762,000,000. And yet, when one thinks over the question in detail, the reasons are on the surface. Let us grasp one important fact. Some apparently productive labour is not productive at all, and though much of the product of this labour is included in the above total and ought to be included in the sum total of national wealth, it does not enter into that wealth in beneficiary use which is the true wealth of a nation.

Let us consider the case of, say, a carpenter working on two jobs, the first for his neighbour, the blacksmith, the other for the landlord who, we shall assume, lives exclusively on rent, or on any of those tolls which the ownership of land deducts from wealth created, without in any way contributing to the production or returning an equivalent.

When the carpenter works for the blacksmith he produces to aid the blacksmith's production,* and he contributes not only to the dead total of wealth in the country, but to the fructifying volume of wealth used in the country. He makes wealth that makes wealth. His products make shorter hours, lower prices,

* If, however, the blacksmith were employed exclusively by the landlord as in the second case which I am to assume, this would not be so, and it is less so in proportion to the time that the blacksmith spends on the landlord's work.

better labour conditions and communal economies and well-being possible. If he discovers a new mode of production that reduces the prices of tables and chairs, he is working in a process that may enable the blacksmith to enjoy a higher standard of comfort and yet reduce the price of horseshoes and coulter sharpenings.

The effect of working for a landlord living on such an income as I have defined is altogether different. The carpenter may produce the same tables and chairs, and may add precisely the same amount of wealth to the sum total held by all the individuals in the country as when he was working for the blacksmith. But he is contributing nothing to the effective wealth of the country, and he himself becomes a parasite on production. He is helping no one to produce another shilling, he is only helping someone to spend shillings abstracted from the volume of production. All that can be said of his work is that it is bringing back into the volume of economically effective wealth parts that had gone astray in the shape of tolls paid to allow production to be carried on. In so far as this carpenter, for this particular part of his work, devised a process of cheap production, it would not have the least effect on general production or prices; it would only enable the toll owner to command more labour, withdraw more services from society and increase the number of parasitic workers. The cheapening of production to our parasitic classes only means that the tolls they take in terms of money or coinage require an ever increasing amount of production to bring them back into the stream of fructifying wealth.

This argument, I know, brings into play much wider and different issues from those strictly involved in the quantitative production of £762,000,000, but it has a direct bearing upon it, and this is, therefore, the place to state it. For the existence of this rent-receiving class, not at all inconsiderable in numbers and very considerable in possessions – this is discussed more fully in the section dealing with distribution – means the existence of an army of workers contributing exclusively to its needs – servants of all kinds, gamekeepers, attendants – whose work adds nothing to visible production – brushing clothes or shooting rabbits – and whose invisible production to society is nil. Their number has to be deducted from that of the producing population. We may include poets and singers in the list of those who add to national products, but not the kitchen maid of the non-service giving person who lives on tolls. Under our present system to make a living is not the same as making wealth.

The figures also disclose the enormous amount of waste labour that capitalism, with its divided interests, requires – the working with inefficient tools because employers for some reason or other cannot or do not install better ones; the overlapping and disorganization of labour in works that may manage to pay to their owners precarious profits, but whose contribution to the sum of products could be made far more economically under better organization; the labour sunk in useless work necessitated by rivalries in production, a striking example of which is the waste involved in the private ownership of wagons on railways with their empty mileage, their shunting and so on; the lack of coordination in the supply of facilities necessary for production, like the frequent shortage of tubs in coal pits; the unproductive labour (so far as total national product is concerned not only unproductive but wasteful, though productive so far as the employing competing firms are concerned) consumed in maintaining the purely competitive machinery of industry, like the armies of commercial travellers going over the same ground with the same kinds of goods, buying agents, clerks, printers employed upon advertisements and all labour engaged uneconomically in competing establishments not big enough to make full economic use of their staffs. Of the 1,000,000 persons in the Census of 1911, classified as being employed in commerce, I doubt if as many as one-half were productively employed. That is one reason why the low figure of £762,000,000 was published in 1907 as the value of the annual production, much to the surprise of people who had been assuming that the business of our people, the advantages of our industry and the favourable circumstances of our country, were being used to the utmost by a capitalism that seemed to be always hustling.

Capitalism has signally failed in its task of producing for the needs of the community both in absolute quantities and in economic ways. The simple and undeniable fact is that it does not contain within it an enduring motive to produce which makes labour an active participant in production. Its inevitable tendency to create great dominating combines is also rightly causing it to forfeit public confidence, as is well stated in the Minority Addendum to the Report on Trusts: 'Where, as is evidently the case in various highly organized capitalist enterprises, competition is being rapidly displaced by combination, largely monopolistic in its structure and powers, and tending to restrict output with a view to raising prices and preventing their fall, we hold that it is contrary to the public interest to allow such enterprises to remain in private hands';* or, in words of strong significance though less committal in proposal, subscribed to by the whole committee: 'We are satisfied that considerable mistrust with regard to their activities exist in the public mind, and that the effect of such mistrust may be equally hurtful to the political and social stability of the State, whether or not the public mistrust or resentment be in fact well-founded.' Capitalism can never be worthy of, nor secure, the confidence of the public if the public would but think. When combined it can crush out all serious rivals or swallow them up, and, with or without tariffs, can defy foreign competition or come to an agreement with foreign competitors. Whether it uses its powers unreasonably or not – it certainly did so during the war – depends upon itself, and no law and no Government supervision can control it. And yet, in the interests of the community, it is not desirable that concentration should be hindered or stopped.† We seem to be on the horns of a dilemma. But are we?

I now turn to the constructive proposals of Socialism.

---

* 'Report', p. 14.

† The importance of this induces me to give a further warning on how combinations exercise power. In an Appendix to the 'Report on Trusts' (p. 27) I find: 'Allegations are made of particular combinations maintaining large secret service funds for the purpose of obtaining subsidies, strengthening their monopoly and acquiring a hold over

Ramsay MacDonald's Political Writings

The Socialist Intellectual Method

It may be well to state categorically first of all that Socialism does not quarrel with history. It does not waste its time and cast doubts upon its intelligence by standing in 1921 and shouting over the broad gulf of past years to 1800 telling of their mistakes and advising them how they ought to have behaved. The Socialist takes historical facts as he finds them, but regards them not as final stages but as conditions that are unstable because they contain impulses that are constantly modifying them by giving them a more complete fulfilment. They are the momentary conditions of processes, and their chief interest to the Socialist lies in the nature of their controlling tendencies, the direction in which they are driving, and the changes which they are making.

Capitalism on its descriptive side presents a fascinating picture, but it is the economic laws which capitalism reveals that concern the Socialist most of all. He has seen production for private gain emerge through a state of competition; he is acquainted with the economic and social theories devised to explain and justify that state; he has traced that state growing out of itself by reason of its own inherent tendencies; he takes the old theories, lays them athwart the actual conditions of today, and knows that they belong to an old order of things; he studies the tendencies now in operation and, with the interest of the whole community as his guide, he makes his constructive proposals

---

the Press by means of bribery and corruption, and of combinations in general exercising great influence where their interests are at stake . . . resulting in the maintenance of prices to the consumer and the direct and indirect influencing of concessions by political and semi-political means, while inability to get information regarding combinations is explained on the ground that there is a great reluctance on the part of individual traders to appear formally in opposition to powerful interests.' This is certainly true of America, and I know of one British combination which gave a member of Parliament a salary and equipped him with an office to look after its interests in Parliament. Tariffs would greatly strengthen this tendency, indeed would make such practices inevitable.

founded not on any abstract Utopias which belong to the free imagination, but on the evolution of functions and institutions in his own time. In that spirit I write, for in that spirit he builds up.

The War

The greatest problem of today is production, its organization and its distribution. The war has changed much – maybe for all time, but it will be years before we can estimate the amount and the permanency of the change. The special advantages which this country's trade enjoyed in the world have gone or are in jeopardy. London as the mart of the trading universe seems to belong to the past. Our carrying predominance has gone. Staggering debts will have to be paid. Germany, whatever its own position may be, is to have much satisfaction in economic revenge. The extravagances, mainly in the form of keeping large classes of non-producers in luxury in our midst, in which we could indulge when the whole world paid us tribute, we shall now indulge at our peril. Above all the war has left behind it a new mentality, the product of the sense of equality in sacrifice and effort called for by the struggle. The decorated wealthy were brought low and the useful humble were exalted. No nation that has gone through a critical struggle for existence can return to where it was when the struggle began. Truly we must settle down to useful and economical labour, scrutinize our industrial machinery lest haply we can improve it, and our waste lest we can eliminate it, and be not afraid to be led by necessity. Production, markets, international peace, economy – these are the pressing needs of this country today. In trying to meet these needs, we must be aware of the great growth of a special kind of property. In its evolution, as I have pointed out, property has grown from being possession in what one has made or uses beneficially to being the holding of a power to exploit other people's labour. Much property is now held as a means of imposing a toll or levying a tax upon products, and the war debt and its burdens has added enormously to this class of property.

This is to have no little effect upon the respect which this generation is to pay to property.

Property as an Incentive to Work

The economics which correspond to the period of production for private gain took it as axiomatic that the motive for working was the acquisition of property. That was the capitalist view, and it suited its own policy and practice. It remained blind to the fact that, as I shall show in the section on distribution, this was purely utopian dreaming as regards 99 per cent of the population. Capitalism provided no 'motive' to work which made work voluntary, and which covered up, with the pleasurable expectation of its reward, any unpleasantness that labour might have. Capitalism offered a certain number of prizes and men worked for them. But in the competition the aspirants outnumbered the prize-winners many times over. To begin with, a prize or two may make scores strive, but the incentive soon weakens. That was all that capitalism offered. The worker worked for the necessities of life, and what he could accumulate was more of the nature of averaging expenditure than of absolute saving. To 'save for a rainy day' is not 'saving' as the economics of property would define it, because when the rainy day has gone, so are the savings. Today, if well-intentioned but innocent persons were to go out to the workers and offer property as a reward for increased production, they would be rightly laughed at. They might offer them better wages, but no one would believe them, and the effect would be nothing.

Immediately after the war an appeal for further production was made, by speech and print, and this bait of higher wages was thrown out. 'If you want more make more' was the chorus. Nothing happened. The appeal did not add to the effort of labour enough to make good the ink and paper used in issuing it. The only extra production was by paper makers and printers. How absurd it now sounds, how cynically comical.

Moreover, were the justification for increased production increased individual property, an equal distribution of the total product can never amount per head to any very considerable quantity, especially in a country which is not drawing heavy tributes from other countries, or which is not peculiarly richly endowed with natural consumable wealth – that is, a country the products of which depend mainly upon the labour efforts of its people – a country like our own. We must dismiss the motives for production upon which capitalist economies are founded. They never really operated; for the remainder of this generation they will operate less than ever. They may have had validity in the earlier stages of capitalism, when capitalists were being made, but that is a century ago or thereabouts. There is no romance and very little envy attached to Carnegies now. Capitalism offers labour wages to enable it to live in return for task work; it offers it neither property nor security.

Communal Property

Here the Socialist can lay down one of the foundation stones of his reconstructed society. The personal enjoyment of property possible to the mass of the people is from collective and not from individual ownership. The significance of this is seen if one considers, say, public parks. Within the administrative county of London there are 4100 acres devoted to parks. These are laid out in woods, arbours, gardens, recreation grounds, walks and so on, and this use is only possible by the massing together of what, on a division into private property, would be millions of mud puddles not big enough to swing a cat by the tail without trespassing. Divided into the number of people who as Londoners really own them, the park area of London only gives a little over four square yards to each. The same is true of museums, picture galleries and such things, where the value of the possessions divided into private property would not, on distribution, allow a new German oleograph to be added to the horrors on our kitchen walls. A very little per head, massed together for common use, puts the discriminating user in a position superior to that of the millionaire. Communal property, however, whilst enlivening the communal interests

Ramsay MacDonald's Political Writings

of the individual and enabling him to understand what community means and how its well-being is his own well-being, is not by itself a sufficient motive for industry. It belongs to a better class of motive than the purely personal one, and we may hope that in time that class will be predominant, but that is not yet.

Socialist Incentives

What, then, are the motives which Socialists trust? Men work to supply needs, their own first of all, but in all societies the communal spirit has some hold and an appeal can always be supplemented by it. The Socialist therefore faces the real conditions, and his first stand is upon this simple truth: 'You have to work to live'. Service is the only claim he recognizes as a title to possession. In a community, service is so varied and so natural that no one able in body and sound in mind ought to try to shirk it, and certainly ought not to be encouraged to do so. Under the pressure of critical need, the Russian Soviet Government made these considerations a justification for forced labour. There is neither law nor principle in a revolution; it is all stopgap work. But the Socialist way is not forced labour in the sense of legal force. The economic constitution of the Socialist State would be such that parasitism would not, and could not, produce incomes, whilst the moral coercion of public opinion would be effective even before the economic changes closed every opportunity for parasitical living.

It must be recognized, however, that if the motive to produce remains on the purely economic or self-regarding level where it now is, and where Socialism still places it in its most universal form, it will be a poor and easily wearied one. It will still impose task work and the community will be little better off than it is now. Life and interest must be given to it. Men ought not only to work, but be interested in work; they ought to use not only their muscles but their hearts in production; and this further motive of interest can never be given by capitalism with its hierarchy of managers and shareholders, and its masses of

210

subordinate and servile workpeople. So natural is it for man to take an interest in the work of his hands, that, despite the haphazard way in which youths are now sent to employment, and the dulling moral and intellectual effect of mere time toil, the workshop and factory as we know them are not totally devoid of this lively interest. The Socialist would enormously increase it, however, by giving the workmen responsibility for workshop control. This is undoubtedly the next step in the evolution of the mechanism of production. Given a fairly good standard of technical instruction, and an education which has enlivened the placid intelligence of labour, and labour can no longer be a hewer of wood and a drawer of water even on good wages – no longer a soldier under a centurion, even if the length of his servitude per day is shortened to eight, seven or six hours. When the workman takes an interest in his work, nothing can prevent him from controlling the conditions of his work. Capital is the dead participant in production; labour is the living participant, and the practical logic of that has to be worked out in industrial conditions.

One of the effects of the war has been to press this problem upon the attention of Socialists. Before the war it was sufficient to create the Socialist mind by explaining the Socialist standpoint and outlook; the war has so revolutionized people's minds and still more their methods (force, violence and short cuts, for the moment at any rate, entering far more than formerly into our thoughts), that the Socialist has now to prepare far more details to meet the expectation of rapid change than was necessary before 1914. Moreover, Socialism or no Socialism, labour is demanding authority in management and will not be placid until it gets it. [. . .]

The Complete Organization of Industry

I now proceed to consequences, for this is only the beginning of the Socialist reconstruction of the mechanism of production. The mistake of the co-operators of the individualistic co-partnership school was that they assumed that reconstruction could come from the independent workshop. The Socialist falls into no such error. Production must be organized; the producing centres must be related to each other; failing an organized industrial nervous system which keeps the whole body in balance, in motion, in unity, in contact with the world in relation to which it has to fulfil its functions, competition is a safeguard to the public. But when evolution has gone so far as to permit of this nerve organization, competition has ceased to be effective and its sphere has not only been narrowed but it itself has become degraded like a deposed king picking up a living. The Socialist builds up his system as a highly organized one, forbidden to tyrannize over the community, not by outside force like law or labour combination, but by the nature of the organization. Social aims become the definite purpose of the system. And it should be remembered that in dealing with human conduct, good organization strengthens spirit, and the strengthened spirit makes better organization possible. Thus Socialism tends to create the conditions of its success.

I have pointed out how capitalist combination has evolved. Everyone who was then aware of world happenings will remember the strange interest taken, about thirty years ago, in that unique monster the Standard Oil Company. It was the Great Eastern Steamship of its time. They will remember how attempt after attempt was made in other industries to create similar monsters, and how from an unbroken preliminary record of failures, an odd success was registered here and an odd success there – mostly abroad. On *a priori* grounds, they will remember how confidently it was prophesied that this country contained no soil for the nourishment of such iniquitous monstrosities. They will remember how various forms of the beast appeared in Germany, especially that species known as *Kartel*. They will remember that one day they became aware that it was actually with us. Perhaps they had some experience of its blasting breath – it was, as a rule, blasting then – upon an investment or a business of their own; perhaps they became acquainted with Mr Macrosty's book on *The Trust Movement in British Industry*, published in 1907, in which it was proved that combinations of

Socialism: Critical and Constructive

various types had already appeared in British industry and were to last 'to control competition'. Those who regarded the movement with disapproval, seeing in it a menace to the freedom of society, may have taken part in agitations to devise ways of strangling the brute, and may have watched brave American legislation from the Sherman Law of 1890 onwards, all so futile, most so mischievously ignorant of economic and industrial forces and resources. The change had come, not by the design of man, but by the inevitable development of industry. All other countries that have attempted anti-Trust legislation have had to record failure or but futile success. The law and order and the tendencies of capitalism defied British traditional economics and the American Legislature. The Socialist looks upon the evolution as an objective manifestation of development which is inevitable, and which, in the end, will contribute to higher states of communal comfort and liberty. For him, the problem it presents is not how to strangle or limit it, but how to control it, and he thinks of control not in any hampering sense, but in that of making it contribute its fullest service to communal advantage. It is, to him, capitalism developing out of itself – becoming an organized system of functions and not of profits.

The Socialist idea of industrial reconstruction is, therefore. one of a more complete combination of productive forces, Whilst he warns against combination controlled by capitalist interests, or by capitalist machinery, he accepts and values the gains of combination itself, and proposes to harness them to communal well-being.

One point remains to be dealt with. Hardly anyone disputes now that the employment of a thousand and one agencies for buying and selling is pure waste. An official committee has recently recommended a union of iron and steel interests for the purpose of securing ore supplies from abroad, and suggests that the union might find it advisable to acquire by purchase or concession the ownership of the deposits. This is necessary to secure not only ample and steady supplies, but prices that do not fluctuate violently. The necessity for combination in manufacturing production is accepted. But the fear is frequently

H

expressed that it will result in an unlovely uniformity, that the life and individuality will go out of goods so made, and that the complete organization proposed by Socialism will make this uniformity wholly intolerable and deadening. A thousand firms working to supply the same market no doubt produce a variety of designs and models, and a thousand shops open for profit allure customers by exhibiting them. In passing, I remark that the bulk of them are unnecessary for anything but whimsical use and are nearly all bad – bad art, bad workmanship. Still, the substance of the objection must be met. If art is to be restored to life, it can be only under conditions of joy and freedom. Combination must produce reasonable variety. The Socialist scheme would certainly not translate standardization into dull uniformity. It would have its artists for design, its engineers for mechanical contrivances, its different managements and workshops for testing the costs and the effectiveness of products. It would both cater for the consumers and be economical in management. Subdivision in work and processes would be determined by the whole united industry, and where private firms now have enough trade to create special departments, none sufficiently equipped perhaps, and none sufficiently large to be economical producing units, the Socialist scheme would provide the best equipment, the greatest variety and the most economical working that the trade as a whole would allow or require. For instance, it has been pointed out again and again what substantial advantage would accrue to engineering if tools and dies were made, not by each workshop, but at great specialized toolshops supplying many workshops. Steps in this direction have indeed been taken by some combinations, who have found that the building of new works and the scrapping and transformation of old ones in order to allow such specialization and coordination have been economical investments of capital. One of the greatest leakages in the economic use of both labour and capital today is the manufacture of subsidiary things by factories that should be exclusively run for other products. The complete organization of production as a national function alone will put an end to this. By far and away the greater bulk of our production can be standardized. But there remains taste in use. That cannot be standardized. For those consumers who wish for specially individualized production, village and other workshops which will arise from the freedom of the people, their capacity to enjoy beautiful work and the co-operative spirit, will cater. These workshops are bound to arise obedient to the spirit of Socialism, and they will be part of the local social organization. For generations ahead of us, the comfort of the people will depend on mass production, however, and their sense of beauty and joy of spirit will grow upon communal property and conditions. Upon the mass and duplicated production a finer sense of taste will be employed, and our stores will be better stocked than ever with things made from the heart by the hands. For, interest in work means an improved quality of work, and service to the whole instead of individual property as the incentive, means that ideas and beauty will be embodied in products.

Standardizationh as its dangers in stereotyping and in preventing improvement, and these would be great if it were in the custody of combined capitalist groups manufacturing for private gain. The Socialist scheme provides the proper and only possible safeguard against that. One of the most important gains of combination is that it alone permits a union on a grand scale of science and art with production. Scientific experiment is not only expensive, but it is a kind of expenditure from which returns are long delayed. It can, therefore, be employed only on large scale production, and only where there is such production has it as a matter of fact been employed. Economic combination was a preliminary to the employment of staffs of chemists in German dye works, and in our own country industries remained without this equipment until they passed under similar control. Scientific knowledge and artistic appreciation are the only powers that can keep industrial processes from becoming stereotyped. Science organized from the universities, or from great technical institutions and attached to the industries where scientific knowledge is important – science, treated not as the handmaiden of capital, but as the brains of industry, can again revolutionize production, both in process and in output, as it revolutionized it by the application of steam. When the complete coordination which Socialism aims at takes place, science will have room to work, it will have opportunities to work. What is now waste will be wealth. In the treatment of coal alone, there will be imperial revenues in smoke, and gold mines in rubbish heaps. The competition between workplace and workplace will not go on the lines of cheapness because everything will be as cheap as possible (concentration and organization having eliminated all but natural differences in costs of production), but in quality, in suitability, in economy. And whereas, under capitalist combinations the consumer is at the mercy of the producer, under Socialist combinations the consumer will control the producer. The consumer will have to be studied, because he will be enfranchised to make effective demands upon a production managed for his enjoyment. So soon as results on the market have revealed the will of the user, the whole machinery of production will be made to respond to it. Experience, scientific knowledge, artistic achievement, statistics, economizing devices can be exchanged throughout, for they will then be the property of the whole function, and not of private interests working in it for their own profit. The will of the consumer will come into direct contact with the object of the producer.

Thus on its purely mechanical side Socialism completes the tentative and limited transformation of capitalism. The economic combinations of capitalism establish the accuracy of Socialist theoretical forecasts. When the world was pooh-poohing the architecture which the Socialist was putting before it, capitalism was silently building a structure of the scouted type.

I can now complete the organization which I left at the workshop. According to the idea now developed, the workshop is but a unit in a great organization and has to fit into that organization. It will be controlled by the co-operation of brain work and hand work, of organizers and labourers, and their unity will be complete. It will be grouped in districts of varying size with kindred workplaces, and its management will co-ordinated accordingly. It will not, therefore, suffer from too much centralization so that no mind or committee can control it, because the people in actual touch with the processes will have freedom and authority to be real managers and not merely agents. It will have all the information necessary to make it effective and precise in its work, and all about its working will be known to its district group. It, therefore, cannot fall behind and cannot stagnate. It must do its required work or cease and its workpeople be absorbed elsewhere. The interests of all are involved in the product of each. Each must come up to a standard in quantity, quality and price. Moreover, the workshop must respond to the trade, and the directors of the trade will not be only workmen and managers, or capitalists with interests as at present, but representatives of the producers, of the scientists and technicians and the consumers. The total production required can be estimated and safe margins always provided for; the capacity of factories will be known; scientific and technical experts will represent the ideas of development and change, and will decide the questions of expansion, re-organization, re-distribution of effort. The trade will provide its own capital, make its own insurances for accidents and unemployment, and thus save, what is now lost to production, the large staffs and financial operations now involved in numerous insurance enterprises. It will be equipped on the one hand with a buying organization, either used by itself or in common with others as circumstances determine, and on the other with a selling and marketing organization which will be international as well as domestic in its activities.

Thus will production reach its maximum efficiency, be freed from the control of special interests and become a true communal concern; thus the true motive to work will be provided, and labour be freed from a servitude that not only kept it inefficient, unhappy and antagonistic but, thereby, damaged the commonwealth.

PARLIAMENT AND
REVOLUTION

Chapter VIII

Parliament

To the man who responds day by day to the call of the factory whistle, Parliament too often appears to be an ineffective thing. And when the man is intelligent and is actively interested in his own affairs, the ineffectiveness is so great that he ceases to believe in Parliament altogether, pronounces a plague upon all political parties and leaders, and lets the world drift so far as political action is concerned. As a rule, such a man becomes a believer in what is called 'Direct Action', or becomes a supporter of the charitable patronage of Tory democracy and a backer of those politicians of social manners who understand his weakness and who pander to them. He becomes blasé. When one applies a microscope to them one sees alarming likenesses between the mental make-up of the chattering Cockney who votes for a scoundrel of fair words and 'understanding', and the revolutionary of set narrow ideas who in times of peace proclaims a 1792 September.

Before we condemn Parliament and political action we must put it in the dock, and pronounce sentence upon it after a patient examination of its faults; and that is what I propose to do in this chapter, with a brevity consistent with the plan of this book.

Parliament itself is a machine of government, and it has been worked hitherto by one section of the community. Labour has voted, but has not run the machine. Whatever the change in electorate may have been, the 'governing classes' have up to now remained pretty much the same. They have had to keep their eye upon the majorities they had to secure, but as they came to understand them, they found that these majorities were moved by no definite idea and sought no definite goal. They lived from hand to mouth. They could be stirred into passion by things which were trivial, they could be easily deceived, they were fond of dramatic representations and were very credulous, mental habits and the world as they found it held them in bondage, they were absolutely tame, very obedient and very suspicious of new leaders and willing to believe anything against them. The danger of thinking things out, of reflecting upon statements so as to come to independent conclusions, did not exist. The masses accepted both statements and conclusions ready made for them, and did not seem to be able to reason as to whether the one and the other hung together or did not. They saw them both in front of them, and they accepted them for reality just as they did a stone on their path. The 'governing classes' have striven to keep things so. They have discovered that the effect of popular education was not to make people intellectually vigorous, but to make them slaves of what they read, and that the effect of having the vote was not to make them consider what they would do with it, but to make them enjoy an election. So the democratic reforms of the past century have been largely changes in forms – like an extended franchise – necessary, undoubtedly, but, in the nature of things, the power given could be abused, used, or played with. Thus, surrounded by democratic reforms, the 'governing classes' have maintained their authority and have used democracy to maintain it.

Therefore, at the very outset, in expressing disappointment with the results of parliamentary government, we must begin by admitting that the first point to be made against it belongs not to itself, but to the masses. They have not been intelligent enough to use it. Now, nothing can take the place of intelligence. We can have a revolution by force, we can have a temporary dictatorship of the intelligent democracy, but continued progress must before long come back to its source in the minds of the masses. We can substitute new forms of government for present ones, but unless the people become 'the governing classes' in fact as well as in name, the rotten foundation will show itself by cracks in the superstructure. Furthermore, we can by an interesting academic analysis show how complicated is modern society, how difficult it is to create one sovereign authority in the State effectively claiming both a political and an economic allegiance, but none of that, nor all of it put together, helps us to get away from the difficulty which the absence of wisdom in the use of power creates. Where there is no intelligence there will be no unity. Where there is no comprehension of unity and no conception of how political action can secure it, a mere change of systems of government is like a change in the style of architecture without discarding the rotten bricks which made the previous building uninhabitable. Socialists, revolutionary or evolutionary, can never get away from this. It dogs them like shadows; it dooms all their efforts and schemes to futility until they change it. If the people do not understand Parliament, better government is not secured by splitting up its functions. If the people cannot construct Socialism in their minds they cannot build it into their institutions.

A mere class consciousness will not guard the nation against this shortcoming, because, however useful it may be to imbue the workers with a sense of their class importance and of their present class subordination, and however clear one may make the facts of the existing class struggle, the political value of this is slight. The shortcoming is intellectual and moral. The self-respect and independence which are to make the workers into a great political power cannot be produced from such thoughts as that, say, 'Local veto maintains the private cellars of the rich whilst it closes the pubs of the poor.' Too much Socialist propaganda has been upon these unsubstantial lines, and the failure of that kind of propaganda was shown when the war came and proved that the most accomplished talkers of brave words were the most ill-prepared for playing their part in the struggle, accepted the most empty of titles, performed with a sense of gratitude and honour the most menial of jobs, and fulfilled with an exemplary faithfulness missions hostile to Labour.

This came at the end of a period of peaceful development when every one of us in Parliament had incurred the suspicion of opportunism, and when it was true that certain working-class leaders were losing their class minds and becoming petty bourgeoisie. What happened soon after the outbreak of war seemed to many to be the natural evolution of this opportunism and of the bourgeois spirit, and political action suffered in reputation accordingly.

This opens up another aspect of the problem: the Labour Party in the House of Commons. The 'governing class' is educated for its business. It comes into public life trained in the habits of team action. One has only to hear the Tory Party cheer in the House of Commons to know its strength as a dominating party. It has the same unity of spirit as a pack of hounds after a fox. It likes the game. The privileges it has enjoyed for many generations have enabled it to acquire the habits which secure the enjoyment. In Parliament, as in its mansions, it is at home. The newcomers are strangers. They have had no practice in the game. They are rent and weakened by hesitancy and jealousy, and they cannot keep these vices in subjection as our ruling classes do. The political education of the workers must not, therefore, be confined to the education of electors, but must extend to that of representatives. The parliamentary machine must not only be worked with know-ledge, but with spirit. These powers are not automatically acquired by people when they are elected, but come by practice. Only when a class feels that it is triumphing can it produce a party with a triumphing spirit. The personality of members helps, of course, and I doubt if the Labour Party has yet dis-covered the best way of selecting candidates. Until selection conferences are wise enough to search for certain qualities rather than accept men of a certain status in local bodies or in organiza-tions whose method of work and training are not those of the House of Commons, the governing machinery will not be captured from the inside.

This fault in Parliament is again not of Parliament, but of Labour outside. If it were properly met it would go a long way to satisfy in a permanent way all that more revolutionary meth-ods – like the domination of the minority – are supposed to satisfy in a temporary way. For the mass is always dominated by a minority – a minority of force, a minority of reason, a minority of the accepted order. A minority of force can appear to do things during a revolution, but it creates a counter-revolution which is serious in proportion to the thoroughness with which the minority proposes to do its work, and if it is to make permanent contributions to progress, it must quickly find sanction in popular support. Though a minority of political intelligence making its voice heard and its will felt through efficient representatives may for a time appear to be proceeding at a tortoise pace, compared with a revolutionary minority of dictators, it will pass the fitful energies of the hare, get to the far goal first, and make itself secure in the possession of its gains.

The parliamentary method must always depend for its success on average, not on special, intelligence or energy. It provokes the specially keen people by its cumbersomeness, but it deals with society and the community, and not with enlightened coteries or associations. Not what a Socialist meeting declares itself anxious to do, but what the community is prepared to do, is the opportunity which the politician has. Parliament deals with the organic change of society, not with satisfying the wisdom of individual minds. A Socialist branch is a totally different thing from the community in which it exists. Were it not so, it would not be a Socialist branch. But our friends are apt to forget this sometimes in criticizing Parliamentary methods. And nothing will ever change that. A revolution only masks it. Nothing will ever relieve the Socialist of the burden of making Socialists, or of persuading the community that his views of affairs are right.

If any scheme of government could be devised to avoid these encumbrances which beset Parliaments I would support it. I have not seen it, however. The encumbrances must just be removed. Short cuts and revolutionary jumps may be possible once in a century, but when these conditions arise the most advantage can be taken of them only when the masses are prepared to allow it, when the politician leads the attack through Parliament in co-operation with the other forces available, and when the counter-revolution can be repelled not by arms and barricades, but by reason and the settled convictions of the people.

In other words, Parliament being the will of the people embodied in an institution, Socialists must work to get the right will and an intelligent will, and to provide the most intimate touch between the two. They are handling a problem of the mass mind, and no trick or kick will enable them to avoid that problem. When a child gets impatient with work which it is doing badly, or of which it has got tired, it smashes it to smithereens and feels relieved, but that does not enable it to accomplish what it set out to do. A policy of such relief is specially bad in public affairs. The gates of heaven are not to be taken by force, nor are the foundations of a new world to be laid in that way. I know that all the emotions of today are impatient with such views. Revolution and the mind of revolution are the progeny of all wars. The reaction would shoot us for safety; some of us would shoot the reaction for righteousness. The tidal waves which follow the earthquake are swishing and swilling everywhere. But we must not launch our galleons, built to carry us on high adventure and exploration, on a tidal wave. [. . .]

Chapter X

Revolution

Revolution is the result of resistance offered to movements that cannot be resisted, not an upset deliberately arranged for by the exponents of some new ideas. Revolution is the product of ideas, but the ideas must be confined in order to be explosive. Until ideas are resisted by force they cannot make revolutions. Of course there are revolutions which are not democratic and which have nothing to do with social revolution. There is the military *coup d'état*, there is the palace conspiracy when one ruler displaces another, there is the revolution of Sidney Street when Ishmael comes into civilization from his wilderness and holds up civilization. Of these I do not speak. I speak of the kind of revolution which some people think to be necessary if capitalism is ever to be supplanted by Socialism; of that revolutionary propaganda and vision which have arisen from the Russian Revolution, and which, discarding the historical, scientific method of Marx, adopt the metaphysical philosophy which Marx and Engels so unmercifully trounced.

A revolution dreamt of and planned, because, logically, an old order must refuse to be transformed, is an absurd thing. Yet, to a very considerable extent such is the position of the 'revolutionary' movement here. Its logic begins by misunderstanding the nature of society, believing it to be a hard resisting structure, an old bottle which contains in physical separateness the new wine, a house in which an increasing family dwells. Whereas the social organization, like the body, is in a constant state of change and of readaptation, responsive to every movement of the human intelligence, sensitive to every change in the mass will. That is so whether 'economic determinism' or 'intellectual

227

determinism' is right, whether progress proceeds by a class struggle or by the readjustment of functions in a society growing in vigour and completeness.

Equally false are its excuses why it should not use democracy. The democracy may be ignorant and unresponsive to truth and new ideas; a revolution will not make it intelligent. Capitalism today may use 'democracy in the mass' for its own ends; cannot governing Labour do the same? Will the seizure of power by a few paralyse for ever the opposition of opponents, or teach the masses the wisdom that nothing else has taught them, or induce them to fit themselves into conditions which now create in their lethargic minds hostility and opposition?

So, the logic I am examining adds to its other faults that of ending its reasoning at the point where it should begin and, having made its criticisms, it tires of its pursuits and leaves its constructive programme to chance. The beginning of the end of its constructive work is: Wait and see. Serious men must protest against such reckless folly. Socialism asks of its friends patient and laborious thought, rectitude, and an ability to handle great affairs. We have had enough revolutions of the sword and the turmoil. Socialism asks for a revolution of the trowel and the disciplined intelligence.

The conception of revolution which I criticize also misunderstands itself. It thinks that revolution can be born from the wills of a select few meeting with the opposition or the lethargy of the many, whereas it can only be created when the weight of pent-up opposition smashes through the barriers which hold it back. It thinks it can make itself; it can only be made by social pressure. It thinks that revolution is a matter of metaphysics and logic; it is a matter of social friction.

With one aspect of the revolutionary impulse I am in complete sympathy. It demands action; it is weary of declarations and resolutions which produce nothing. We have all had this feeling enlivened by the work of the Second International. It met at Berne, and declared its position on the great international interests of the day – the Treaty of Peace, national boundaries, the League of Nations; and it resolved to send a deputation of inquiry into Russia. Nothing has happened. Its wisdom has been treated with contempt by the Governments; its request for passports has met with denial casually given. Its Permanent Commission has met in Amsterdam and again in Lucerne. It has repeated its wisdom and the Governments have repeated their rebuffs. Never has a more ample supply of crumbs been thrown from the masters' table; never with more insult has Labour been refused a place at the feast. Its power in small things has been increased; in the large affairs and policies of States it is as weak today as ever it was. In these times of critical action when decisions are to determine the fate of generations this weakness is a special grievance. No one requires to come and tell me, by marshalled argument and indignant rhetoric, of the humiliation under which Labour suffers. It cuts like a thong into one's soul. It is the putting up of barriers against ideas which makes ideas revolutionary.

But, obviously, whoever longs for action cannot long for any action – for the forlorn splash of the topmost ripples over the barriers. When we think of it, the inaction which is so galling is the inaction of those feeding on the crumbs under the table. It is inaction because the leverage for action is not there. True, some leaders are partly to blame for this. The action, for instance, of the French minority at the meetings of the International could not be otherwise if they were a wing of the Governments serving the interests of the Governments. That, however, is not the determining factor. The Socialist is not in authority; his guns are too far off for him to plant his shells in the midst of the enemy's camp. The only action which is possible at the moment is that of changing opinion and awakening intelligence. There may be strikes for this and riots for that, and this may be gained and that may be won. It is true that Labour in an unsettled frame of mind and in an ugly temper makes Governments careful, but where does that bring us? All these things are only checks. When we come to consider the position of the Miners' Federation in relation to mining affairs we are in the presence of a different set of conditions. Here we have a body of men well knit together in their own interests, who come to

Ramsay MacDonald's Political Writings

resolutions and who can act upon them because of their organization. Thus it has come about that thoughtless persons are always telling the miners that they should strike for this course and for that, forgetting all the time that the Miners' Federation is not an association of general human regeneration formed for the purpose of making it unnecessary for those who would advise it to take upon their own shoulders the burdens of their advice.

I doubt if any model of political action is more misunderstood, both by friend and foe alike, than is the Miners' Federation. It is a mining organization formed for industrial purposes; its membership is confined to mine workers, its immediate objects are concerned with pits. In these days of interlaced influence and concern such a body must have a hand in politics, and if the worker industrially organized were called upon to save his nation by industrial action, the Federation would be expected to play its part, and, no doubt, would do it. But it is not the instrument of action such as I am now discussing. When the representatives of the Second International go to the Governments, they have no body behind them such as Mr Smillie has when he asks for a Coal Commission. If they had, they would produce action. The intelligence of the people has never yet translated their potentialities of power into power itself, and therefore the conditions of effective action such as is asked for do not exist, and before we have action they must exist. To create it without them is only playing at revolution. Any man can raise a standard, but it requires a disciplined crowd to win the battle.

Therefore, when people impatiently demand action they ought to see first of all that the conditions of action are present; if they are not they should help to create them. Only when that is done can they reasonably blame leaders. When they do that work they will find that the weapon which they have been fashioning for use is, in this country, at any rate, not a revolutionary, but a political one. As the conditions of a revolution are created they will filter into Parliament, and there the action will take place. Again, I appeal to our active spirits to go in for real politics and not to be content to indulge in metaphysical ones.

Parliament and Revolution

Fight and educate; educate and fight. It is true that in the mean-time the hateful reaction will be in authority, but the reaction knows that the most ominous thing it has to face is a steadily growing beleaguering army.

We must analyse revolution into its stages. The Socialist stage of the Russian revolution followed the political stage, and consists of two sections – that of programme and that of method. I leave out of account the Terror and similar incidents, not only because most of them are mere fabrications,* but because they belong to the counter-revolution and have nothing to do with the political colour of the party in power. Besides, Lenin abhors them, whereas Koltchak glories in them. The programme is such, on the whole, as any Socialist government would put into operation, though its land policy would be stronger in this country and, with some preliminary preparation, its proposals regarding wealth conscription would have been less crude. The distinctive revolutionary feature was therefore that of method. Now, the method depended solely upon the fact that a political revolution had been necessary, and that the country was bankrupt and in a state of political and industrial collapse.

In this country we have had our political revolution. Everyone who has come into touch with the revolutionaries of the non-democratic countries of Europe must have been struck with the limited nature of their intentions. How often have I heard

* The number of times that Kropotkin and other people whose names are known in Great Britain have been shot, has become a joke, but the prettiest of all the tales is one which, so far, I have only seen in foreign newspapers. When Maria Spiridonovna was tried for characterizing one of Tchicherine's notes to the Allies as 'a base betrayal of the Russian workers', the Stockholm newspaper manufactory of atrocities reported that she had been sentenced to be shot and our newspapers displayed the news with appropriate moral disgust. The fact is that this revolutionary showed by her behaviour in the Court that she was terribly overstrung (revolution with her had not been a pastime), and the 'sentence' actually passed on her was a year in a sanatorium, with a rider added that it was hoped she might enjoy her rest to gain new strength 'through healthy physical and mental work'.

British Socialists comment that they were only liberals or at best radicals. Thus, so far as this country is concerned, we have reached the stage when the Socialist programme is a matter of political fighting. A parliamentary election will give us all the power that Lenin had to get by a revolution, and such a majority can proceed to effect the transition from capitalism to Socialism with the co-operation of the people, and not merely by edict. More than that, a country which has gained already all that a political revolution can give it, cannot begin its social revolution as Russia began its. To have an election followed by a revolution for the purpose of carrying out the programme of the defeated minority belongs to the world of playfully fanciful romance, not to that of serious politics. I can imagine that a Socialist government in Parliament may be met by obstruction, and in the country by agitation. But if that government has the country behind it, it will stand no humbug in Parliament; if it has not the country behind it, it can neither work Parliament nor create a revolution. It certainly should be bold; if as a result of this boldness, Parliament began to work and the opposition were overawed into decency – good and well; if not, a revolution would still be a thing which could not be pulled off. Of course, if it came to be that we had a bankrupt country, a demoralized and disorganized people, and anarchy, either active or latent, from one end of a ruined nation to the other, a Committee of Public Safety might well step into Whitehall and make up its mind to impose a New Order upon an Old Chaos, but the origin and circumstances of that revolution would not be those of the committee room, the book logic, the minority intellectual wisdom which our present-day anti-Parliamentarians offer as a means of Socialist progress. Therefore, I conclude that for a progressive movement here to try and copy Russian methods, or create Russian conditions, is to go back upon our own evolution, and that if the design were successful it would only bring us face to face with the very same difficulties as parliamentary methods have to meet.

This consideration does not weigh however with those who have abandoned political action. They say that chaos must come and that it ought to be created, because only then will the vigour of Socialism manifest itself as it did in Russia after the fall of Kerensky. These people value vigour for its own sake, not for its results, and yet strangely enough this most metaphysical of all conceptions of social change is held by those who are specially fond of calling themselves 'scientific'. The adjective would be given to them by no one else but themselves.

Will Socialist forces act better under revolutionary than under parliamentary conditions? The greatest weakness of Socialist forces is their tendency to split up and to dissipate their spirit in internal disputes just at the moment of apparent success. Ever since I have been a member of the Independent Labour Party this curse has troubled it. The religious disputes on grace and salvation which have always weakened religious revolutions, crop up to this day amongst political pioneers. A revolution would be a signal not for closing ranks but for opening them up. Its unsettlement affects the revolutionists themselves. Whoever has followed events in revolutionary Europe during the past twelve months must be convinced that the divisions in the Socialist ranks must have brought Socialist power to a speedy termination were it not that defeat in the field during the war had completely demoralized the counter-revolution and deprived it of all chance of an immediate rally. The treatment that the Social Revolutionaries have had at the hands of the Bolshevists, the fratricidal conflicts in Germany, the divisions in Hungary, should be studied not as evidence that there are Socialists who are not Socialists, but that revolutions disrupt the parties that ought to benefit by them. So do parliamentary methods, but their consequences are nothing compared with the other. The reason for this must be apparent to everyone. Fear always shadows revolution; suspicion sits at the table with every Committee of Public Safety. A revolution presents every Socialist problem for simultaneous settlement; it is the road of maximum difficulty; it is also the occasion both of minimum confidence and co-operation and of the necessity of concentrating power in the hands of a few. Only reckless folly would deliberately choose this way of minimum chance of bringing Socialism about and of establishing the Socialist State.

233

Every Socialist relationship is so interdependent, that under the most favourable conditions much failure must attend the first schemes of socialization. No one could preach a better sermon on that text than Lenin, unless it were Bela Kun. When these failures have to be faced in one nation alone they are trying enough; when they are attended by a revolution which draws upon itself the enmity of the world, they will break the ablest and the most devoted men. For a revolution, by destroying, or at any rate paralysing for the time being, the ordinary economic life of a nation makes that nation dependent upon foreign states. It must, therefore, receive foreign sympathy and support. So long as the world is ruled by capitalism this support will not be forthcoming. A Socialist revolution in this country could be starved out by America much more easily than the Socialist revolution in Russia can be fought out by the Allies.

No wise Socialist need plot and plan a revolution. If bankruptcy ends the present order in disaster and disgrace, if the meanness of mind of our politicians who for momentary triumphs degrade public life and mislead the country like demagogues and charlatans until Parliament has forfeited respect and neither persons nor institutions wield moral or political authority, if prices of commodities keep high and life becomes harder, if we continue to be made the prey of profiteers and plunderers and the evidences of their illgotten gains are to be flaunted in the face of the distressed people, if the mind of the mass is the subject of daily misrepresentation in a contemptible press, and if the desire of the best thought of democracy to find expression and to be consulted as a responsible authority is thwarted by tricksters and cheap jacks, then Labour troubles will become chronic, restlessness will defy reason, anarchy will spread, and social cohesion will be destroyed. Then also the duty of Socialists will be clear. That will be the friction which causes revolution, that will be the hindrance which makes ideas explosive. The Socialists alone can then save the State, and a decisive act of commanding will will be required to do it. It may be a minority that will have to act, but, in this process of creating revolutionary conditions, the majority will have been deprived of its authority, of its intelligence, of its defences, of justice. It will have been weakened by fear, and be made cowardly by its own sense of its criminality and unworthiness.

Chapter XI

The Independent Labour Party

I cannot conceive that the end of good government is to make society stagnant by its excellence and to lull the individual into quiescence by the security he feels under it. Nor can I conceive of any rational theory of progress that depends upon periodic and violent revolution as a means. Every day comes with its own revolution in a progressive society just as a series of explosions produces motion and a series of impacts produces harmony. The individual, energetic in mind and in action, is too valuable to his community to be lulled to sleep or to be condemned if he occasionally produces trouble and inconvenience. The revolutionary and exploring spirit will always be necessary to keep society from stagnating. It is not a menace to society; it is the life of society. Therefore, whilst the Socialist conception of society remains fixed, its creeds and methods must never sink into infallible dogma and its gospels become closed books. It is said of Marx that he was once overheard muttering to himself, 'Thank God, I am no Marxist', and his great protagonist, Clara Zetkin, has written, 'When the pen fell from Marx's hand, the last word on Socialism had not been written.'

In maintaining this revolutionary and critical mind, it is futile to scurry about from feverish dream to feverish dream. The minds which do this are generally those which live on superficialities – now the panacea of a new electoral system, now the Gileadite test of some phrase or dogma, now the heaven-disclosed evangel of a new thought. Nothing is of any use till it is digested and set into the system of action in which it is to play a part, and the homage done to the Russian Revolution by an uncritical adoption of its phases and its phrases is not one worthy of acceptance by those to whom it is offered.

The Russian Revolution has been one of the greatest events in the history of the world, and the attacks that have been made upon it by frightened ruling classes and hostile capitalism should rally to its defence everyone who cares for political liberty and freedom of thought. But it is Russian. Its historical setting and parentage is Russia; the economic State in which it is is Russia. Moreover, it is still in its eruptive stage, and has hardly passed under the moulding hand of evolution. What it is to become, who can say? All we can do is to see that it has a chance of becoming something, and not die away like the Peace Night flares that are gleaming in the sky as I write this. To cry as flare after flare goes up: 'This is the permanent pillar of fire which is to light us to Canaan,' is certainly not common sense. We know that some expedients have been purely temporary; we know that others cannot bear close and detailed examination.* For them the comprehensive excuse, which is a justification under the circumstances, can be made that they belong to the stress of revolution. History may justify their authors, but it certainly will not their copiers. Lenin in this respect is too big a man to be a Leninite, as he told Bela Kun when Hungary passed under Soviet Government.

Political action remains the normal method of transforming the structure of communities, both politically and socially. The problem of adapting it to its work is far from being solved, that of mass action is only beginning to be understood. Treatises on the subject written by the last great school of political theorists, the radicals, are out of date. The task of the Socialist is to make enlightenment come quick – but it must be enlightenment; to coordinate in a movement all the forces that make for organic change such as he wishes; to concentrate, in this time of unsettled minds and habits, upon great essentials, as the Miners' Federation is doing in its own concerns; and to prevent the

* I commend a careful study of Mr Ransome's book, *Six Weeks in Russia in 1919*, to everyone who really wishes to understand Russian events.

world from being closed to new ideas and experiments like those now coming from Russia.

If this is said to be slow, I reply that it need not be so, but that, if it is, it is so by the nature of society, and no revolutionary action can be planned to avoid the slowness. All short cuts swing round in a circuit to where they started. The footpath is for the individual, the high road for the crowd. It is hard for Socialists to fight capitalism; it is much harder for them to fight Nature. Whether by revolution or without it, the transformation of the economic structure of society is no easy undertaking, as Lenin is now confessing, and the success of the venture must depend in a very great measure upon the spirit in which it is undertaken. One kind of spirit which appeals to the impatience of the time is, I believe, to lead Socialism into disaster proportionate to the simplicity with which it presents our problems and the dogmatic logic with which it supports them. To such minds force and authority are the characteristic modes of thought and expedients for action. They deal with book logic, and not with society; they begin their researches by writing their conclusions; and their political method is at enmity with liberty. In every country, though especially in those governed tyrannically, the revolutionary type is bred. It is there the salt of the earth. It lives like hunted beasts; its life is constantly in its hands; it is defiant and untamable; it acquires the psychology of the powers with which it is at war; it would leap into police offices, as they have leaped into them, and turn upon rulers the captured machine, as soldiers turn captured guns upon their late owners. Without these men, Europe today would be a filthy, stagnant pool. But it is quite different with imitators who in peaceful streets try to feel like them, who use imagination to surround themselves with the hardships in which the originals live, and who in humdrum lives find romance in revolutionary dogmas. This pseudo-revolutionism has nothing in common with the real thing – and certainly nothing in common with Socialism. It subverts Socialism; it distracts it and disrupts it; it gives it no personalities who can be relied upon and no guidance which is illuminating. It is particularly destructive amongst the youth who start with a gay spurt up the hill of life – may they never do otherwise! – and leaves them when their first wind has been exhausted on a trackless country.

The Socialist spirit is that of liberty, of discussion. It is historical and not cataclysmic. It is objective as well as subjective; it can understand as well as feel. It can admire even when it does not agree. Such admiration is part of the capacity to transform society, because that transformation depends upon a relationship between the mind of the reformer and his social circumstances. It knows that there are various roads leading to the same trysting place; that the Russian comrades may come one way and the British come another way; that the method of success is the co-operation of differences within Socialism rather than a formal unity which gives full freedom of advance to no section. Today it recognizes that there is one tactic possible to the people of defeated countries, another possible to people the political fabric of whose States has fallen to the earth, another to the people whose nations are dancing through victory celebrations and as military conquerors are emerging from the psychology of war to meet the problems of peace. A tactic which claims universal uniformity as a characteristic is self-condemned.

Above all it discards lightning changes as the way to realize itself. It knows that no system of government or of society can rest upon anything but common consent – the consent of passive minds, or the consent of active minds. The latter kind of consent is the only one it values. The idea of a revolution transforming the structure of Society by the will of a minority must seem as utopian to it as the ideas of the Owenites and of all who sought to create an oasis of peace in the wilderness of the capitalist system. It believes in democracy, not only as a moral creed which alone is consistent with its views of humanity, but because it is the only practical creed. It knows that, revolutions or no revolutions, public consent is the basis of all social order and that the good builder makes his foundations sound before he puts up his storeys.

The Independent Labour Party is a product of British history and British conditions. It is neither Russian, nor German, nor

American. It found the radical movement as one ancestor, the trade union movement as another, the intellectual proletarian movement – Chartism and the earlier Socialist thinkers like Owen, Hall, Thompson – as another; the Continental Socialists – especially Marx – as still another. It has gathered up its inheritance and has produced from it an historical movement of its own, political in its method, free in its spirit, economic in its purpose. It comes after the liberal political revolution, and it therefore joins democracy to Socialism, carrying on in this respect the work of Marx. It knows that opinion must always precede reconstruction, but it also knows that the harvest of Socialism does not ripen in a night and has therefore to be gathered at one cutting, but that every day brings something to fruition, that the moments as they go bring us nearer to Socialism by their products of Socialist thought and experiment which have to be seized and embodied in the transforming structure of society, not in a bunch, but bit by bit. It believes in the class conflict as a descriptive fact, but it does not regard it as supplying a political method. It strives to transform through education, through raising the standards of mental and moral qualities, through the acceptance of programmes by reason of their justice, rationality and wisdom. it trusts to no regeneration by trick or force. Founding itself on the common sense of everyday experience, it knows that, come enthusiasm or depression, impatience or lethargy, the enlightened State can be built up and maintained only by enlightened citizens. It walks with the map of Socialism in front of it and guides its steps by the compass of democracy. It issues from the past, it deals with the present, it has a clear conception of the future; it unites these relationships into a great living movement. In the International it co-operates with its kindred. Upon its consistency with itself depends its success, and upon its success depends the future of Socialism in this country.

PARLIAMENT AND
DEMOCRACY

Chapter IV

The Functional Society

The most important problem of all that arises out of representation is: How is the representative body to be kept in touch with the needs of the represented, and how are the represented to be kept interested in their responsibilities? How is the will of the Parliament to be kept identical with the will of the mass? For representation does not only refer to opinion but to action. The representative body must not only agree, it must act.

The Guild Socialist is trying to construct a political scheme in accordance with which society is to be divided into various industrial and social functions, and these functions are to be made the basis of representation. The argument is that I, in society, am a complex of interests, that no one can represent me in my complexity but only in my separate simplicities, and that consequently I, for representative purposes, must divide myself into as many groups, and be represented by as many representatives as I have functions. Moreover, just as I cannot have one representative, so the State cannot have one representative sovereign authority. The political structure which this school would build up has not been officially decided yet, and is being pulled about and frequently readjusted. It is like a machine in the hands of the experimenter. But we can see its general outlines. The overwhelming impression they give is of hopeless confusion and unworkable complexity.

In the conception of government by function there is a simple but deadly error. The process of reasoning is this: society is a coordination of functions and is therefore complicated. Each functional association has a comparatively simple aim; therefore, as we ought to proceed from the simple to the more complex, we should begin with the representation and the enfranchisement of functions, and thus by building up from the function we shall best attain to the whole society which function serves.

That is not true, and the difficulties in which this school finds itself in building up a structure to suit its theories prove that it is not true.* On paper, as Mr Cole says, a function is the specific work which associations were formed to do. But that specific work, say the profession of teaching, by no means produces a simple organization, with simple objects, which enable any teacher to represent adequately any other teacher; all specific work is not capable of being performed by associations acting apart or with reference to their own specific function, but can be done only by combinations of functions and associations, sometimes the whole of associations and sometimes only parts or aspects of them. Thus the transport workers cannot manage the transport system alone but only jointly with the representative of, say, miners (for coal), consumers (for passenger traffic), and so on. A function is not always assignable to one organ or association; it is often the 'specific work' of an organization of associations, like transport.

These conclusions seem to be sound:

1. *The attempt to build up a social structure from specific functions must fail because society is not composed of a mosaic combination of functions but is itself a unity in which the functions find their purpose and utility.*

By analysing the organization of society, we resolve it into functions, but society itself is not the sum of these functions working alongside of each other. It is the controlling personality, so to speak, which sets the functions in a system and imposes upon them the higher utilities of communal life. Mr Cole, in his *Social Theory*, begins by defining functional associations as being the creations of individuals, and goes on to admit that they may be anti-social though they should be 'social purposes selected and placed in coherent relationship'. If these words have any meaning it must be that the control of the function is

* Cf. *Social Theory* by G. D. H. Cole, especially the chapter on 'The Principles of Function'.

not within itself but is in the social unity which all the functions serve, e.g., society itself. Begun for purely personal ends (the workman, simply as a workman, works for himself, just as the capitalist, simply as a capitalist, works for himself, and both workman and capitalist in an industrial organization may work, as they have worked, against the community), at no point in their own special interests can functional organizations become communal organizations and be directed by either communal morality or economics. We all know how easy it is for trade unionism, for instance, to become anti-social and, by looking after the immediate interests of its own members, sacrifice a more general well-being. The whole trend of recent progressive thought is to destroy the merely functional spirit of trade unionism and make it social.

2. *If it is impossible for anyone to represent the individual in his civic opinions because they are not sufficiently simple and detached one from another, neither are the opinions and wishes of an individual in his functioning organization single and detached even when that organization is working alone; much less do we get simplicity when the function is performed by combinations of organizations and functions.*

A social system is not made up of simple functional groups, but of groupings of these groups. That means that the representation in that system has to be indirect and not direct. The engineers', the teachers', the miners' functions operate only in relation to each other and to the whole community. Their work is all of the nature of a derived authority. A printers' guild may run the printing presses, but it is not independent of the papermakers, and it must have some relations not only with publishing but with the guilds of literary producers. Now each of those points of contact widens the activities of the various functions beyond themselves, necessitates coordinate functions and destroys the claims that 'each function can get on with its own job'. Its job is a communal job, and so soon as the functional body concerns itself with its real social business it is more than a mere functional body (as this school of theorists define it), and the representatives who act for it cease to represent anybody but themselves or perhaps the committee that appointed them. The result is that a scheme which is introduced by pointing out that representation is impossible under our present methods ends by creating a system which throws over democratic representation altogether. The necessity of coordinating functions compels the abandonment of the idea that the representatives on the co-ordinations express the wishes of the rank and file. Indirect, undemocratic and non-responsible representation is an inevitable feature of the society which the functionalists visualize.

3. *Although the 'functionalists' admit that functions should work for social ends they can provide no coordinating social authority.*

The individual who joins the various associations can unite all their functioning in his own will. Functioning, say, in the association of engineers, he is not only an engineer but a citizen, and his actions and thoughts as an engineer are really determined by his intellectual and economic relations to his society. Therefore the engineering functional association is either something that contemplates the whole of society from an engineering point of view, or it contemplates engineering interests only. Here is a dilemma from which there is no escape for Guild Socialists who believe that they have not merely made valuable suggestions regarding industrial administration under nationalization, but that, in addition, they have discovered a better conception of society and a more scientific organization of the State itself. If the former is the true view, then the representation of the engineering function is just as difficult ('impossible' the Guild Socialists would say) as the civic constituency, and the functioning group is the microcosm of the whole of society; if the latter view be true, at no point in functional organization does the whole interest of society appear at all.* In this conception

* Obviously the reply to this, that there will be joint meetings of representatives of various functional organizations, is no reply at all. (1) The representative who goes from various organizations to co-ordinate their work cannot represent any simple aim of a function and so violates the only conditions of representation which the Guild Socialist as politician will accept. (2) The Union of separate functions cannot deal with any wider interest than the sum of the functions

of social organization the engineer can be represented and all the other separate functions which a man performs can be organized, but the whole political unity of the man* is organized and represented in nothing.

This consideration is important for practical reasons as well. A social system based on functions is a system that is likely to be worked primarily in the interests of functions. In order to make its working even conceivable the most disputable assumptions are made, for instance, that guilds once formed will not develop the same type of conservatism and anti-social policy which their prototypes of the Middle Ages did, and which there is good reason for assuming they will do if they are absolutely self-governing. A workman or a professional man in control of his own function in society *may* develop so much of the social mind that he will involuntarily put himself wholeheartedly at the disposal of society. But that assumption is a very insecure basis upon which to found social structure. Capitalism has so divided society and so disrupted social cohesion that the habit of social service has been sadly weakened. When it grows, it will not demand the absolute self-government of the Guild Socialists, but a just relationship to all other social services.

The whole idea of society as a group of functions is as inadequate as that of the body as a group of organs. The life of the whole is left out. It has no coordinating power, and is therefore chaotic and anarchist; it disrupts the social mind and conception; it multiplies infinitely small and ineffective groupings, pretending to be definite in their function but all mere indefinable abstractions; with these vague groupings it must create a special judiciary to settle what they are to be, how authoritative they are to be, and what functions are to be obedient to them;

---

represented, and that is much short of all the social interests. For instance, a combination of labour and capital, as in the historical bedstead makers' case, was not a combination which represented a wider social interest than the functional one of the parties.

* I am not thinking of the whole unity of the man, but only his political unity which is represented today in the sovereign political State.

it multiplies enormously the complications of 'law' and increases the problems of arbitrators and judges on matters of interpretation and validity, whilst it weakens at the same time the authority of these functionaries. It is bound to create a massive weight and confused entanglement of written constitutions and an enormous army of committee men and bureaucrats, each attached to numerous small functional states within society.

Political social policy must start with the conception of a general unity of which functions are contributing parts, and apart from which function has no meaning. The Guild Socialist, as politician, starts at the other end and arrives nowhere. He not only divides society into two unfusible unities – the political and the industrial – and creates many quasi-sovereign authorities both in national and in local government, but in trying to produce a scheme by which they are to operate he assumes a smoothness of working which all experience warns us cannot be secured, but a lack of which would bring down the flimsy structure like a house of cards.

In this chapter I have dealt only with the political proposals of the Guild Socialist, and my opposition to them must not be taken to indicate an opposition to all that Guild Socialism stands for. The Guild Socialist has made most valuable contributions to the solution of the problems of Socialist administration, and by virtue of these he has gained a permanent place in the history of the development of Socialist theory and practice.

Chapter VI

The Industrial State

A belief that the political State representative of the full civic life of the community must retain final authority in the organization of production does not mean, as it is so often taken to mean, the control of industry by politicians or by a civil service bureaucracy.

The Socialist who believes in the State is not necessarily what is technically known as 'a State Socialist'. Hitherto, I have disagreed with the Guild Socialist, but now I am to find myself in pretty complete agreement with him. When the Guild Socialist tries to construct an organization of industry on the principle of the direct responsibility of the workers (of course, including the management and the scientific and technical workers) he does great service to Socialism, and his contribution to the problem of how nationalized industry can be administered is invaluable. He has advanced practical Socialism a substantial stage.

The Socialist demand for nationalization and municipalization marked a new departure in social thought; bringing that demand within the scope of practical politics marked a new stage in social evolution. At first, however, it was only an operative idea. Naturally, its first form was that of State Socialism, but many who were content to advocate it in that form knew that that could only be provisional. The instinct of the Independent Labour Party was always urging for a more liberal conception of nationalized administration, and, consequently, the Party hospitably received the ideas and proposals of the Guild Socialists regarding workshop management and the control of industry. These ideas are now sufficiently clear and well defined to enable the Party to state them in accordance with its own position and embody them definitely in its programme. Nationalized industry is not to be bureaucratically controlled by a Civil Service. The State is to delegate its industrial responsibility to industrial associations just as it delegates its municipal responsibilities to local government bodies. If it be observed that the relations between these local bodies and the central authorities are unsatisfactory and that the liberty of the former is not sufficiently ample, we admit it. A State inspired by the democratic spirit of Socialism would be more liberal, and for a long time the Independent Labour Party has been committed to giving much greater authority to municipal bodies. I am only concerned here with the principle.

Upon an industry becoming nationalized, the State by Act of Parliament and administrative order will at once set up a body of administration with properly defined duties. It will be composed in the main of the workers of all grades concerned, and may constitute itself into workshop, regional and national committees to enable it to do its work. That work will be, in the main, production, and so the body need not be complicated in its composition by the representation of consumers or any other interest, except that the State, when the owner of the industrial capital employed, must be represented in those parts of the general organization where its interests are involved.

The needs of production are briefly as follows: (1) the supply of raw material; (2) day to day working, including machinery for dealing with disputes and other questions involved in working as they arise; (3) management, promotion, including efficiency working, etc.; (4) scientific and technical investigation in connection with the different processes, and their application when completed.

The first requires an organization which must vary from trade to trade. In most cases, it is not a matter which affects the labour to be employed upon the raw material, and would have to be dealt with by skilled agents working under directions of a Central Committee of Supply which would be divided into departments, e.g., cotton, ferrous and non-ferrous metals, and so on.

The second is purely a matter for the workers (again, I emphasize *all* grades) employed. A workshop or a mine committee of responsible workers, chosen as shop stewards, foremen, managers, would see to this, and the same committee would consider and formulate demands, carry them out when they concerned the workshop alone or were within their jurisdiction, and bring them to the notice of the proper authorities if they themselves could not deal with them. This would include such questions as wages and hours of labour, both of which obviously concern the whole industry in the first place, but also affect the balance of social exchange and the relation of any one industry to the rest. The workshop would formulate them in the first instance, the trade guild or committee would have to discuss them and give them their final form as a demand, but obviously some higher authority would have to sanction them.

We must observe that this function would have to be performed under two different conditions – the transition State, when only some industries would be socially organized, and the complete Socialist State. Under the latter, wages problems would have completely changed their character and would be concerned with how the national product was to be divided. The product would be amply sufficient to secure men in life and human comfort, and its precise division, provided each gets a satisfactory minimum, would not trouble people. Insecurity alone makes a scramble for income inevitable and the reward of greed useful.

But in the transition State, wages problems will continue to be troublesome and the intelligent wage-earner will seek with more and more keenness to take all pure profit to himself. Thus, the miners are now (June 1920) refusing to allow the Government to make large profits from the sale of coal to ease the taxpayer, and are asking that part of the surplus should be added to their wages and the rest used for the reduction of prices. In this transition State and, at first, in the nationalized industries, wages might well be paid on a standard minimum (not necessarily the same for all trades and certainly not the same for all grades) with additions based on piece rates. That would be the simplest way for securing to the workers the maximum share in the products of their labour, and at the same time it would reduce the wages problem to the simple one of ascertaining facts as to what is the most equitable way under certain given conditions for dividing the available production. The general question, then, would be: 'Is the industry supporting itself' (if it be a productive one), or: 'Is the service receiving its just share of social charges?'

The third need is one in which the workshop should be dealt with by the guild committee of the industry but in which the higher authority of supply has also an interest, and the fourth is in the same position.

Such is the work to be done. What organization is required to do it? First of all, the question arises as to what the higher authority of supply should be, and how it should be composed. It should be the body which should estimate the complete needs of the community from time to time, present its mandates for production to the various industrial guilds or committees, receive from them their demands for raw material, and satisfy itself that the whole machinery of production was being run. This department should also deal with the organization of transport (the actual working of transport being managed on the same general plan as production), for transport belongs to the responsibility of supply and not of production. It might also have to deal with the general conditions of industry and apportion to each trade its collective share in the available wealth, though this might well be dealt with by a separate body similarly constituted. From this conspectus of duties, the composition of the body becomes clear. It must be a part of the political State and be subject to parliamentary control. Its work may be public, and its subordinate staff must belong to the Civil Service. On it, and on all its operative committees, there must be representatives of production – labour, managerial, scientific and technical. It must be able to create *ad hoc* advisory committees properly representative in view of the functions they have to perform. In a word, it must be at once the great wholesale of the industrial State, the clearing-house for all requirements that need national consideration, and it should act as the industrial financial agent for the State.

Put in this way, one may gather the impression of great centralization; as a matter of fact that will not be so. Centralization we must have, and because of an ignorant and ill-thought-out cry against it we must not be frightened away from it. Bureaucratic it may even seem, but again, as a matter of fact, bureaucratic it is not. We must organize the purely mechanical side of administration so as to make it an efficient machine, but in control of the machine should be free initiative in direct touch with the affairs with which it deals. Bureaucracy divides the machine from its work; Socialist administration puts the life and experience of the work in command of the machine. Also, in order to reap the full benefits of centralization, it must be run with, and not be exclusive of, a large delegation of power to localities and associations; it must give liberty to the workers and responsibility to their associations. Indeed, it will be to a great extent a watching department asking for results rather than interfering with the getting of them. A healthy body is not conscious of its organs, but it knows at once if they are out of order, and it alone can tell when they are diseased.

The scheme of organization which grows in one's mind by relating and coordinating the various stages in the process of an organized industrial State is in outline as follows:

The actual workshop management and the responsibility for seeing that each workplace contributes its proper quota to the necessary national total will be in the hands of the workers: the coordination of workplaces in districts and the concern for generally efficient management will be in the hands of district committees, upon which the managerial and technical sides will be strongly represented: the general concerns of the separate trades, the scientific requirements, the most up-to-date methods, research connected with them, and the skill and knowledge which go to make the trade organization and technique as perfect as can be, will be looked after by national trade boards upon which all the trade interests will be represented: a central body will be in control of the necessary national supply and will see that the various industrial organizations are working satisfactorily. When the community has advanced so far in nationalization and control of industry as to be free to fix wages – that is, the share of the producers and service givers in the national product – one of the functions of this central body will be to assign to each industrial group its share in the national product and allow its own Guild or Council to fix the wages of its grades and services. That, in general outline, is the plan upon which the industrial State might organize itself, assigning the various needs and duties to appropriate organizations of the people and interests concerned.

Obviously the Central Economic Council for which this scheme provides is of the greatest importance, and when its duties and possibilities are thought over it may appear to be far too important to be a mere Department of State. I shall return to this in the next chapter, but in the meantime shall try to indicate what change this conception of industrial organization will necessitate in the two existing democratic combinations formed by the producers and consumers to protect themselves within the capitalist State.

What is to become of the trade union and Co-operative movements should industrial evolution follow these or similar lines?

There will always be work for associations of labour, managers, technicians, but as our Trade Unions change their present functions of being watchdogs against the encroachments of capitalism, or aggressive bodies constantly invading the territory of capitalism in the interests of those they represent, and become organizations through which capitalist control is to be transmuted into social control (acting, of course, with the political State) their activities will change and they will become the associations through which labour will function in the administration of the new industrial State. They will be the links binding workshop with workshop and trade with trade, so their craft* character may disappear and they may become simply

* It is quite possible that craft organizations may survive, because they will be required for the representation of workmen in the separate

industrial, and watch that organization and machinery generally do not encroach upon the interest and the liberty of the workman. The managerial and technical associations will perform like functions for their own clientele, but will also be concerned with the further interests of their own efficiency. They will thus take over the work now done by some of the technical institutes – like those of the Civil Engineers or of Applied Chemistry – and keep alive experiment, investigation, initiative. Socialist conditions will be a great stimulus to technical intelligence, and these professional associations will become real institutions for the advancement of applied science, and not mere instruments for securing professional advantages.

The Co-operative movement presents a much more complicated problem. Started in a competitive capitalist society and working in such a society, it has had to develop itself as an industrial State within an alien industrial State. It has therefore had to invade the realms of production, ownership of raw material, transport, and finally banking. The consumer's interest cannot be separated from other interests if it is to be safeguarded. The organization which begins with the consumer must extend and extend until it controls every activity which enters into production and exchange. The Co-operative purpose under capitalism cannot be fulfilled by looking after distribution alone.

Therefore, when the community has reached the stage when it must begin to protect itself and its freedom by the organization of its production, it must absorb into its system the voluntary organizations which have been formed for similar purposes by groups in the capitalist community. What does this mean to the Co-operative movement as we know it?

To discuss this subject in the detail which it deserves would require a separate volume, and in the exploration of the social policy of the Independent Labour Party this ought to be prepared. Here, and for my present purpose, I need only refer to some of the broader facts.

---

trades, and it must be remembered that the tactical advantages of forming industrial Unions to fight capitalism will disappear in the Socialist State and a new need will arise for craft organization.

I ought to say to begin with that I reject the idea that without altering its relation to the political State the Co-operative movement can supplant capitalism, and, by the engrafting of the administrative ideas of Guild Socialism, can become the great organ of social production, distribution, and exchange for a completely Co-operative community. An application of the conclusions which I have argued out in the chapter on the political proposals of Guild Socialism will explain why I hold this view on principle; whoever studies the conflict between Co-operation and capitalism and surveys the position of both in the world today must see why, as a practical proposal, the Co-operative movement, in spite of its marvellous success, must fail to supersede capitalism.

In the State which I have in mind an organization representing consumers is as essential as are organizations for carrying on production. The State should at once use the existing machinery of Co-operation in every way possible for distribution of supplies, and scientific lines of demarcation between municipal trading and Co-operative enterprise should be drawn. The municipality should supply the communal needs – like trams, electricity and so on – which concern good government, public health and other matters of communal efficiency; the Co-operative organization should deal with the more individual needs of consumers. Thus if Co-operation under capitalism has developed in directions which will be barred to it under democratic Socialism, so in like fashion municipal trading has developed under capitalism on lines which really belong to guilds of consumers. The Co-operative movement should be used for foreign trading relations, and on all industrial committees such as those I have been describing when distribution, transport and consumers' interests have to be dealt with, Co-operation should be the organization recognized.

Thus in the end the Co-operative movement would become what it was intended to be – a function in the industrial state, and its protective outworks of production and transport would be absorbed in the organizations to which they belong. It should be regarded as the basis of the organization of distribution in the industrial state, and should be transformed accordingly. It will, when complete, be no longer a society of members, but will include all adults in the localities which its stores serve; it will remain democratic in its control, and it will be organized in immediate localities, in districts and nationally, each widening circle having its appropriate duties to perform in the efficient working of the distributive scheme.

Select Bibliography

ARON, R., *Main Currents in Sociological Thought*, Weidenfeld & Nicolson, 1965

AVINERI, S., *The Social and Political Thought of Karl Marx*, Cambridge University Press, 1969

BEER, M., *History of British Socialism* (1919), Norton, 1940

BOWLE, J., *Politics and Opinion in the Nineteenth Century*, Cape, 1954

BURROW, J. W., *Evolution and Society: A Study in Victorian Social Theory*, Cambridge University Press, 1966

BURY, J. B., *The Idea of Progress*, London, 1932; Dover Books, 1960

COMTE, A., *A System of Positive Polity* (1851), B. Franklin, 1966

DUNCAN, D., *Life and Letters of Herbert Spencer*, Methuen, 1908

HOBSON, J. A., *Confessions of an Economic Heretic*, Macmillan, 1938

HOBSON, J. A., *The Evolution of Modern Capitalism: A Study of Machine Production*, Contemporary Science Series, Walter Scott, 1894

HOBSON, J. A., *John Ruskin, Social Reformer*, Nisbet, 1898

HOBSON, J. A., *The Science of Wealth*, Home University Library, Williams & Norgate, 1911

KIRKUP, T., *A History of Socialism*, A. & C. Black, 1892

MACDONALD, J. R., *Parliament and Democracy*, National Labour Press, 1920

MACDONALD, J. R., *Parliament and Revolution*, National Labour Press, 1919

MACDONALD, J. R., *A Policy for the Labour Party*, Leonard Parsons, 1920

MACDONALD, J. R., *The Social Unrest: Its Cause and Solution*, Independent Labour Party, 1913

MACDONALD, J. R., *Socialism after the War*, National Labour Press, 1917

Select Bibliography

MACDONALD, J. R., *Socialism,* Social Problems Series, ed. O. Smeaton, T. C. & E. C. Jack, 1907

MACDONALD, J. R., *Socialism: Critical and Constructive* (1921), Cassell, 1924

MACDONALD, J. R., *Socialism and Government* (2 vols.), Independent Labour Party, 1909

MACDONALD, J. R., *Socialism and Society,* Independent Labour Party, 1905

MACDONALD, J. R., *The Socialist Movement,* Independent Labour Party, 1911

MACDONALD, J. R., *Syndicalism: A Critical Examination,* Constable, 1912

MACDONALD, J. R., Preface to Enrico Ferri's *Socialism and Positive Science,* Socialist Library, 1909

MARKHAM, F. M. H., *Selected Writings of Saint-Simon,* Oxford University Press, 1952

MARX, K., and ENGELS, F., *Selected Works,* Foreign Languages Publishing House, 1962

MCBRIAR, A. M., *Fabian Socialism and English Politics,* Cambridge University Press, 1962

MILL, J. S., *Autobiography,* ed. Helen Taylor, London, 1873

PEASE, E. R., *A History of the Fabian Society,* A. C. Fifield, 1918

PORTER, B., *Critics of Empire,* Macmillan, 1968

RITCHIE, D. G., *Darwinism and Politics,* Swan Sonnenschein, 1889

RUSKIN, J., *Unto this Last: Four Essays on the First Principles of Political Economy* (1862), Smith, Elder & Co., 1900

SPENCER, H., *Essays: Scientific, Political and Speculative,* Williams & Norgate, 1891

SPENCER, H., *First Principles: A System of Synthetic Philosophy,* Williams & Norgate, 1963

WEBB, S., *Socialism in England,* Swan Sonnenschein, 1890